Axis Diplomats
in American Custody

Axis Diplomats in American Custody

*The Housing of Enemy Representatives
and Their Exchange
for American Counterparts,
1941–1945*

LANDON ALFRIEND DUNN
and TIMOTHY J. RYAN

McFarland & Company, Inc., Publishers
Jefferson, North Carolina

LIBRARY OF CONGRESS CATALOGUING-IN-PUBLICATION DATA

Names: Dunn, Landon Alfriend, 1956– author. |
Ryan, Timothy J., 1954– author.
Title: Axis diplomats in American custody : the housing of enemy
representatives and their exchange for American counterparts,
1941–1945 / Landon Alfriend Dunn and Timothy J. Ryan.
Description: Jefferson, N.C. : McFarland & Company, Inc., 2016. |
Includes bibliographical references and index.
Identifiers: LCCN 2016033648 | ISBN 9781476664866
(softcover : acid free paper) ∞
Subjects: LCSH: World War, 1939–1945—Prisoners and prisons,
American. | World War, 1939–1945—Diplomatic history. |
World War, 1939–1945—United States. | Diplomats—
United States—History—20th century. | Germans—Relocation—
United States—History—20th century. | Italians—Relocation—
United States—History—20th century. | Japanese—Relocation—
United States—History—20th century.
Classification: LCC D769.8.A5 D86 2016 | DDC 940.53/2—dc23
LC record available at https://lccn.loc.gov/2016033648

BRITISH LIBRARY CATALOGUING DATA ARE AVAILABLE

**ISBN (print) 978-1-4766-6486-6
ISBN (ebook) 978-1-4766-2539-3**

© 2016 Landon Alfriend Dunn and Timothy J. Ryan.
All rights reserved

*No part of this book may be reproduced or transmitted in any form
or by any means, electronic or mechanical, including photocopying
or recording, or by any information storage and retrieval system,
without permission in writing from the publisher.*

Front cover image of the Greenbrier Hotel (White Sulphur Springs,
West Virginia), Detroit Publishing Co. (Library of Congress)

Printed in the United States of America

*McFarland & Company, Inc., Publishers
Box 611, Jefferson, North Carolina 28640
www.mcfarlandpub.com*

Table of Contents

Preface	1
Introduction	6
One—The Hotels Are Selected	17
Two—The Round-Up	28
Three—Daily Routine	41
Four—Musical Chairs	54
Five—Negotiations for Exchange	66
Six—Be Careful What You Wish For	80
Seven—The Actual Exchange	95
Eight—End Games	107
Nine—Vichy French at the Hotel Hershey	121
Ten—Diplomats Captured in North Africa During the War	131
Eleven—Japanese Captured in Europe Near the End of the War	144
Conclusion	153
Chapter Notes	157
Bibliography	177
Index	199

Preface

This book deals with an obscure facet of World War II history—the four separate exchanges of Axis diplomats held in the United States for U.S. diplomats held overseas. The first and largest exchange dealt with the temporary housing in "grand hotels" of German, Italian, and Japanese diplomats who had been kicked out of their Washington, D.C., embassies after Pearl Harbor and who would eventually be exchanged for U.S. diplomats similarly stranded in Berlin, Rome and Tokyo.

The German, Italian, and Hungarian diplomats were sent to the Greenbrier Hotel in West Virginia and the Japanese to the Homestead in Virginia. On President Roosevelt's insistence, the Japanese diplomats from the Honolulu consulate, whom he suspected of spying, were taken to a remote Arizona dude ranch. As this initial group of approximately 800 settled in, the State Department, terrified of sabotage and insurgency in the Western Hemisphere and not trusting the Central American and South American governments, demanded that Axis diplomats in these Central and South American countries be brought to the U.S. before being sent on to their home countries. This plan was fiercely resisted not only by the belligerent countries and by the Latin American countries but also by the British.

However, by bullying and bribery, the United States prevailed, and another 900 people began to arrive—much more than anticipated, as some South American countries took the opportunity to purge those whom they considered "undesirables." Peru, for example, deported a group of middle-age Japanese tailors because—according to the Peruvian government—they could contribute to the enemy's war effort. Hundreds of such "dangerous" and "subversive" individuals, including women and children, were crammed into U.S. Military transports and

Preface

sent to the United States for transit on to their home countries. However, negotiations for the exchange moved slowly. The Latin Americans continued to arrive, including a group of 500 who were stuck for three weeks in the top four floors of a downtown Cincinnati hotel.

As the hotels became overcrowded, the Homestead, unwilling to lose its summer season, refused to extend its lease, and other hotels declined to accept the Japanese diplomats. The State Department began a frantic search for a new location and looked at an unused weather observatory on the top of a mountain, as well as resorts at Lake Placid and on the Florida beaches. One recommendation was to keep the South Americans on the vessel and moor it in the harbor at Savannah.

The Grove Park Inn (NC) was leased, and in an intricate game of musical chairs, the Japanese were moved from the Homestead to the Greenbrier and the Italians and Hungarians were moved from the Greenbrier to the Grove Park. Almost immediately, the Germans, who were left at the Greenbrier, clashed with the Japanese. The FBI turned informants—both hotel staff who spied on each other and detainees who spied on other detainees. As the detainees settled into long stretches of boredom interspersed with "the most sexually promiscuous part[ies]," intense negotiations went on regarding the diplomatic exchange. Although these negotiations are described, the focus of the book is on the activity at the hotel and in the towns.

In midsummer 1942, the first group of "bona fide" diplomats were exchanged. However, the South American countries continued to deport ethnic Japanese. The Grove Park Inn negotiated a better lease with the navy, which wanted the hotel for a convalescent center. The State Department selected the Assembly Inn at Montreat, North Carolina, and moved the South American group from the Grove Park and the remaining Germans from the Greenbrier to this remote location. Friction with the Inn's management began almost immediately, including a complaint by the German legation to the international YWCA about the living conditions. The detainees stayed nearly a year, with some gaining parole and some getting berths on the next exchange vessels. However, many of the South American Japanese, who had been grouped with the "bona fide" diplomats arriving from South America, were, in a bureaucratic sleight of hand, reclassified from this pseudo-diplomatic status to that of "an alien without a visa," and were shipped

Preface

off to detention camps run by the War Relocation Authority. The first diplomatic exchange was over.

The second diplomatic exchange began a few months later, in November of 1942, with the closing of the Washington embassy of Vichy France. The French ambassador and legation, a total of around two hundred and fifty people, were moved to a hotel in Pennsylvania. For the next fourteen months, as many of the entourage sought parole and asylum in the United States, the ambassador was moved from hotel to hotel until he and sixteen die-hard supporters were exchanged for U.S. diplomats who had been captured in Europe when the Vichy government fell.

Another exchange involved approximately forty German and Italian diplomats who had been captured in North Africa, then flown to the United States and hosted in a series of hotels in Virginia. They too would become bargaining chips in the negotiations for the American diplomats held when the Vichy government collapsed. When the Italian government fell, the Italian diplomats lost their value as bargaining chips. They, instead of wanting a return to Italy, now wanted to stay in the U.S., but their wishes were ignored. As they were loaded onto planes at the start of their journey back to Italy, they pleaded with the U.S. to provide them protection once they arrived, fearful of the fate that befell Mussolini.

The last exchange occurred in midsummer 1945 and started when the Japanese ambassador to Germany and other Japanese officials, about one hundred and eighty people in all, were caught as the Allied army advanced towards Berlin. The State Department and the War Department debated whether they should be treated as war criminals or diplomats. The State Department prevailed, not so much on the merits of the case, but because the diplomats and others could be traded if the U.S. got an opportunity to deal for General Wainwright and other U.S. officers held by the Japanese. The group was to be housed in a hotel in Virginia but met with bitter opposition from the local townspeople. These people included maimed soldiers from the Pacific and the family and friends of soldiers who lost their lives fighting the Japanese. The situation is so tense that authorities were unsure, in the event of a riot or other incident, if local law enforcement or the military would have jurisdiction. Nevertheless, the State Department moved

Preface

ahead with the hotel. While they were interned, the war ended, and America had to decide what to do with them.

Our work is based primarily on FBI reports, State Department reports, newspaper clippings, examination of documents held at the various hotels, and autobiographies and oral histories. We have visited the National Archives, West Virginia State Archives, the law library at the University of Virginia, and various historical societies as well as most of the hotels.

The book includes extensive quotations from the daily activity reports of the FBI agents and State Department officials who were at the hotels. Similarly, the texts of telegrams and memoranda from officials of the State Department are presented. Although we read newspaper reports, we have been careful about these. There appears to have been something of a news blackout about the activities. It is unclear if this was voluntary or required by the authorities. Most of what information we found in the local papers was strictly about the movement of the parties outside the hotels and was typically published several days after the event. There are several articles, usually from a syndicated source, of what we would consider yellow journalism. These stories tended to describe activities inside the hotels. We tended to discount these reports and to identify them as such if we included them in the book. We did include numerous quotations from local papers that were from letters to the editor or editorials, as these, we feel, give a sense of what the community felt. At the Greenbrier and the Homestead, the head clerk and the general manager respectively wrote short synopses of the diplomats' stay a few weeks after the last detainee had departed, and we were able to obtain copies of these. We were also able to locate testimonials and firsthand accounts from a few of the detainees. These were either in published autobiographies or were on the Internet.

The book does not dwell on the internment of Japanese Americans on the West Coast. It does not deal with Axis POWs held in camps across the United States. It alludes to but does not go into detail about the American diplomats at Baden-Baden. The story of the actual ocean voyage of the *Gripsholm* or *Drottningholm* is left for others. Although background is given about the Nazi presence in South America and about the political situation in Peru, Colombia, and other countries, these are not the focus of our work.

Preface

The exchanges included not only high-level diplomats but also wives, children, cooks, and drivers. Schools were set up, babies were born, and weddings took place. At the Arizona dude ranch, one of the Border Patrol guards held an Easter egg hunt for the children. An Italian diplomat at the Greenbrier who was in love with an American woman became a snitch for the FBI in return for a promise that he could stay in the United States, an agreement that violated the terms of the proposed exchange. At the Ingleside Hotel in Virginia, the townspeople became irate that the detainees were served sumptuous meals while they dealt with rationed meat and butter and became more irate when the American flag was removed from the dining hall. There are dozens of these stories.

Introduction

The Greenbrier Hotel is located in the town of White Sulphur Springs, West Virginia, about two hundred and fifty miles west of Washington. In the early 1940s it had 600 rooms and a staff-to-guest ratio of one to two and prided itself on being a "grand resort"—a place where affluent guests wore dinner jackets and evening gowns to dinner, played croquet, enjoyed golf, or rode—English style—on well-groomed trails through the ten-square-mile grounds.

About twenty-five miles away is Quinwood, West Virginia, a coal town of a few hundred people. The 1940 census shows that Ernest Angle, age 18, was the oldest of seven brothers and sisters, had an eighth-grade education, and was employed as a miner. Within a year, he managed to escape the mountains, and a backbreaking job, by enlisting in the navy. Somehow he got stationed in Hawaii—imagine him sending a postcard showing a palm tree, or maybe a hula dancer, to his friends back home.

On December 6, 1941, "approximately 15 minutes into the attack, a Japanese high-level bomber dropped a 1,760-pound (800 kg) naval projectile that had been specially converted, onto the USS *Arizona*. The bomb penetrated the forward deck of the ship about 40 feet in from the bow. The resulting explosion ignited aviation fuel stores and the powder magazines for the 14-inch guns, instantly separating most of the bow from the ship and lifting the 33,000-ton vessel out of the water.... The explosion and subsequent fires killed 1,177 sailors and marines instantly."[1]

Fireman Second Class Angle was one of the casualties.

Ten days later, an obscure agency of the State Department called the Special War Problems Division contacted the directors of the C&O railroad, which owned the Greenbrier. Within hours the framework

Introduction

for a short-term, exclusive lease was worked out. Hotel management was informed the next day, and a town hall meeting was held just after that. On December 19, 1941, Axis diplomats who had been kicked out of their Washington embassies arrived by train in White Sulphur Springs and were escorted through town to the hotel by State Department personnel, agents of the FBI and of the Immigration Service, and officers of the West Virginia State Highway Patrol. It is not known whether the diplomats walked up like guests or like conquerors.

This book is about the approximately 2,000 Axis diplomats, embassy personnel and staffs, family members, and assorted other quasi-officials and hangers-on who were housed in luxury resorts on the East Coast by the U.S. State Department for approximately 200 days as arrangements were made to exchange them for U.S. diplomats who had been similarly stranded in U.S. embassies in Europe and Asia. The book also describes three other exchanges of enemy diplomats handled by the Special War Problems Division. When the Washington embassy of Vichy France was closed in November 1942, the ambassador and legation, a total of around 250 people, were moved to a hotel in Pennsylvania. Another exchange involved approximately 40 German and Italian diplomats who had been captured in North Africa, then flown to the U.S. and hosted in a series of hotels in Virginia. Finally, in midsummer 1945, the Japanese ambassador to Germany and other Japanese officials, about 180 people in all, were caught as the Allied army advanced towards Berlin. They were taken to a small hotel in Pennsylvania and held. While they were interned, the war ended, and America had to decide what to do with them.

There seems to be no generally accepted name for what happened to the diplomats. As historian Erika Dreifus points out: "A caveat: it must be emphasized that in virtually ever[y] respect, 'diplomatic internment' was the absolute antithesis of any other detention experience normally associated with the Second World War ... [the diplomats] were not military prisoners-of-war. They did not suffer the miseries of Japanese and Japanese-Americans in the United States, or the indignities borne by other civilian 'alien enemies.'"[2]

A letter from the FBI refers to the use of hotels as "a place of assembly." The assistant secretary of state refers to "assembling and safeguarding" the diplomats. Some authors say that the diplomats were

Introduction

"confined" to the various hotels. The Greenbrier was called a temporary "holding facility," and the diplomats were "sequestered." A publication put out by the Diplomatic Corps refers to "Diplomatic Detentions During Wartime." A member of the Japanese government describes its diplomats as being "blocked" in the USA. An Italian official talks about the lack of a "status of liberty" of its people. The German government calls the U.S. diplomats which it holds as "the exchange group." An Italian minister complains about being in "psychological captivity." A Department of State memo refers to "civilian internees and other persons in an analogous situation."

Tensions Rise

In a 1938 memo, Mr. Nathaniel P. Davis, chief of the Division of Foreign Service Personnel, concerned about the many problems a war in Europe or the Pacific could bring, suggested the creation of a new group to be called the Special War Problems Division. It was intended to deal with location and welfare issues, that is, to help find out the status of Americans stranded in hostile territory if war broke out.

> Another important function which was added to the new Division was the representation of the interests of various belligerent governments that requested this service of the United States. Representation of this sort requires the taking charge of the represented government's diplomatic and consular property and archives, the handling of whereabouts and welfare inquiries in respect to its citizens, the receipt and payment of funds to them, and the providing for their repatriation when possible.[3]

Additionally, the Division was tasked with dealing with "the exchange of official and non-official American and Axis powers personnel ... the granting by the United States of safe conducts for travel of enemy nationals between neutral points ... the transmission of documents or messages to or from enemy territory ... and other special war problems."[4]

During 1940, relations between Germany and the United States deteriorated. The Germans regularly accused the U.S. diplomats at the Berlin embassy and at the various American consulates in Germany of sabotage and spying. In the United States, the State Department accused the German diplomats in the Washington embassy and various consulates across the country of the same things.

Introduction

At this time, spying and espionage were more benign. They did not necessarily involve cloak and dagger stuff—no guns, electronic equipment, blackmail, or payoffs. Much of the activity was what today we would consider to be commercial espionage or even market research. Newspapers were studied. Dry statistical documents from government and trade sources about industrial and agricultural production were closely monitored. Trade shows were attended and factories toured. Personal contact was critical to obtain inside information. Peter Riedel, a famous German glider pilot, gave amazing displays of acrobatics at air shows—reportedly his glider "sported a red and black Nazi swastika on its rudder."[5] His title was Air Attaché for the German government and he was friends with aeronautical engineers and given VIP tours of aircraft factories. He later would be interned at the Greenbrier and considered a spy.

A memorandum from the FBI notes that "the German espionage system has manifested a keen interest in various trade journals, technical periodicals and other publications, particularly those containing information concerning the economic welfare and national defense of the nation."[6] These publications included the *Daily Freight Register*, *Army and Navy Journal*, *Iron Age*, *Business Week*, *Federal Reserve Bulletin*, the *Explosives Engineer*, *The Official Gazette of the United States Patent Office*, *The Oil and Gas Journal*, *Journal of the Aeronautical Sciences*, *Flying* and *Popular Aviation* as well as many other publications readily available at newsstands or through subscription.

In June 1941, President Roosevelt instructed the State Department to demand that all German nationals connected with the German Library of Information in New York, the German Railway and Tourist agencies, and the Transoceanic News Service be sent back to Europe. He also requested that most of the consulates of Germany across America be shut down and that all consular officers, agents, clerks, and employees of German nationality be expelled by July 10, 1941. At this time the Germans had consulates in nine cities. Each location had a large staff. For example, the Chicago consulate had a chancellor, first consular secretary, seven clerks, and three stenographers. Many of the personnel were there with family, as well as maids and drivers. All were to be expelled from the country.

Germany returned the favor. On June 19, 1941, the American

Introduction

Chargé d'Affaires, Leland Morris, was informed that due to suspicion of spying and of spreading malicious information, the consular offices of America needed to be closed and all consular personnel sent out of Germany. (President Roosevelt had withdrawn the last ambassador in 1938 to protest Kristallnacht—the night of broken glass when Jews were systematically attacked by Nazis throughout Germany.) Consulates were closed in Berlin, Bremen, Frankfort, Munich, and six other cities. Similarly, the Italians had the United States close consulates in Florence, Genoa, Milan, and four other cities. The United States responded by closing the Italian consulates in Detroit and Newark. Relations worsened with the Italian government, and in midsummer, it ordered all U.S. consulates in Italy to be closed. The Americans promptly demanded that the Italians close all of their consulates in the United States and remove all their consular people. By fall, the State Department had sent close to five hundred German and Italian consulate staff packing, which represented a little less than half of the German and Italian diplomatic personnel in the United States at the time. The Italian and German embassies in Washington stayed open, and some consulate members were transferred to them. In Europe, over 300 U.S. diplomatic personnel were expelled, including those from Norway, occupied France, Greece, Luxemburg, Denmark, Netherlands, Belgium, and Yugoslavia as well as Germany and Italy. In America, although all Italian consulates had closed, several German consulates stayed open. Moreover, German and Italians journalists, and certain special envoys and high-level business executives, remained in the country. No Japanese embassies or consulates were affected.

War

When J. Edgar Hoover heard of the Pearl Harbor attack, he immediately dispatched his men to surround the various Axis embassies and remaining consulates. Under long-standing tradition, diplomats cannot be imprisoned. Their embassies cannot be entered. They, technically, should have free movement and, for example, be able to go to their homes or go shopping. They should be able to communicate with whomever they want both inside the United States and overseas,

Introduction

receive and send packages or mail without inspection, and have visitors. Moreover, their safety and that of their staff and families continue to be the responsibility of the United States government.

The State Department received a message through the Swiss Foreign Office on December 11, 1941, from Joseph C. Grew, the American ambassador in Tokyo, that American personnel had been confined to the embassy but were safe. The American delegation in Germany and Rome also relayed that they were well.

In Washington, the treatment of the European Axis diplomats was slightly different from that of the Japanese diplomats. A December 12, 1941, *Washington Times Herald* article reads, "[T]he German staff along with that at the Italian embassy had been permitted to come and go at will. In contrast the Japanese embassy staff had been 'imprisoned' within the embassy walls since the unexpected Jap attack on the Hawaiian Islands. A large squad of Government agents, reinforced by Metropolitan Police details, have enforced the confinement order there, permitting no one to leave the building without legitimate reason, and then they are accompanied on their mission by two Government agents."[7] This different treatment may or may not have been a racial or ethnic issue, but most likely it was because of the seething anger over the Pearl Harbor attack. The authorities may have just been prudent—who knows what could have happened to an unescorted Japanese out on the street. The Germans seem to have kept a low profile. The Italians seemed to come and go as they please, continuing to dine out and to go shopping.

Reciprocity

The suddenness of the start of the war created an unprecedented set of problems for the State Department. In the First World War, a succession of threats and ultimatums were given before the shooting war broke out, allowing diplomatic personnel to evacuate as embassies were shut down or left with a skeleton staff. In 1914, *The London Times* reported:

> As soon as it became clear that Great Britain and Germany were enemy countries, Sir Neville Henderson, the British Ambassador, prepared to leave Germany with

Introduction

the Embassy staff, entrusting their affairs to the United States Embassy. In London the German (Chargé d'Affaires) went yesterday to the Swiss Legation to ask them to take over, and later arranged to leave London from Victoria. A later report makes clear that Henderson and all his staff left Germany by special train on September 4th. On the same day, (the German Chargé d'Affaires) and a group of Embassy staff and businessmen left Victoria at just after 7 pm: their train took them to Gravesend where they embarked for Rotterdam on the Dutch steamer Batavia.[8]

In the United States, "the 1941 detention of Axis diplomats differed sharply from what had occurred during World War One when Chief Special Agent Joseph Nye personally escorted the German Ambassador until his departure."[9]

The German ambassadors' gentle departures from London and from Washington at the start of the First World War was in contrast to the situation faced by the State Department in December 1941— hundreds of enemy diplomats stranded in Washington and other cities, similar numbers of U.S. diplomats stranded in the capitals of belligerent countries, and the sea lanes a shooting gallery filled with battleships, destroyers, and submarines.

Various cables and memorandums had been sent during 1940 and 1941 to diplomats around the world dealing with what actions to take if war was declared. However, a sneak attack and an instantaneous war footing had not been anticipated. There was no contingency plan for this, no blueprint that could be dusted off or precedents to follow.

Moreover, the "diplomats" involved in these exchanges included more than just the ambassador and his officials. Legations included those at the embassy and also the various consulates. Lists of those eventually exchanged include the following descriptions: ambassador, minister plenipotentiary, first secretary, attachés, 3rd secretary, 1st interpreter, chancellors, chief of military mission, military attachés, commercial attachés, consular agents, typists, clerks, wives, children, mothers, governesses, nurses, drivers, maids, servants, cooks, chauffeurs, auxiliary employees, students, academics, journalists, press photographers, and film producers. Also included were what the Japanese called "Trade Merchants" and the Germans referred to as Chamber of Commerce representatives. These people were non-governmental personnel such as bankers and businessmen at the top levels of companies like Mitsubishi or Siemens, as well as technical experts such as

Introduction

chemists, engineers, and shipping agents of these large corporations who were posted overseas.

In approaching any swap of diplomats, the Special War Problems Division of the State Department was guided by two principles: the standards of existing protocols, which focused on safety and immunity, and by the concept of reciprocity. As Arnold M. Krammer writes,

> American law concerning the protection of foreign diplomats, whether in peacetime or war, is clearly spelled out in the U.S. Statute of 1790. Simply stated, Sections 252–254 of Title 22, United States Code, accords complete immunity from criminal, civil and administrative jurisdiction to all foreign nationals who are ... assigned the proper nonimmigrant visa status in the employment of any embassy in Washington DC. This law ... extends even to private servants in the household of a diplomat. Without question, then, the enemy diplomats and their families and staffs were to be protected by the American government until their safe repatriation could be accomplished.[10]

The concept of reciprocity was the simple tit-for-tat treatment of the diplomats. The State Department, from the very beginning, decided to host Axis diplomats in the best accommodations and provide them with the best treatment possible in expectation—or at least the hope—that these standards would be mirrored by the Axis governments. This decision was made unilaterally, that is, at the time this decision was made, we did not know how the Germans, Italians, or Japanese would treat our people.

However, Cordell Hull, the secretary of state, in a letter to Francis Biddle, the attorney general, made clear the priorities of the United States. He wrote, "As you know, we have followed a policy of reciprocity in the treatment in the United States of the former representatives of the governments with which we are now at war. However, the question of reciprocity was always a secondary consideration. The primary factory has been the security of the United States."[11]

Initial Moves

With closure of the various embassies and consulates, communication between the hostile parties became difficult. An agreement was made that Switzerland, a neutral country, would act as liaison between the U.S. and the European Axis parties, and that Spain, another neutral,

Introduction

would perform the same duties for Japan. These "protective powers" were not postmen, nor did they function as a package delivery system. If the State Department wished to communicate with the enemy, a letter or telegram would actually be written to the Swiss or Spanish legations, with a request that they convey the information in the letter to the enemy, that is, the Swiss or Spanish delegate would write a letter paraphrasing or quoting the United States' letter.

The protective powers often labeled the notes they wrote to add meaning outside the written word. "Mutatis mutandis" means "the necessary changes having been made." An "aide-memoire" is a proposed agreement or a negotiating text circulated informally among delegations for discussion without committing the originating delegation's country to the contents. "Officieusement" means "unofficially." A "note verbale" is "a diplomatic communication prepared in the third person and unsigned. It is less formal than a note but more formal than an aide-memoire." (The above from Wikipedia.) Often the protective power would relay information in an informal setting, and the related "memorandum of conversation" would note this. Who called the meetings, whose office was used, and the urgency of the meeting were duly noted. All discussions however, were one step removed in that, for example, the U.S. State Department never directly spoke with their German, Italian or Japanese counterparts but instead always communicated through a Swiss or Spanish intermediary.

Adding to the difficulties of communication were the language barriers and the disruption of telephone, telegraph, and courier services due to the war. Often, messages were delayed. A proposed sailing list for the first Japanese exchange was sent by the State Department to the Spanish Embassy in Washington, which sent it on to Madrid, which then sent it on to Tokyo, taking a total of nineteen days. The list was reviewed, modified, and returned in the same manner, taking over six weeks in elapsed time. Communications were often received out of order, and the diplomats had to sort through exactly which communiqué was referenced. A telegram from the Swiss to the secretary of state begins:

> American Interests—Germany. Department's 485, February 19. Swiss Foreign Office note March 3 forwards copy note February 29 addressed to Swiss Legation, Berlin, by German Foreign Office of which the following is translated "Ministry

Introduction

Foreign Affairs in reference to notes verbales 38, January 10, 48, January 12, 131, January 30 and 213, February 12, from Swiss Legation regarding extensions and changes in proposals of American government...."[12]

The protective power had many other duties, such as winding down the personal affairs of the individual diplomats by selling furniture, closing out leases and mortgages, and dealing with personal banking issues. The protective power also provided stewardship of the now empty embassy and consulate buildings. For example, there is a large file in the National Archives dealing with Swiss efforts to repair a faulty heating system at the abandoned German embassy. Another file details the Spanish efforts to sell four automobiles owned by the Japanese delegation in Washington.

The State Department initially believed that two exchanges—one for the American diplomats in Europe and another for the American diplomats in Asia—would be needed. The exchanges were expected to take place no later than March or early April 1942. In the meantime, the Axis diplomats would need to be kept in a safe location until the terms of the exchange were agreed upon between the warring parties and until safe passage across hostile oceans could be worked out. In addition, as the destinations for the exchange vessels would be in ports of neutral countries, the cooperation of these countries would be needed. Almost from the beginning, the assumptions were that the European Axis personnel would be exchanged in Lisbon and that the Japanese would be exchanged on the east coast of Africa in Lourenço Marques, Portuguese East Africa (now Mozambique). The State Department believed that one large vessel could make the European exchange, return to the United States, and then embark to make the Japanese exchange. The number of Axis diplomats expected to be exchanged varied greatly. It was unknown how many Axis diplomats were in South America, if any would transit through the United States as part of some hemispheric pact, or if each South American nation would broker independent exchanges with Germany, Italy, and Japan without U.S. involvement.

Sometime around December 14, 1941, Berlin announced that the U.S. diplomats under their control had been taken to Bad Nauheim, about twenty miles north of Frankfort. (The German word Bad translates roughly to "the baths" or "spa.") It was a world-famous resort,

Introduction

noted for its salt springs, which were used to treat heart and nerve diseases.

At Bad Nauheim, the U.S. legation stayed at the Jeschke's Grand Hotel.

> The hotel had been closed with the outbreak of war in Europe in September 1939 and its staff had dispersed. The hotel director, Gustav Zorn, had remained in residence since its closing, but without staff ... the hotel had burst water pipes, no heat, no electricity. Furniture, linens, silver and curtains as well as other accoutrements, were placed in storage. The hotel was not prepared for sudden wartime occupancy.... The hotel lacked the plant and the coal for proper heating. The temperature in January 1942, dropped to below zero.... [The local Gestapo agent] used his position to commandeer supplies supposedly meant for a neighboring town.[13]

In the Orient, although the State Department knew the status of its personnel at the Tokyo embassy, it had been anxiously waiting to hear from the 24 consulates scattered throughout the region. Gradually word came in from Canton, Singapore, Hong Kong, and the many other locations that all were safe. Some of the State Department's people were already under escort and on their way to Tokyo. Others were under house arrest enforced by Japanese soldiers. At Kobe, "the staff was transferred to Consul Warner's home. Guards installed themselves in the house, using freely any furniture they desired and helping themselves to foodstuff and coal supplies. On several occasions, the guards conducted themselves in a highly objectionably manner, one guard getting drunk and roaming through the house brandishing a sword."[14]

The Mussolini government had gathered up the diplomats from the U.S. embassy and housed them in a hotel in Rome. With its people accounted for, the State Department began a search for a place for the diplomats of the belligerent countries.

ONE

The Hotels Are Selected

The State Department began a search for suitable accommodations. The hotel or lodge needed to be located on the East Coast, preferably reasonably near Washington, and secluded but close to a rail line. Security was a concern. It had to be ready for immediate occupation, have no other guests, and be available for an estimated two to three months. First-class accommodations were wanted. Other criteria included the general appearance of the hotel, interior arrangement of lobbies and rooms, type and condition of furniture, number of baths and room plan, the general condition of the hotel and rooms, heating facilities, season of normal operations, type of meals served generally by the hotel to normal patrons, the extent of the outside grounds, whether the terrain was level (for purposes of guarding the premises), what recreational facilities were available, the location of highways, the availability of a hospital and medical facilities, and the proximity of shops.

The early memos between State Department officials assumed that the diplomats of all the hostile countries would be held at the same place, but estimates of the size of the group differed widely, ranging from 500 to 900. The FBI and State Department had solid numbers for Axis diplomats, staff, families, and other designated individuals in the United States. However, Axis diplomats also resided in the countries of Latin American. The State Department was negotiating to include these in any exchange program, but whether this would be successful, and the number of these diplomats and size of their legations, was unclear. Also unknown was the number, if any, of non-credentialed Axis nationals that might be included as part of the diplomatic exchange.

Axis Diplomats in American Custody

State Department Special Agent Bannerman writes in a memo dated December 16, 1941:

> In view of the fact that there will be about 500 officials, members of their families, clerks and servants in the Diplomatic and Consular missions of Japan, Germany, Italy, Rumania and Bulgaria, the selection of a suitable hotel to accommodate such a group has narrowed down to two principal hotels, The Greenbrier Hotel at White Sulphur Springs, West Virginia and the Homestead Hotel at Hot Springs, Virginia. Each have 600 rooms, adequate ground space and hotel facilities and are near enough to Washington to be within immediate reach of the department. The officials of the above nations could not object to the class of accommodations offered by these two hotels.... This is the off season for these two hotels and it is believed that either hotel could easily be obtained for the exclusive use by the Department on this occasion.[1]

He mentions another possibility: "The Ocean Forest Hotel at Myrtle Beach, S.C. is now closed but can be opened by January 15th or a little earlier. This hotel has only 220 rooms but adequate ground space. It is not, however, considered to be a first class hotel in the standing of the Greenbrier and the Homestead.... There are no other hotels near Washington that can be used to accommodate such a large group and which will allow the Department to exercise the necessary control over the movements of the party."[2]

As it turned out, the State Department leased both the Greenbrier and the Homestead resorts, perhaps to allow a separation of the diplomats from the different Axis countries, or perhaps because each hotel alone was bumping up against the potential number of detainees. There may, however, have been a simpler explanation. At this time, the army and navy were leasing whatever hotels they could find. In fact, the army, which needed training facilities, hospitals, and convalescent centers, would end up in control of over 900 hotels with over 50,000 rooms by the end of the war. The State Department may have felt it would be out of options if it did not secure both locations, especially given the uncertainty regarding the potential number of detainees from South America.

The Greenbrier was in the Allegheny Mountains, about halfway between Charleston, WV, and Richmond, VA. It was the largest and virtually only employer in the area. It had 650 rooms, numerous separate cottages, ten square miles of grounds, a golf course, tennis courts, horse trails, and walking trails. Nearby streams offered trout fishing,

One. The Hotels Are Selected

the lowlands were good for pheasant and quail hunts, and deer were plentiful in the heavily forested mountains. The hotel was a self-sufficient town with a post office, drug store, telegraph office, linen shop, dress shop, gift store, candy store, beauty salon, barber shop, and newsstand. It had a complete laundry as well as dry-cleaning facilities. It boasted a huge indoor pool, almost one hundred yards long, located inside an ornate marble building. The hotel, known for its curative spring waters, also included an extensive health area with baths and therapy rooms. Its beautiful setting, antebellum buildings, fine food, and unsurpassed service had attracted a blue-blood guest list for decades.

The Homestead Hotel in Hot Springs, two hours east of the Greenbrier, was a similar "grand resort." It had close to 600 rooms, was famous for its dining and service, and also claimed healing powers for the water from its natural spring. An article in *Life Magazine* refers to the Homestead's staff of 700 waiters, maids, bellboys, porters, chauffeurs, gardeners, chefs, butchers, bakers, laundresses, craftsmen, game wardens, masseurs, and hostlers, the "vast white-pillared dining hall, the palms in the long lobby," and its "fashionable shops and pool." According to the magazine, the Homestead even boasted its own silversmith and pheasant hatchery.[3]

At both the Greenbrier and at the Homestead, the State Department paid an approximate lease rate of $9.00 per day per guest. Children were charged slightly less. A discount was given for State Department officials and FBI agents. The Border Patrol guards were charged even less, as they were usually crowded into cottages or staff dorms as opposed to rooms in the main building. Meals, including wine and liquor, and all bar tabs and room service, were included in the fee. Tips were not, but it was suggested that the diplomats would provide a lump sum, to be paid weekly, to be divided amongst the staff. The contracts stipulated that standard wear and tear were included, but any vandalism or major damages would be added to the bill, as would any upfits to the hotel, such as outdoor lighting, guard shacks, or improved telephone system.

Each hotel was promised a target number of guests and provided with an estimated number of days that the lease would run. Both hotels priced the contracts at less than the standard rate, not necessarily out of patriotism, but because it was the winter season and very few rooms were taken. Both hotels were assured that the detainees would be gone in a few months and certainly before Easter, which was the traditional beginning of the high season.

Hotel Management Is Informed

According to the personal notes of Roy Sibold, the chief clerk of the Greenbrier:

> On December 17th, 1941, shortly after lunch, the Management received a telephone call at the request of certain individuals of our State Department, from a representative of the C&O railroad company for the purpose of ascertaining whether or not the Greenbrier would be interested in housing the personnel of certain Axis Diplomats and Nationals numbering some 400 or 500 beginning within ten days and lasting for from one to three months. This representative was told that the matter would receive prompt and serious consideration and that he would informed at the earliest possible moment because the staff here was, at that time, at a minimum and the usual winter clearing and repair work had just begun.
> At exactly 10:30 o'clock this same evening the management was contacted a second time and told that an order had been issued by the President to an official of the State Department, to the effect that the Diplomats who were then in Washington, some two hundred, must be removed from their embassies within forty-eight hours. Well, that was a very short notice and exacting information, so the management got busy and concluded that the Greenbrier had an opportunity to serve our Government at a time when they needed it most, therefore, the very next morning, December 18, 1941, the officials of our State Department were advised that the Greenbrier was only too happy to serve and would endeavor to do the best possible job under their direction because the responsibility rested entirely on their shoulders.[4]

Per Sibold, the FBI agents arrived almost immediately after that. Fay Ingalls, the president of the Homestead, writes an almost identical story:

> At about midnight on the eighteenth of December, 1941, we received a telephone message from Washington that the State Department had approached the Chesapeake and Ohio Railway representative to learn if it would be possible to use the Homestead and the Greenbrier to house the Axis diplomatic and consular personnel and certain commercial aliens who were caught in this country by the commencement of war with the Axis powers. This gentleman, in posing the information, left no doubt that the request for these two hotels to be made available was in the nature of a command.[5]

One. The Hotels Are Selected

On December 19, 1941, the Swiss were requested by the State Department to inform the German government as follows: "For their greater comfort and protection all of this personnel and their dependents [at the embassy] have today been accommodated in a first class resort hotel where there will be more space available and larger grounds at their disposal."[6]

On December 17, 1941, the American people were told in a newspaper article:

> The State Department tonight announced a reciprocal plan under which German, Japanese and Hungarian diplomats and some nationals will be accorded certain privileges in exchange for comparable treatment of American officials and nationals in their countries.... This government has decided to move members of the German embassy staff to a "comfortable hotel in another location," and that pending the departure they have been requested to "confine themselves to their embassy building." German correspondents in custody pending an investigation will accompany the embassy staff and will be lodged with them.... The American government has been guided in its attitude towards the representatives of the power with which it is now at war in accordance with the rules of international law and on the basis of reciprocity.... [These steps] are a part of the process for a reciprocal exchange for American officers abroad.[7]

Reaction of the Townspeople

At the Greenbrier, it is impossible to determine if any of the staff knew Ernest Angle, the sailor killed in Hawaii, personally, but maybe they heard that a local boy had been killed. As with big cities and small communities across the country, the world had changed with the sneak attack. The *White Sulphur Springs Sentinel* was issued weekly. The front page for December 12, 1941—the first edition since Pearl Harbor—includes three stories.

One is titled "Large Crowd At Defense Meeting." Close to five hundred people attended—about one-quarter of the town's population. The article describes an angry crowd. There is talk of the "stab-in-the-back"[8] method of the "Japs." (Author's note: "Japs" was the word that was used at the time.)

Another article is "Gala New Year is Planned at Resort." It states that the celebration would provide "the right kind of adieu to 1941 and the welcoming salute to a new and is to be hoped, a better new year."[9]

The locals, reading this, must have shaken their heads, knowing the event would inevitably be cancelled—no one was in a mood for festivities, and all looked upon the upcoming year with foreboding.

The third article is only two sentences long and is titled "Internments." It reads: "The 'Sentinel' is trying to comply with the wishes of the Federal authorities relative to publishing the rumors of internment of Aliens during the crises.... At such time as the State Department makes such releases we shall be glad to publish (the) same."[10]

Sibold writes:

> Everyone entrusted with the operation here immediately realized that grave responsibility existed and that we were to be educated in many phases of the workings of our government. For instance, everyone was cautioned most emphatically that those people to be cared for were without a doubt avowed agents of a hostile government and, undoubtedly, the directing heads of fifth column activities in this country directed by their respective governments. Nevertheless, according to International Law, which we learned from the Protocol Division of the State Department, when such people are caught in a country with which their homelands are at war, they are entitled to living conditions according to their customary standard pending their return home. Our people, at the time, living in foreign countries, were to be accorded the same treatment.... There are of course limitations as to privileges. There must be in order to prevent engaging in any activities other than the interest of the country in which they are detained.[11]

Basic Rules

In Washington, a meeting was held on December 20, 1941, with Attorney General Francis Biddle, Stanley Woodward of the State Department, Major Lemmel Schofield of the Immigration and Naturalization Service, and J. Edgar Hoover of the FBI. They established basic rules:

(1) All of the members of the [legation] ... will be confined within the limits of the hotel proper and will not be allowed on the hotel grounds except under such specific surveillance as may later be determined.

(2) None of the members of the embassy and legation will be permitted to communicate with any outside person in any way with the exceptions hereinafter determined. This includes outside communications with wives or other members of their families.

(3) The Swiss ... who are transacting business for the Germans ... shall designate the persons who shall transact the business at the hotel and shall furnish the State Department with the names of such persons.... Each representative shall be furnished identifying credentials. They shall be assigned a room where all conferences shall take [place] and shall be permitted to talk with any of the persons confined without supervision.

(4) There will be no short wave receiving or sending sets in the hotel; no long wave sending sets.

(5) All written communications, including mail and telegrams, destined for the persons confined, shall first be cleared with the State Department. This does not include mail sent by the Swiss or Swedish Legations in the diplomatic pouches.

(6) The Swiss ... shall be permitted to communicate by direct wire to the chiefs of the missions at the Greenbrier or their designate representative and vice versus.[12]

Officials Take Over the Hotels

Overall responsibility for the management and coordination of the internment program was given to State Department Chief Special Agent Thomas A. Fitch. He, in turn, designated Special Agent Robert L. Bannerman to handle day-to-day responsibility for running the program. Bannerman moved quickly to establish procedures at the hotel. He would oversee several other State Department agents and act as liaison with the FBI, the Border Patrol, and hotel management. The FBI was on the lookout for subversive and covert activities by the detainees. The Border Patrol, a division of the Immigration and Naturalization Service of the State Department, was charged with the actual guarding of the detainees. FBI Agent A.N. Carlblom writes in a memo dated December 23, 1941:

> It has been determined that various governmental agencies have had or presently have representatives in the Greenbrier Hotel.... District Supervisor, Miami Field Division, of the Bureau of Immigration and Naturalization, and who is presently at the Greenbrier and head of approximately 56 men, whom he has assigned to

Axis Diplomats in American Custody

various duties, that he expects some 40 more men to work under him thus making a total of approximately 75 men to accomplish the various guard duties and such other tasks as have been agreed to come under his domain. There has been at the Greenbrier until last night (redacted) of the Division of Protocol, Department of State, whose superior is believed to be (redacted) of the Department of State. He has been present to attend to the many details in which the Department of State would naturally be concerned with in a situation such as this. Also from the Department of State there have been (redacted) and (redacted). The former left Greenbrier last night but is expected to return tonight with more individuals to be kept at the hotel, which individuals he apparently is accompanying from Ellis Island, New York Harbor. (Redacted) has been here since our arrival and the intention is to have him continue residing at the Greenbrier as a representative, and apparently the sole one, of the Department of State. There has also been present (redacted) of the Swiss Legation which is handling matters for the Germans, who left tonight to return to Washington DC. He does not intend to return and likely there will [be] no Swiss Legation member in residence.... Prior to the installation of the guard force of the Bureau of Immigration and Naturalization there were 16 members of the West Virginia State Police patrolling the grounds and doing guard duty. Presently there are no members of the State Police on the premises of the Greenbrier Hotel. The Greenbrier has a police force of its own consisting of 15 men operating under (redacted) Chief, and who guarded the premises night and day performing the usual duties of a private police force. Of course there are the three Special Agents of the FBI present at the Greenbrier according to your instructions.[13]

A front-page article in the December 26, 1941, edition of *The White Sulphur Springs Sentinel* is titled "Axis Officials Interned Here." It states that the staff of the German embassy and the Hungarian legation had arrived and goes on:

> Folks of the mountains and plateaus of Greenbrier county have lodged such strenuous complaint against the presence of the German and Hungarian diplomatic corps here that a representative of the U.S. State Department came to Lewisburg (a nearby town) to address a public meeting.... Criticism has been outspoken throughout the county, whose population is largely descendants of Revolutionary war families, ever since the special train of nearly 200 German and Hungarian pulled in this week on the Greenbrier hotel's special siding.[14]

The same edition of the paper has another article, dated two days later (the newspaper is published weekly) titled "Greenbrier Denies Alien Objection." It states:

> Townsfolk of White Sulphur Springs, in whose midst the government temporarily has interned 159 alien diplomats and newsmen, disclaimed through their mayor today any feeling of animosity over the action in the face of reports to the contrary.... [The mayor stated that].... We, and I speak for every person in our town,

are happy to have this privilege of doing our part during the war crises ... in his statement, which [the mayor] said has the approval of the State Department, the mayor declared "our whole tradition here in White Sulphur Springs is one of patriotism and support of our government."[15]

Employees Are Checked Out

The FBI compiled a list of employees of the Greenbrier, about 350 at this time, and began to investigate them. An initial step was to send the list of names to Washington to be compared to their many indices of subversives and troublemakers.

The FBI also interviewed all employees. From a letter from FBI Agent Carlblom to Director Hoover:

> I want to assure you that immediate steps were taken to expeditiously conduct investigation of each of the employees of the Greenbrier Hotel to determine their backgrounds, reputations, activities, and conduct.... I have been advised by Agent (redacted) that the hotel records are meager. I have instructed Agent (redacted) to interview each of the employees for the purpose of securing from the employee his background and activities and to photograph and fingerprint each of the employees when interviewed.... Agent (redacted) will endeavor to have the employees voluntarily submit to interview, photographing and fingerprinting and it is my belief that if an employee does not voluntarily submit he will be evidencing a lack of cooperation with the FBI and a lack of the proper attitude toward the United States. I believe any reluctance on their part to fully cooperate will be in itself very suspicious and probably evidence enough to hold them since they are in direct contact with members of the German, Italian and Japanese embassies.... A number of the employees of the hotel have resigned since the government started using the hotel as a place to hold aliens and these former employees will also be thoroughly investigated.[16]

The Homestead employed about 500 workers. Mr. Ingalls writes, "Rapidly the FBI investigated the personnel of the Homestead which naturally had to come in contact with the Japanese. It is a matter of great satisfaction to management that although these investigations were minute to the last degree and extended not only to the individual but to his background, in not one single instance was the loyalty or the integrity of any employee of the Homestead questioned by the FBI."[17]

At the Greenbrier, the FBI's investigation turned out differently. Mr. Joseph Krautlegger was a waiter who had worked at the hotel since

Axis Diplomats in American Custody

1925. He was born in Germany in 1908. The FBI investigation determined that he and some other employees "organized themselves into a pro–Germany group, having their headquarters in Room No. 54, Servant's Quarters, Greenbrier Hotel, ... which room was decorated with four Swastika emblems, a picture of Hitler, and German propaganda. In this room they are reported to hold meetings and celebrate German victories."[18] This same individual was already on the FBI watch list from its Huntington, West Virginia, district office. These files carried a report that Mr. Krautlegger, early in the summer of 1941, "upon receiving a questionnaire from his Local Selective Service Board ... started swearing, making the statement in public that he would never serve in the United States Army nor fight for this country. He also stated that he was a Fifth Columnist and didn't care who knew it.... [Witnesses also] quoted Krautlegger as follows: 'It would be better for the whole world for Hitler to take it over. Everybody would be better off if he did.'"[19] The hotel terminated Mr. Krautlegger's employment.

In its background checks, the FBI found that six German waiters and one Italian baker were in the United States illegally. They ranged in age from 33 to 52. Most had been in the United States for years. Per the *White Sulfur Springs Sentinel*, "Some of the waiters had worked at hotels here, in Florida and in New York since coming to this country between 1925 and 1933. Two have brothers in the German army. The Italian had worked at the resort since coming to the United States in 1904 or 1904."[20] All were fired.

The FBI also checked out Mr. Slosson, the general manager of the Homestead, upon finding out that his wife was born in Munich. She had been in the United States for over twenty years and her loyalty to the U.S. was unquestioned, but the FBI did note that she had no relatives in this country, some relatives in Germany who were anti–Nazi, and one sister who was pro–Nazi. FBI Agent Morgan writes, "The above information was obtained by the writer in general conversation with Mr. Slosson and Jon Rudall, clerk at the Homestead, without any direct inquiries. The conversation grew out of [German-Americans] born in the United States at the present time and their unquestioned loyalty in the United States, and most of the information was volunteered by Slosson."[21] He was able to keep his job.

One. The Hotels Are Selected

Guests Are Kicked Out

Winter was the slow season for both hotels, even around Christmastime. Often repair work and large redecorating projects were undertaken. The Homestead had a handful of guests, the Greenbrier the same. They were all sent away and all reservations through Easter cancelled, except for one.

J. Edgar Hoover writes to Attorney General Biddle in a memo dated January 7, 1942:

> The acting manager of the Greenbrier Hotel has advised that all guests have been turned away: however, the hotel management desires that an exception be made concerning an individual named Mary A. Murphy, RFD #2, Bangor, Maine. She is seventy-five years of age and has been coming to White Sulphur Springs for the past six years to take sulphur baths. This woman has a maid to look after her and usually stays [at] the Greenbrier Hotel during the winter seasons. She plans to stay at the hotel if permitted for approximately the next three months. She is a widow and, according to the management of this hotel, her reputation is spotless. My position is that no guests should be permitted at the hotel however, I will, of course, be guided by your desires as to whether Mrs. Murphy should be permitted to come to the hotel.[22]

In a handwritten response, the attorney general wrote back, refusing to make the decision, forcing it back upon his FBI Director. The Attorney General writes, "I think, as a matter of precedent, it is unwise to make exceptions to the rule; however, if on the understanding that no more be asked I should approve this one, only if you think it advisable."[23]

To which, in a handwritten reply, came the response, "I do not think it advisable,"[24] signed with a heavy-handed capital letter "H." Mrs. Murphy was not allowed to come to the hotel.

Two

The Round-Up

A total of 159 Germans, Italians, Hungarians, and Bulgarians left Washington on December 20, 1941, travelled by train to White Sulphur Springs, then walked approximately a quarter-mile to the hotel. They were escorted by sixteen members of the West Virginia State Highway Patrol. Little notice was given to them by the townspeople.

The Japanese diplomats spent an additional ten days at their embassy in Washington. On December 29, 1941, the entourage gathered in the large hall of the embassy, then pushed through a jeering crowd of onlookers and boarded a caravan of cars and buses. Gwen Terasaki, who was the American wife of a Japanese diplomat, wrote of her departure from Washington: "At Union Station, all was confusion, flash bulbs popping, and people staring and shouting."[1] Upon arriving at the Homestead, she wrote:

> I was taken aback to discover a huge crowd assembled to watch us come in.... I was curious and somewhat fearful to see how they would react. There was not a sound, only silent, unfriendly faces. It was a relief when Mr. Muri, of the State Department, informed me that there was a car waiting to take us to the hotel. The men were to walk to the hotel and I know that it must have been an anxious time for the FBI men who were responsible for getting them safely there. The safety of the Japanese was in their hand, and they well knew that if one Japanese official should be killed or injured some American interned in Tokyo would suffer for it.... We were assembled in the vast lobby to be assigned rooms and to try to fish out our luggage from the mountains of trunks, valises, suitcase[s] piled there.... I noticed the official table was placed just inside the main door. Here sat the FBI agents, immigration officials, State Department people and a Swiss representative to serve as a liaison between the two governments.[2]

The arrival of the Axis diplomats at the hotels was covered in local and syndicated news reports. Most articles are brief, as news about the new war dominated the headlines. There were no demonstrations in

Two. The Round-Up

White Sulphur Springs or Hot Springs. At the hotels, employees came to work, and vendors and contractors continued with their business. A few protest letters arrived at the Homestead:

> To the Japanese Ambassador. There was a time when nations declared war and then met their enemy in fair open battle. Then back-stabbing cowards thought up the idea of cutting down a peaceful people without warning and then declaring war after this happened.... But remember you back-stabbing, underhanded, smiling assassins, when we get through with you and yours, you will wish you had never copied the Hitler gangster. Not one single warship of yours will be left on the seas, every plane will be destroyed and for the lives you took at Hawaii we will take 100,000, alone for that outrage. Your Island will be reduced to ashes and you will become slaves to the Chinese. Remember this, you dirty, stinking, underhanded, double-crossing snake, and take this message back to your stupid emperor.[3]

Triangle T Guest Ranch

By mid–January 1942, virtually all of the Axis diplomats were at the two hotels, with the exception of the diplomats who had been assigned to the Japanese consulate in Honolulu. The consulate staff was arrested on the morning of December 7, 1941, initially by the local police, but soon the FBI took over. The staff was confined to the consulate for about ten days as the State Department mulled what to do with them. They were not allowed any communication of any kind. These actions were on the edge of violating the protections traditionally provided diplomats. Historian Jane Eppinga explains the government's actions: "J. Edgar Hoover protested that the Honolulu Japanese should be kept separate from other Japanese because of their involvement in subversive espionage activities and the Pearl Harbor bombing. He insisted that the place chosen for their detainment should be only where they could be watched and their activities closely monitored."[4] Hoover was not being vindictive. His agents had reported to him that the Japanese had been seen burning papers on the grounds of the consulate in the weeks prior to the attack. The Honolulu Japanese may have had knowledge about the attack or its planning which could be useful to the Japanese government. The Japanese at the Homestead had the ability to communicate with Tokyo via the Spanish representative powers.

Axis Diplomats in American Custody

The State Department began to look for an isolated location for the Honolulu diplomats. Personnel briefly considered the Lake Tahoe area then, for unknown reasons they fixated on lodging somewhere in the Phoenix or Tucson area. They put together a list of ten possible guest ranches and also reached out to a local postmaster, who was a friend of Special Agent Bannerman from the time early in Bannerman's career when he was a postal inspector. After a frantic search, the local State Department agent reported to Bannerman that he had contacted "all known owners of ranches equipped to handle thirty people.... The tourist season now at peak and majority ranches have permanent and regular guests and will not consider proposition in view of exclusion of other guest feature and indefinite period angle.... Would you consider dividing group between two places?"[5] In addition, the State Department was warned by the local postmaster that "most places near Phoenix or Tucson would not be considered isolated even though outside city. There would be neighboring ranches and houses within mile or two. Also it would be extremely hot during summer months.... If isolation and comfort desired I believe district North of Phoenix vicinity Wickenburg or Prescott only territory for consideration. In my opinion Tucson and Patagonia district too near Mexican Border."[6]

In the meantime, the Japanese left Honolulu aboard the USS *President Hayes*, traveling in first-class staterooms, arriving at San Diego on February 17, 1942. They went by bus to the train station, traveled to Los Angeles, changed trains, traveled through Tucson, and then the train made a stop at the small station at Dragoon, Arizona, a town of about forty inhabitants. They set out in thirty cars and two buses and rode into the desert for about a hundred miles, arriving at the Triangle T, a dude ranch run by Donald Huntingo and Marjori Murfree plus five servants, who were never officially told who their guests were.

These twenty-three diplomats, who, according to normal protocols, should have been allowed to contact their country's protective power, were held incommunicado:

> The removal from the ship and transfer to Los Angeles was effected without any publicity whatever and without anyone knowing the ultimate destination or purpose of this move. The railroad officials gave complete cooperation.... The Japanese Consular representatives know only that they are someplace in Arizona and

Two. The Round-Up

do not know the place where they are located.... No person concerned with this movement, such as railroad officials, porters and so forth, know where these Japanese originally came from as this is not known to anyone outside of the Immigration and Navy officials. Even the owner of the ranch does not know where these Japanese are from. To make certain that no information as to the fact that these people were from Honolulu should become known, all labels on the baggage of the Japanese indicating Honolulu or Hawaii were removed from their baggage.... They are, of course, denied the use of radios, newspapers, magazines and other such material that would give them any information as to what is going on or where they may be located. All signs and papers at the ranch were carefully gone over and removed that would in any way give the Japanese an inkling as to where they are located.[7]

A terse note was sent by the State Department via the Spanish in their role as the representative power to inform the Japanese government that the consulate staff from Honolulu was being held in an appropriate but secret location. The Japanese do not seem to have pursued the matter any further, and the Spanish never investigated the ranch. There was a brief mention in a local newspaper that Japanese had arrived at the ranch, but no connection seems to have been made to Honolulu, perhaps because the mass internment of ethnic Japanese was beginning along the West Coast.

The ranch was occasionally used as base of operations by Hollywood filmmakers who shot Westerns. It is located in a pass in the mountains and stretches out over 300 acres. It is isolated from public view and contact.

> On the ranch there is a main house containing a large recreation room, a central dining room and kitchen. The quarters for the Japanese are contained in four cottages, three of which have double rooms with connection baths which adequately cares for three families with children and servants. The fourth house contains five large rooms, of which two rooms have a connecting bath, and the other three rooms have private baths. The furnishings in these quarters are excellent and very comfortable. In each bathroom there is a stove for hot water and heating purposes. Each room has a large open fireplace and in each room there is an oil stove also for heating purposes.... There is a fifth building located near the main building containing quarters for Immigration Guards and the owner and his wife. To the rear of the main building are bunk houses containing quarters for the servants of the ranch....
>
> The meals served on the ranch are simple, but of excellent quality. There is no choice as to the meals as just a straight meal is served; however, efforts have been made to serve those foods that the Japanese party like....
>
> The immediate area surrounding the main house and the cottages contains about three acres in the form of a square and is surrounded by a barbed wire

fence, within which limits the Japanese are allowed to exercise. This ground area contains a tennis court, croquet court, ping pong table and a sun deck with chairs.[8]

The party consisted of the consul general and his wife, their sons ages seven and five, lesser officials, servants, gardeners, and wives and children, a total of 23 people. The ranch charged $1135 per week—$900 for the Japanese, $200 for the guards, and a $35 tip for the staff.

Additional Arrivals of Diplomats from Across the USA

At the Greenbrier, another 183 Axis official personnel were rounded up from across the country by the FBI and escorted by them to the Greenbrier. Within a few days, another 41 Japanese arrived at the Homestead. These diplomats were from various consulates from across the country plus individuals from press offices and universities. The FBI had been keeping lists of these people for years, and local FBI agents contacted the diplomats to let them know what the arrangements were. Either an FBI agent or a representative of the Naturalization and Immigration Service travelled with the group. According to most reports, the diplomats and families were given one or two days' notification to put their personal affairs in order. Baggage was generally forwarded to the train station, they would rendezvous at the consulate, and then the FBI or Immigration and Naturalization Service officers would escort the group by bus or a taxi caravan to the train station. There is no report of any members of the diplomatic legations going missing. A few families requested some extra time to settle their affairs, but these were usually denied, with the exception of several individuals who were hospitalized.

The FBI was very careful about the travel arrangements. A memo dated December 24, 1941, and titled "Instructions for Representatives of Former Hungarian Consulate New York, New York" provides details about the trip to the Greenbrier:

> 10:00 am December 29, 1941 All baggage should be ready and will be collected at this time.
> 1:45 PM December 30, 1941—All Hungarian representatives in New York

Two. The Round-Up

should be at the Consulate and ready to leave at that time for the Pennsylvania station, where a special train will be waiting for them. Buses will be provided to take them from the Consulate to the station. They will depart on the Pennsylvania Railroad at 3 PM for White Sulphur Springs, West Virginia.... The Hungarian representatives at New York will travel on this same special train with Japanese.... The Hungarian representatives at New York should be instructed to prepare immediately a baggage list of those places from which baggage is to be collected. This list will be called for by a Special Agent of the Secretary of State.[9]

Many of the diplomats and staff had family with them. One agent reports a horrendous choice facing one such family. Robert Minner was a German citizen who had worked for the German News Bureau, and as a credentialed foreign correspondent, he was automatically part of the exchange group. He was transported from New York to the Greenbrier. His wife was an American citizen, and they had two young children, both born in America. The wife and children were not part of the exchange unless they volunteered. The wife and children, on their own, went to White Sulphur Springs, to be with Mr. Minner at least until the time the exchange vessel would leave, which was still months away. However, she was told that if they entered the grounds of the hotel, they would not be allowed to leave and the four of them would be sent to Germany. She was surprised at this restriction and didn't know if she wanted to enter the Greenbrier under these circumstances. The FBI agent on the scene compromised, allowing her and the children to enter, but "gave her until December 29, 1941 to make up her mind whether to stay or not."[10] On December 29, 1941, she decided to leave her husband and go back to New York with the children.

In another family, the wife of the Hungarian consul general from New York, "is at the Greenbrier with her husband, and is going to return to Hungary with him. She is an American citizen. Their two sons [young boys] are presently in Chicago with relatives, and the plans are that the boys will stay in the United States."[11]

Another couple did not seem to be facing such difficult choices. An FBI agent reported on the arrival of Annemarie Stumbke, secretary to Kurt Sell, a German diplomat, "Upon her arrival early morning of January 27, 1942, they fondly embraced each other in the lobby of the hotel, and after Kurt Sell had kissed her on both cheeks, he then pressed his lips to her lips. They both appeared to be delighted over the reunion.

Since her arrival here, they have been inseparable.... From the above facts, it appears that there is more than a mere employer-employee relationship existing between the two."[12]

First Arrivals from South and Central America

A newsreel produced by the office of the Coordinator of Inter-American Affairs mentions some of the strategic materials sourced from South America—items that were in short supply due to the disruption of normal trade patterns and due to the heavy demand for war production. They include tin from Bolivia, copper from Chile, hemp (for rope) from Haiti, rubber from Brazil, quinine (for malaria treatment) from Honduras, nitrate from Chile (for explosives and fertilizer), and quartz crystals (for radios), mahogany, and balsa from Brazil. President Roosevelt was anxious to maintain access to these strategic materials. The vulnerability of the Panama Canal was another concern. A State Department official in Panama warned him, "I am seriously worried at the potential danger to the Canal inherent in the continued presence in Panama of the personnel of the German, Italian and Japanese legations.... Despite efforts of the Panamanian police to keep these people under surveillance they manage to elude the police and move about in the city and environs. They would be able in case of an air raid to guide planes by radio signals and flares."[13] President Roosevelt also wanted to avoid any possible staging area in, for example, Cuba. He also had an eye on Brazil, with the possibility of establishing air bases to potentially support airlift operations to North Africa.

The influence of Axis powers in Latin America varied by country. "[A]bout one million Brazilians were of German ancestry and about one-fifth of these in 1938 were German-born. Almost all were concentrated in the southern part of the country. There were over two thousand German social organizations in the country, and the Nazis controlled most of them."[14]

"[Axis interests] presented problems for Colombian policy. The most important of these was the German administration of the nation's major airline, many of whose pilots and technicians were German....

Two. The Round-Up

The United States perceived threats to her security in the aerial surveys of Colombia, including the approaches to the Canal that were taken by German personnel of the airline, and in its extensive radio network, which was also under German control."[15]

In June 1939, President Roosevelt issued a directive pertaining to who had jurisdiction over counter-espionage, sabotage, and other security issues. He divided responsibility between the FBI, the office of Naval Intelligence, and the Army Military Intelligence Division. "President Roosevelt's directive further defined the FBI's responsibilities to include investigating foreign agents and activities at U.S. posts overseas."[16] Or, as an another writer put it, "By 1940 the United States had become directly involved with security in Latin America. After the European war erupted in 1939, the government posted FBI agents in United States embassies in Latin America to compile information on Axis nationals and sympathizers."[17] The FBI agents posed as attaches and consulate members. Reportedly few spoke Spanish or German, let alone Japanese.

Through a series of treaties, agreements, and conferences, starting in the mid–1930s, the United States applied gentle and not-so-gentle pressure to the countries of Central and South America. They were reminded that the United States could be a giant trading partner given its voracious appetite for raw materials to feed its factories, which were churning out war materials. They were reminded that trade with Europe had essentially stopped. They were not offered U.S. troops—these would be needed for the active war zones—but promises were made for armaments to be sent, plus the protection of the U.S. Navy. Airfields needed for refueling stations would be built, especially in Northern Brazil. Generous terms were offered for lend-lease arrangements. Loans were made available.

In a memo dated May 4, 1942, Joseph Green of the State Department writes:

> For many years the Department of State has recognized the growing necessity for the elimination of improper Axis influence in the other American Republics....
> This Government negotiated informal agreements with the governments of all of the other American Republics except Argentina and Chile by which Axis officials, Axis political agents and other dangerous Axis nationals within their jurisdictions were to be repatriated and offered to include such persons in the reciprocal repatriation agreements being negotiated with the Axis Powers. The Governments of

Axis Diplomats in American Custody

> Brazil and Uruguay informed this Government that they adhered fully to the policy initiated by this Government but that they desired to negotiate separate repatriation agreements with the European members of the Axis. The Government of Paraguay joined with Brazil in these negotiations. All of the other American Republics concerned accepted the invitation of this government.[18]

When Pearl Harbor was attacked and the United States entered the war, certain South American and Central American countries immediately put Axis diplomats into custody and moved them to the United States as quickly as possible. For example, 44 Germans from Guatemala arrived in New York Harbor on the USS *Jamaica* on December 28, 1941. They were taken off the vessel by a Coast Guard cutter, taken by bus to the Baltimore and Ohio station at Jersey City, and went by special train to White Sulphur Springs, arriving at the Greenbrier on December 29, 1941.

On January 11, 1942, 17 Italians from Guatemala were moved to the Greenbrier, and, on the same day, from a separate boat, 11 Germans arrived from Costa Rica. Mexico sent four Germans via Laredo, Texas, to the Greenbrier. They arrived on January 16, 1942. On January 18, 1942, 20 Germans, 13 Italians, and three Japanese arrived in New Orleans from Panama. In the next few days more diplomats and families arrive from Haiti, Nicaragua, San Salvador, Cuba, and other countries. In this first wave of arrivals, 418 European Axis diplomats, staff, and families were sent to the Greenbrier. Sixty-seven Japanese were sent to the Homestead.

However, not all American republics cooperated with the United States. The countries of Brazil, Uruguay, and Paraguay pushed back. An article dated January 22, 1942, from the International News Service in Rio de Janeiro reads:

> Axis diplomats throughout the length and breadth of South America began packing their bags today in realization that by Monday at the latest they will be persona non grata in this hemisphere. Foreign ministers of 21 American nations represented at the inter-American conference were to meet at 4 pm to consider a resolution severing all relations with Germany, Italy and Japan. There appeared to be no doubt that it would be adopted unanimously.... The only South American capital where totalitarian representatives are likely to have ample time to say farewell is Buenos Aires. The agreement reached last night permits Argentina, if she wishes, to delay rupture of relations until her congress convenes in May. It is considered likely however that Acting President Ramon S. Castillo will break relations in March immediately after the presidential elections.[19]

Two. The Round-Up

By late January 1942, the exchange program seemed to be going well. There were twenty-three people at the Triangle T from the Japanese Honolulu consulate. The Homestead had approximately 290 Japanese from the Washington embassy and consulates in the United States as well as those kicked out of some of the American republics. The Greenbrier had 342 embassy and consulate people, mostly German, but also Hungarians, Bulgarians, and Italians. These also came from Washington and some American republics. All Axis power embassies and consulates in the United States had been shut down. The buildings were in the control of the protective powers. The huge Washington embassies had caretakers but other than that stood empty. The personal bank accounts of the diplomats were frozen, as were embassy funds. Personal possessions were placed into storage, or arrangements were made to sell them. A few families, those with American wives and children, had split up, but in most cases entire families now lived at one of the hotels. The detainees included not just the ambassadors and other high officials, but clerks, typists, governesses, chauffeurs, and servants as well as family members.

In South America, the United States backed off pressuring Brazil, Paraguay, and Uruguay to send their Japanese and European Axis diplomats to the United States. Instead, the United States agreed that these three countries could send them directly back to their homelands, that is, the three countries could arrange their own exchange programs. The United States was insistent, however, that all Axis diplomats be in fact expelled from these countries, and arrangements were made to verify their departure.

With the other American republics, the United States not only insisted that the Axis diplomats be expelled, it demanded that they transit through the United States. The United States envisioned an exchange wherein all the belligerent diplomats of all the countries in the Western Hemisphere except for Brazil, Uruguay, and Paraguay, would be exchanged as a group. Moreover, the United States strongly suggested to the countries of Central and South America that those Axis nationals who were identified as potentially dangerous also be sent on to the United States, where they could also be included in the negotiations with Germany, Italy, and Japan.

Regarding these civilians, the South American countries were offered

Axis Diplomats in American Custody

a unique arrangement. In a letter written by Joachim Marggraff, a member of the German legation to Colombia, the program was explained:

> When, after Colombia had broken off relations with Germany, the German Legation at Bogota prepared to return home via the United States of America, the Colombian Government informed the German colony that there was an opportunity for a limited number of persons to attach themselves to the party of the German minister. This possibility, namely, to return to Germany by effecting a transit through enemy country during a time of war, seemed to the writer to be so without precedence that he required further details from Mr. G. de Ojeda, Spanish Minister to Bogota, representative of German interests in Colombia.
>
> He informed the writer that the voyage had been guaranteed in a safe-conduct by the Government of the United States and Great Britain covering without doubt all particulars, i.e., non-official person attached to the party of the German Minister. The writer still not satisfied, however, requested that the Spanish Minister should call the American Ambassador for still further details. Mr. Spruille Braden confirmed that without any exception all persons traveling together with the German minister were covered by the safe-conduct. The writer as well as the whole group which intended to attach itself to the party of the German Legation now were fully convinced that they would reach their country without difficulty....
> [Later] Mr. Spruille Braden had confirmed again his assurance given in Bogota that our status had been recognized as semi-diplomatic as preferred for repatriation.[20]

The commitment by the United States that it would be simply a way-station as Axis personnel were removed from the South American countries on their way back to their homelands was emphasized in another memo:

> While the first group of Axis Nationals expelled from Guatemala and Costa Rica may not have been brought to this country under a specific understanding that they are to be repatriated, the German, Italian and Japanese Government has intimated that it considers as an indispensable condition of the exchange of German, Italian and Japanese nationals for the nationals of the United State and the other American Republics the early repatriation of all those German, Italian and Japanese nationals who have been brought here from across the other American Republics. We have, of course, retain[ed] the right to withhold from repatriation those few individuals whose return to Germany, Italy and Japan is found contrary to the national interest.... If we do not repatriate the Germans, Italians and Japanese received from Costa Rica, Guatemala and Panama who were not sent here specifically for repatriation, the Germans, Italians and Japanese will retaliate (1) against us by holding out of the exchange a corresponding number of United States nationals and (2) against Costa Rica, Guatemala and Panama by holding back as many Costa Rican, Guatemalan and Panamanian national[s] as possible. Therefore while the Department of State may not have been a party to the arrangements whereby all these persons reached this country, it has a specific interest in the disposition to be made of them.[21]

Two. The Round-Up

The other South American countries each agreed to the State Department's request to expel the Axis diplomats and legations. However, the details of the various agreements were not nailed down—or perhaps they were left purposely vague to facilitate the approval of the deal. Some South American countries, in particular Peru, began to interpret the agreements in ways that would create trouble for the State Department. Other South American countries, although nominally agreeing to the repatriation pact, faced enormous internal pressure to ignore or at least slow-walk the process as it related to Germans within their borders. A memorandum from the United States legation in Bolivia states:

> As reported in [a previous telegram] it is only during the past week that the Bolivian Government has evinced any interest in the repatriation of Axis non-officials and it has done little or nothing to effect that of the real undesirables. On March 25 the Minister of Government was unofficially given a list of 35 names prepared by the Legation, comprising the most dangerous enemy elements in the country. Later, in interviews with the President and the Ministers of Foreign Relations and Government, I stressed the importance of expelling such aliens, and was assured by Minister Anee Matienzo that this would be done, even to the extent of shipping out such highly influential persons as the Eleners and the Bauers. However, it is feared that heavy influence will be brought to bear by the more important Nazis and that only a few of the lesser propagandists may be expelled. If this point is brought up in a Cabinet meeting, as seems likely, the Minister of Foreign Relations will most probably be outvoted.[22]

Although the internal politics of each American republic differed, the proposals offered to them by the United States were consistent. A memorandum prepared by the State Department that lays out in some detail the terms of the exchange for the Peruvian government begins:

> The American government has given assurances to the Protecting Power regarding the repatriation of Axis officials and nationals. This guaranty covers persons and effects and assures that they will not examined or detained by American or British authorities but will be transposed immediately on the exchange vessels from New York to Lisbon, and in the case of Japanese to Lourenco Marques.... Persons embarking on the S.S. Acadia or Etolin [ships sent by the State Department to South America] will proceed directly across the United States to New York without detention.... Non-official Axis nationals will be embarked at New York on the official exchange vessel.... Safe conducts issued by the Ecuadoran Foreign Office to Axis officials and nationals will be fully honored by the American and British Governments.[23]

Axis Diplomats in American Custody

Up until now, the exchange program had been about credentialed officials and their staff and families. This memo reflects a new direction that the State Department adopted. Now any German, Italian, or Japanese citizen residing in a Latin American country could be included in the exchange program. The United States had its sights on Axis nationals involved in espionage, subversion, or contraband. It broadened the exchange program in expectation of removing these people from the hemisphere. However, some South American countries would exploit this expansion for their own purposes.

Three

Daily Routine

At the Homestead, the State Department issued guidelines for the Japanese. They were to have use of the East Wing of the hotel, including the North Porch and part of the North Main Lobby and the Italian Gardens and stores in the Main Building. Part of the outside grounds would be available for recreation at designated times. Communication with any outside person, or any visitors, was forbidden. A representative of Spain would be given a room at the hotel. He would be allowed to speak with any of the Japanese at any time without supervision. No transmitting sets or short wave receiving sets were permitted. Uncensored mail was allowed between the Spanish embassy and the former Japanese ambassador. The Spanish embassy would have unrestricted telephone communication with the former Japanese ambassador. No other persons were allowed to make or receive phone calls. A daily head count would be made if deemed necessary. Similar guidelines were issued at the Greenbrier.

Security

Roy Sibold at the Greenbrier writes:

> Arrangements for the care of guarding were complicated to the extreme. The personnel of the hotel were investigated and each and every one given a pass card or identification card to show who they were and were also fingerprinted; in fact, everything about them appearing on the card, permitted them to go or come in the course of their duties. Little guard houses were constructed by our Engineering Department and placed all around the building and at all entrances. At all times a guard was on duty in these guard houses. Lights were erected about the grounds which stayed on all night. There were approximately eighty-eight guards in all, some thirty-eight of which were made up by local enlistment. Only two

entrances to the property could be used—the front gate and employees' entrance or watch-box.[1]

At the Homestead, Mr. Ingalls reports a similar arrangement:

Three members of the FBI were continuously at the Homestead during the whole time the Japanese were here. They were on twenty-four hour duty with one man always at the telephone. It was their task to see that no communication of any sort was held by these Japanese with anyone without the bounds of their place of isolation. They censored all mail and put in elaborate precautions to prevent the use of other means of communication such as conventional telephone or the use of radio of any sort or manner whatsoever.[2]

At the Greenbrier:

The FBI, in addition to their many other duties, censored all mail going and coming including telegrams or anything in the form of a communication. Anyone attempting to come inside the property was investigated and unless on urgent business—other than with the internees—were not allowed.... For the period of time in which the internees were here they had marked off and guarded a specific area where they could go walking each day between certain appointed hours. This area, of course, was on the property immediately surrounding the building. They were finally granted permission to use the tennis courts and they made very good use of them [because] golf, horseback riding and other recreational features were prohibited.[3]

There were three FBI agents at each hotel, and they soon settled into a daily routine. One describes his typical day:

The writer alternates with [another Special Agent] on day and night duty ... [and they] shift from day to night duty each week. The duties performed by the writer, and the approximate amount of time devoted to each duty per average day are as follows;

Ten hours per day are devoted to the maintenance of technical surveillance being conducted on the activities of certain internees. The Bureau has instructed that this surveillance be maintained twenty-four hours per day. The writer is on duty twelve hours per day, less two hours for meals.

During hours when there is a minimum of activity the writer performs the following other functions:

One hour daily reviewing second class mail, newspapers, magazines, etc. and sorting same. These items have been passed by censor, but contain many possible sources of information of an intelligence nature. Two hours daily transcribing recordings in English and preparing special memorandums re: information obtained from the strictly confidential sources of information. Two hours daily assisting in the clerical detail, examining and listing internees outgoing mail and preparing memorandum on same.

One-half hour daily examining packages [express and freight] delivered to the hotel and consigned to various internees in order to know their content and clear

Three. Daily Routine

only such items as do not affect the security of the mission. One half-hour daily wrapping and mailing packages for transmittal to Bureau.

During hours outside of the period when the writer is maintaining the technical surveillances and at other times when relieved by [another Special Agent] the writer performs the following functions: Two hours daily maintaining contacts in the Village of White Sulphur Springs which contacts are valuable in carrying out the mission successfully. One hour daily maintaining contacts with certain of the internees for the purpose of developing them either with or without their knowledge into informants.

Three hours daily maintain contacts with employees of the hotel and of the medical and bath departments for the purpose of developing informant[s] and obtaining such information from these employees as they may gather during their regular duties. It is noted that the personnel of the bath departments come into very close contact with most of the more important of the internees inasmuch as they are the ones who are able to afford the medical bath treatments which are too expensive for the people who hold the lower paid positions.

One hour daily performing investigative work in connection with the mission. Such investigative tasks are assigned to the writer by [another Special Agent] and consists chiefly of necessary investigations, which because of pressure of other matter, it would be impossible for him to attend to promptly.

Two hours daily performing the general duties of the mission on those occasions when the best interest of the mission necessitates [other Special Agents] being in confidential conference or temporarily absent from the hotel proper.[4]

The informants the FBI turned were not just the internees. During the first few hectic days of arrival, an employee at the Greenbrier mistakenly mailed letters for a German. An FBI agent threatened him with loss of his job and perhaps worse. The agent writes:

> He [the desk clerk] lost his wife one month ago and he has a child three years old.... He agreed to be on the alert and furnish the Writer with any information which would be of interest to this detail here as it related to the conduct of the waiters and waitresses in the dining room. I pointed out during the course of my interview the gravity of such a situation and [the individual] stated that he would upon his oath promise never to do such an act again and would do everything possible to offset his incident by furnishing the Writer with data as to the activities of dining room attendants. [The individual] is a captain in the dining room.[5]

Another informant had his own motives for cooperation. Piero Saporiti was a correspondent for an Italian newspaper who had been based in Washington. He initiated contact with FBI agent Lawler and volunteered to be an informant. Saporiti suggested he knew of Nazi agents in New York and also that he was willing to pass on information about his fellow detainees at the Greenbrier. He also "advised

Axis Diplomats in American Custody

the writer [Lawler] that he had ninety-five chances out of one hundred to be placed in Lisbon as a foreign correspondent for his Italian Newspaper [after the exchange of diplomats]. He stated he would be in constant contact with Axis officials, diplomats and newspaper men in Lisbon and that he would be glad to make a report concerning any information that may develop that would be of interest to this government."[6]

Saporiti told Lawler of his motivation for helping the FBI.

> He advised that he would be open and frank and lay all of the facts in the case open to me. He related that about five years ago he had met Mrs. Jocklyn Busch Gonzales in Ethiopia. At that time he was in charge of the Italian News Agency in Africa and that Catalono Gonzales, the husband of this woman, was the "number one fascist" in Africa and was in charge of Italian propaganda in Africa. About three years ago, because of domestic difficulties, Mrs. Gonzales returned to the United States leaving her husband and child in Africa. In order to join Mrs. Gonzales he gave up his position and obtained a foreign correspondent job for an Italian newspaper in New York. In the meantime, Mr. Gonzales was recalled to Rome and is now in charge of all Italian colonial possessions and is characterized as a "big fascist." He stated that Mrs. Gonzales is an American girl from 12 Charles Street, Boston Massachusetts. He related that she has arranged to be exchanged under the condition that she wants to join her husband and child in Rome, but in fact she wants to be near Saporiti. He plans to remain in Lisbon and to have her do likewise. He wants her to come to the Greenbrier Hotel and be married by a Justice of the Peace as she is obtaining a divorce on March 9, 1942 in New York City. Her name has been placed on the exchange list. Saporiti state[d] that as soon as the war is over he plans to return to [t]his country as his marriage in Italy would not be valid. However, Mrs. Gonzales is going to endeavor to have her present marriage annulled. He state[d] that he would like to be helpful to the American people in so far as it was not harmful to his country as he wished to some day make a new life in this country and he asked to act as a confidential informant for the F.B.I. I told Saporiti we could make no promise to him but that we would accept any information he had to offer.[7]

At the Homestead, a schism was immediately apparent within the Japanese contingent. Gwen Terasaki, reminiscing about her time at the Homestead, relates:

> The officers in our group, immediately feeling the dominance of the military at the outbreak of war, took it upon themselves to give orders to the diplomats. Perhaps they had nurtured a jealousy through the long period of subordination to the civilian officials whose advisers they were.... They set up a schedule for calisthenics in the mornings for everyone and posted it in the lobby and the dining room. [My husband] announced publicly [he] would have nothing to do with it,

Three. Daily Routine

nor his family.... One morning, while taking a stroll, we passed the calisthenics grounds where the motley group of men, women and children were responding in awkward fashion to the curt directions of a lieutenant. One of the officers ordered us into line, to do deep knee bends with the rest. [My husband] told him the idea was absurd. [The officer] came up to [my husband] to lecture him and to my shocked surprise my husband slapped him in the face. The astonished man turned to the group and asked if they were going to let Terasaki-san do that to him. He got no reply [and] thereafter, the number of people showing up for calisthenics dropped off sharply.[8]

Mr. Terasaki was initially designated by the Japanese to be their representative to the Spanish in matters regarding the hotel. However, he soon met with Mr. Morgan of the FBI and told him of his "resignation." Terasaki explained that "the other first secretaries for the Japanese Embassy were jealous of the fact that he was acting as liaison officer for Ambassador Nomur and that for the good of all concerned that he had tendered his resignation. He indicated to [Mr. Morgan] that there was no other reason for his resignation than the feeling the others had against him which was one of pure jealousy."[9]

Terasaki was replaced by Sadao Iguchi, Counselor of the Japanese Embassy. He was "of the opinion that the Japanese here are enjoying too many luxuries, especially the servant class and suggested, for instance, that the servants be removed to a separate dining room, that the menu be made simpler, and that the afternoon musical concert be removed from the main lobby to another part of the hotel."[10]

Although Mr. Terasaki was never an informer to the extent of Saporiti at the Greenbrier, he met occasionally with Mr. Morgan to discuss the general state of affairs within the hotel. This information was not of a particularly secretive or salacious nature. Mr. Morgan describes one individual, Kyusuke Hoshide, as a confidential informant, but he did not provide any inside information.

The agents of the State Department and the members of the Border Patrol had day-to-day responsibility for guard duties. An FBI agent, hearing from a housekeeper that a bed sheet had gone missing from a room, quickly informed the Immigration Service. "The incident has been reported to C.C. Courtney, who is in charge of the Immigration and Naturalization Service Detail at the Greenbrier as it is believed any logical purpose on [the Germans'] part in taking such bedsheet insofar as the situation involves safety and security of internees would probably

Axis Diplomats in American Custody

be one of interest to his service which is charged with the responsibility of guarding those interned here."[11]

The Immigration Service personnel spent much of their time dealing with complaints. In one meeting, a Hungarian diplomat at the Greenbrier took issue that they were not let out during a rainstorm, newspapers were not delivered on time, books that had been ordered had not arrived. He was not satisfied with types of books allowed for the children, he did not want to sit around all the time and play cards, he wanted a bigger outside area to walk. He complained that representatives of the FBI told him one thing and the State Department said something else, he complained that he had no money, that he did not know when he was leaving, and finally complained that an American citizen was refused permission to make a personal visit to one of the Hungarian diplomatic detainees.

Although the security routine seemed overblow, it was effective. In May 1942, a newsstand worker at the Greenbrier became suspicious when a waiter, who had gone to a back part of the newsstand that was prohibited to the Germans, purchased two copies of a magazine called *The Mercury*. She reported her concerns to an FBI agent, who confronted the waiter, Alfred Rudolf Nerz. He confessed to passing one of the magazines to a German. Eventually, J. Edgar Hoover himself wrote a letter to Mr. Morgan, the FBI agent in charge, which says in part,

> It is desired that this information be brought to the attention of [the manager of the hotel] with the request that he take appropriate action to fully insure that Nerz will have no further opportunity to transmit messages or articles to the internees at the Greenbrier Hotel in violation of the rules.... This matter should be handled immediately and the Bureau fully informed of any development.... For your further information, the facts in this matter have been brought to the attention of the Attorney General with the suggestion that denaturalization proceedings be instituted concerning Nerz. The facts in this case have also been brought to the attention of the Department of State and Immigration and Naturalization Service. Signed.... J. Edgar Hoover.[12]

This incident demonstrates that government officials at the highest level were heavily involved not only with planning and policy issues, but also with monitoring day-to-day activity at the hotels closely. In addition, the incident highlights the government's firmness about rules and procedures. There were no warning or verbal reprimands. Mr. Nerz broke a rule and was fired.

Three. Daily Routine

There were approximately 60 guards at the Homestead and about 80 at the Greenbrier. The guards were members of the U.S. Border Patrol, which reported to the Immigration and Naturalization Service of the State Department. The FBI did not provide guard service. J. Edgar Hoover was adamant about this, saying that his men were stationed at the hotel only to make sure that the diplomats did not communicate with the outside world. Many of the Border Patrol agents had been pulled from assignments at border crossings with Canada.

Mr. Ingalls writes:

> The guard system extended beyond the confines of The Homestead and our grounds. At all times there were Department of Justice cars parked in front of The Homestead and from time to time these cars were used to cruise within a radius of a number of miles from The Homestead. No car could be stopped on the road within a considerable distance of Hot Springs for more than a short period before one of the Department of Justice cars would pull up and investigate the occupants. Even the walking paths about The Homestead were patrolled from time to time and persons on them were apt to be called upon to show their credentials, even when over a mile from The Homestead.[13]

The Border Patrol provided guard service twenty-four hours a day, seven days a week. Technically, within the Border Patrol there were Patrol Inspectors and guards. In addition, a few locals were hired to augment the security force. At both the Homestead and Greenbrier, a series of sheds were erected, as the temperature was dipping to below zero.

At the Triangle T, three Border Patrolmen split shifts, two on, one off, keeping guard twenty-four hours a day, seven days a week. Roland A. Fleagle was one of the guards. In a memoir, his wife writes, "Roland didn't get home for Easter that time because he was coloring Easter Eggs for the Japanese children out there. The Negro cook they had at the time got after Roland because he was hiding the Easter Eggs in the cactus and she scolded him for that. And he said, 'Oh its good for them, will give them something to do.'"[14]

The Press

At times the press seemed to sensationalize the internees. At other times it seemed that the press was too compliant with the FBI and the

Axis Diplomats in American Custody

State Department. A "Memorandum for the Director" dated January 6, 1942, from Hot Springs, Virginia, relates a story about a fistfight involving an off-duty Border Patrol agent and a local who worked as a vegetable cook at the hotel. The agent may have pulled out a blackjack, and the local ended up in the hospital, suffering from a concussion. R.L. Morgan, the FBI Special Agent in Charge, writes that no statements or documents regarding the fault or responsibility for this altercation would be generated by the FBI. He goes on, "In view of the fact that this matter might receive publicity and that [the Border Patrol agent] be mistaken for a Bureau agent, [the manager of the Homestead] was contacted and he advised that the only newspaper in the county is a weekly which is partially owned by the Homestead. He stated that inasmuch as the incident might give the hotel unfavorable publicity, he intended to see that the paper carry no account of it."[15]

The *White Sulphur Springs Sentinel* very early on wrote:

> In connection with the alleged movements of [diplomats] from one location to another, the Sentinel wishes to continue its policy of complete cooperation with the federal government and the Greenbrier hotel management as regards its war efforts. The federal authorities do not desire publicity pertaining to [such movements and until] they see fit to release this information we see no useful purpose that can be served and great harm may result from any premature disclosure of such information.... Therefore in the interest of national defense this paper will not publish any data that is not in accord with government wishes.[16]

Other newspapers sensationalized the diplomats. A syndicated *Times Herald* article reports about a time "when a foursome veered off into the woods after the eighteenth hole and the time the horseback rider just couldn't seem to keep his horse on the bridle path."[17] The only problem was that at the time, the diplomats were not allowed use of the golf course and were never allowed use of the stables. A *News Syndicate* article about the Greenbrier describes how the Germans were going to the local cobbler to hoard leather soles for shoes, to the grocer to buy up flour, cornmeal, and canned goods, and that the luggage storerooms of the hotel were filled with crates and boxes of goods the guests hope to take along when they left. The article describes how the hotel shops "are doing a land-office business. Soap, cosmetics, drugs, suits, dresses and frocks, coats, furs, shoes and goodness knows what else are being packed into newly bought luggage in the hope that customs agents won't forget the courtesy usually afforded diplomats.

Three. Daily Routine

The Germans have stocked up heavily on silk and nylon stockings but the Japanese apparently feel there's no use carrying coals to Newcastle."[18] None of this was possible. The only stores available were in the hotel's concourse, were controlled by the hotels, and were under the watchful eyes of the Border Patrol and FBI.

Medical

Whether in the desert of Arizona or the luxurious hotels of the East, the State Department demonstrated extreme vigilance over the health of the internees. A memorandum issued by the State Department states, "Under Article 14 of the Prisoner of War Convention of July 27, 1929, which we have agreed to apply to civilian internees, the detaining power is obligated to provide free medical attention and hospital care for the persons in its custody."[19] A note attached to this memo reads "It seems to me this should be done even though the Japs are not doing it for our people."[20]

An FBI daily reports state that Ursula Martin was a youngster confined at the C&O Hospital who was critically ill and not expected to live. A subsequent memo from the Border Patrol, however, provides good news. "It is recalled that Ursula Martin is the three (3) year old child presently at the C&O Hospital at Clifton Forge, Virginia and this child has been critically ill from a spinal trouble. According to Dr. Sennhenn and Dr. Caldwell the child is progressing nicely and if the present progress continues the child may within a few days be completely recovered from the critical stage. Both Dr. Sennhenn and Dr. Caldwell advised the Writer that the critical condition of the child was due to the taking of the spinal fluid for the purpose of a laboratory examination."[21]

In Arizona, Hana Kusanoba was rushed to the Tucson Hospital, where an emergency appendectomy was performed. The doctors and nurses were sworn to secrecy as Border Patrol agents stood vigil outside her room. Other memoranda deal with routine doctor visits and dentist visits. One incident involved Mr. George Linzboth, who "was transferred to a local institution. It seems that his dipsomaniacal proclivities have caused a recurrence of a stomach condition which necessitates

Axis Diplomats in American Custody

hospitalization. They are considering the Appalachian Hall, an institution for alcoholics."[22]

Food

While at the Greenbrier and the Homestead, the detainees enjoyed some of the best and most lavish meals available in America. The hotels, with the State Department's encouragement, seemed to put on a display of American opulence and excess. Perhaps this was a propaganda ploy. Perhaps it was to encourage reciprocity. However, in February, a disturbing report came from the American diplomats held in Germany. Leland Morris, the Chargé d'Affaires, reports:

> ... unsatisfactory conditions relative to our detention.... In general, purchases of food for this hotel have been based during the period of our detention here on an allotment amounting to one and a half times the normal German civilian ration. This allotment is insufficient.... Formally meat is served at nine meals per week, although as will be seen below quantities are quite inadequate. The other five main meals are meatless and on 2 days a week no meat at all is served.... No fresh eggs have ever been served.... On meatless days, poor quality fish was served.... The Food in general consists of soups mostly of a flour or thin meat stock.... Sweets are provided in the form of puddings of indifferent composition, some of which have a rice basis and others of which appeared to be of synthetic composition.... Since the middle of January the portions served are totally inadequate, consisting always of one very thin slice of meat and second helping[s] are not serve[d]. Twice a week the meal specified one of the so-called Feldkuchengericht, or soldier's field ratio[n]. This is a single dish usually composed of potatoes and cabbage with small piece of meat on top. This, together with the bread, is the whole meal. This civilian Feldkuchengericht is admittedly smaller in calorie content than that served to the troops and civilians are asked to restrict themselves to it as a patriotic duty.... This ration has resulted in a marked reduction in weight, diminution of energy and deterioration of well-being throughout the group.[23]

A dinner menu from the time at the Homestead includes Cream of Lettuce Soup or Fresh Tomato Broth, followed by Filet of Sole, Fried in Butter, or Half Broiled Chicken on Toast, with Green Peas in Butter or Fondant Potato. Similar meals are served at the Greenbrier. An often-told story is that the State Department sent the Swiss an actual menu from the Greenbrier, which was passed on to the Germans, and that within a few weeks, the food situation at Bad Nauheim improved,

Three. Daily Routine

although it was never close to that available at the Greenbrier or Homestead.

A Lot of Reading

From Mr. Sibold's personal notes about the Greenbrier:

> They did a lot [of] reading. Of course the only newspaper available to them was the New York Times. They played Chess, Backgammon, Checkers, Ping Pong, spend a lot of time in the Haberdasher store, the Drug Store buying articles of various kinds. Finally they were given permission to order by mail, COD which was to go through the Travel Bureau—from there to the private office and finally checked by the FBI and went out. When the packages arrived they were checked again and a notice was sent to the individual who went to the Post Office, paid for the good and received the parcel.[24]

The news stand, haberdasher, drug store and post office are all in the concourse area of the hotel.

At the Homestead, Mr. Ingalls describes a similar situation.

> The Japanese played cards, chess, Chinese checkers, backgammon, ping-pong and read. They were allowed to select only one newspaper which they might have and chose the New York Times. They were not allowed to buy current magazines or novels.... They spent largely, purchasing toilet articles from our drug store and from the various shops in The Homestead, particularly wearing apparel and such articles as watches, clocks and the like from the jewelry store.[25]

At the Triangle T, life settled down quickly to a routine. Border Patrol agents had enclosed about three acres in the center of the three-hundred-acre ranch with a barbed-wire fence. "Within these limits, the Japanese could exercise, play tennis, croquet or Ping Pong or relax in deck chairs.... All entrances to the ranch were blocked off except for one gate where an Immigration service guard was posted.... The only telephone was in the manager's office."[26] In a memo, one of the Border Patrol agents writes, "The members have been assiduously trapping for the past two months. To date the bag has been one bird which eventually languished and died. Further efforts along these lines will be discouraged."[27]

Peter Riedel, the glider ace, began to study Russian, stating that he figured that Germany would defeat them and Germany would rule the country or vice versa, and either way he would be better off knowing the language. Others requested books with titles like *America's 60 Families*, *Democracy in American Life*, *Pardon My Harvard Accent*, and *Spirit of American Democracy*. The requests were denied. It is hard to imagine how these diplomats, people who had big jobs, and were accustomed to dealing with important issues, could adjust to their confinement. They, of course, knew the war was raging, yet even the *New York Times* editions they received were heavily redacted. Radios were not allowed. The staff of the hotel were instructed not to speak to them about the outside world.

Those detained were not all high-level people. There were maids, servants, and drivers who had composed the staffs of the closed embassies and consulates. Turukiti Handa was a cook with the Japanese group arriving from Columbia and stayed at both the Homestead and Greenbrier. How, one wonders, did she spend her days?

Hitler's Birthday

A newspaper, in one of their sensational but made-up articles, reports on the Germans celebrating Hitler's birthday: "It was a hilarious party, replete with cases of whiskey, barrels of beer and what one waiter described as 'a Hell of a hail of heils'. The next day the dining room looked as though it had been through the Battle of Flanders. Swastikas were scrawled on the walls, the tablecloths, and even on the cushions of valuable petit-point chairs. Furniture was smashed and broken glass was everywhere. No offer was made to pay for the damage."[28] No FBI report substantiates this event.

Von Stempel's Birthday Party

An FBI agent reports:

> On March 9, confidential informant GB1 advised the Writer that on the evening of March 8, 1942, he had been invited to the birthday party of VON STEMPEL. The informant related that this is the first German party that he has attended in the evenings. He state[d] that it was the most sexually promiscuous party he had ever been to. He stated that the woman came slightly dressed and that all of the individuals sat on the floor and drank very heavily and that there was a continual switching and swapping of wives and a promiscuous handling of the private parts

Three. Daily Routine

of the bodies of many of the outstanding diplomat's wives here. He stated that it was one of the most unsightly parties of a diplomatic gathering that he had ever attended in his life.

He related that Hans Wolfram had played with various intimate parts of Mrs. Hans Thomsen's body and after embracing on several occasions left the room to visit in Hans Wolfram's room for over half an hour. The informant stated that he did not know what occurred but he did not believe that they went there for him to wash his hands. He stated that [Mrs.] Thomsen came into the party in a carriage, with her legs wide open and the private parts of her body could easily be seen. He stated that this was an unsightly scene for the Number One lady of the German group here to display.... The informant related that while the Germans are very correct and very strait-lace[d] on the outside, that after they have had a few drinks, they are sexually the most promiscuous individuals that he has ever come in contact with. He stated that many reports prevailed as to the sexual promiscuity going on among the Germans here at the Hotel at the present time. In this connection Mr. Halfel told the barber here that he was hopeful that his wife would not rejoin him soon as he could sleep with a different woman each night. It is recalled that Mrs. Halfel was gone for a tonsillectomy. The Maids complain that it is necessary to change the bed linens on most of the beds daily because of the resultant efforts of sexual intercourse.[29]

Domestic Difficulties

A FBI activity report reads:

On March 17, 1942, Confidential Informant GB1 advised the Writer that on the evening of March 16, 1942, Mr. Sievernich had informed his wife that he would be unable to attend the motion picture show that evening as he was going to engage in a poker game in Mr. Rea's room When Mrs. Sievernich left her husband, she proceeded through the lobby and there observed Mr. Rea. She asked Mr. Rea if he was not going to play poker with her husband that evening where upon Mr. Rea explained his unawareness of such a poker game. Mrs. Sievernich suspected illicit relations existing between her husband and on[e of] the German Embassy's secretaries here, so she proceeded to the secretary's room. Upon hearing sounds of love affairs and conversations going on in the room of this young woman, she knocked upon the door and the young lady answered the door in the nude.[30]

Four

Musical Chairs

Although the Japanese, Germans, and Italians were allies, they did not get along well. As early as January 12, 1942, in a State Department memorandum of a conversation with a member of the Swiss legation, Assistant Secretary of State Long notes that one of the Swiss confided in him:

> that the Italians do not desire to be assembled at the Greenbrier [and that] if they were to be confined at some place that he [Prince Colonna] hoped they would be confined in a place other than the place where the Germans were confined, and that a hotel other than at White Sulphur Springs would be selected.... As to the question of other hotels, I explained to the Minister that there were practically no hotels available, that all the hotels [in] the southern part of the United States were now enjoying their winter season, and that all the guests would have to be put out of the hotel to make places for those to be confined, because they could not have visitors and casual contacts with those confined. As regards the hotels in the north, there seemed to be none available. The administrative problem was largely aided by having all of the diplomats in the general neighborhood, some at Hot Springs and some at White Sulphur Springs, that all that remained was the hotel at White Sulphur Springs. And I assured him that we would give them decent and comfortable treatment and that we would secure some assembly room other than that used by the Germans and would try to arrange for their exercise in a part of the park different from that used by the Germans.[1]

An FBI agents reports that "as a matter of fact, [the Italian representative] hates the Germans with all his well being. He pointed out that in the beginning the Germans and Italians were very clannish and frequented each other's parties but in the recent past it has been noted that neither the Germans or the Italians visit one another, each have their own locations in the hotel and the only parties that they frequent together are the official ones for the obvious purposes."[2]

Four. Musical Chairs

The Management of the Homestead Is Unhappy

By February 1942, the State Department was facing several problems. In addition to the squabbling between the Italians and the Germans at the Greenbrier, the number of people anticipated to be sent from South America far exceeded anyone's expectations. Moreover, negotiations for the actual exchange were dragging, both for the European exchange and the Japanese exchange. The delay had cost them a large vessel, the MS *Kungsholm*, capable of carrying over 1,500 passengers, which the State Department had in mind for the exchange ship, but its owners instead chartered it to the War Shipping Administration for use as a troop transport. Besides losing the ship, the delay meant that the original detainees had not embarked for Europe or the Orient, and consequently, their rooms were not available for the arriving Latin American detainees.

But the most immediate concern of the State Department was with the Homestead. The management of the hotel was very unhappy:

> Immediately upon the arrival of the Japanese it became obvious to the management that while we could profitably take this business during the quiet winter months, with the only loss the interruption of our long history of continuous operation and a certain amount of ill-will from those who did not understand the situation and felt we were favoring enemy aliens, it would be ruinous to the Homestead if our spring season, the time of year when we must make money to carry us over the dull period, was to be lost. Hence the Japanese had hardly arrived at the Homestead before we began active measures to secure their removal from the Homestead.... No contract had been arranged with the Homestead when the Japanese arrived. When the first party came, accompanied by a representative of the Protocol Division, immediately a contract was negotiated under which the subsequent business arrangements were carried out. This contract provided that it was only to extend until March fifteenth.... Our contract, further, provided that when the number of Japanese (which we had been led to expect in the beginning would reach 400) passed 250 the rates would be reduced by 10 percent. On January twenty-fourth this figure was passed by one and our compensation decreased, but not until February twenty-second do we receive the materially increased number which the original contract contemplated.[3]

In fact, the first guest did not arrive until December 28, 1941, and as such, the hotel made no money for six days, when they'd been expecting revenues of over $20,000. In addition, the first arrivals totaled only 55 people, not the 400 promised. The 400-guest complement was never reached. The high attendance was around 350. Finally, the stay began to lengthen. Although at first this seems like a positive for the hotel, the reality was that the rate was extremely low compared to the normal seasonal rate, which began around Easter. The Homestead may have entered into the agreement for patriotic reasons, or it may not have really been given a choice by the State Department, but as spring approached, it tried to renegotiate the contract. Management asked for a higher rate to reflect the lower head count and a definite date when the Japanese would leave. The State Department ignored both requests.

The hotel industry in the spring of 1942 faced issues of gasoline rationing, food rationing, and labor shortages, as well as curtailment of leisure time activities due to the war mobilization. Nevertheless, as the high season approached, the Homestead management was distressed that it was unable to inform potential guests—either families or businesses who were planning conferences and meetings—exactly when the Japanese would be leaving. With Easter, a traditionally huge weekend at the hotel, coming early that year, the Homestead began to reach out to other hotels to see if they would be interested in taking the diplomats.

The Homestead was also reaching out for help from high places. General Manager Ingalls expressed the following:

> Getting rid of the Japs had its dramatic moments. The highlight came when I went to a prominent member of Congress and asked him to put pressure on the State Department to move them elsewhere. We had a good case, as there had been verbal assurance that the hotel would be released to us by spring, and we had alternative places of residence to suggest, but things moved slowly. While I was in my friend's office he called the State Department and got an Assistant Secretary on the phone. Of course I only heard one end of the conversation but watched the Congressman getting more and more testy as the talk went on, and then heard his final shot. "I don't give a damn what you do about Heaven and Earth. What I want is for you to move those Japs."[4]

A Search for More Rooms

A memo dated February 10, 1942, from Special Agent Bannerman describes his efforts to locate a hotel to replace the Homestead. He

Four. Musical Chairs

writes, "A rather thorough survey of hotel accommodations suitable to house the Japanese party has been made of the entire Eastern section of the country from Maine to Florida."[5] Bannerman specifically discusses the merits and drawbacks of sixteen hotels, noting their ability to house a group numbering close to 600, the standard of comfort, size of grounds, the ability to ensure security, and the proximity to defense works. These hotels include The Mount Washington Hotel at Bretton Woods, New Hampshire, The Saranac Inn at Saranac Lake, New York, the Miami Biltmore Hotel in Coral Gables, Florida, The Breakers Hotel in Palm Beach, Florida, and The United States Hotel in Saratoga Springs, New York. He concludes, "The most suitable hotel located appears to be the Bon Air Hotel at Augusta, GA."[6]

Later that same day, Mr. Bannerman reports on a phone call he had with Mr. Brandon of the Bon Air Hotel. Mr. Brandon indicates a willingness to discuss the lease of the hotel, they need only three days notice to be ready, and the hotel is available for the State Department's exclusive use. He states that the rate would be between seven and ten dollars per adult per day, but Mr. Bannerman notes that it is possible that a lower rate could be negotiated. He says that the hotel has 400 rooms, which can accommodate 600 people, that two dormitories are located on the grounds that could accommodate the guards, that the main dining room can seat 750, and that there are large public rooms which could function as game rooms, meeting rooms or be converted at night to a theater. The grounds exceed 11 acres.[7]

The management of the Homestead contacted another hotel, the Lake Placid Club, about the situation, and they phoned Mr. Bannerman. Located in upstate New York, the hotel consisted of a main building with 278 rooms, which could accommodate close to 600 people, plus forty cottages, which could house from three to thirty people each. Bannerman relates that the manager of the Lake Placid Club talked about the large areas inside the main building: "This is mentioned because at the present time the temperature is 2 degrees below zero."[8] The manager accepts that "the Department would want a rate lower than that which we are now paying to the Homestead, and ... a figure of around $7.50 per person, American plan, would probably be acceptable."[9]

In the next few weeks the State Department seems to have made up its mind that the Japanese will be moved from the Homestead and

Axis Diplomats in American Custody

that they will go to the Bon Air. A memo dated March 3, 1942, from Bannerman has the subject title "Movement of Japanese from Homestead Hotel, Hot Springs, Virginia to the Bon Air Hotel, Augusta, Georgia, tentatively fixed for March 12." It begins: "On Sunday night, March 8, Special Agents Bannerman and Hastable will go to Hot Springs, the former to confer with Special Agent Poole with reference to details of the transfer of the Japanese, and the latter to remain at Hot Springs until departure of the second and last train carrying Japanese on March 12th.... There will be two agents on each train, Bannerman and one Agent on the first train, and Poole and another agent on the second train."[10]

However, the move to Augusta fell apart. No clear-cut reason is mentioned in any of the correspondence or memos in any of the FBI or State Department files. A sentence in a March 11, 1942, letter from Bannerman states, "At the moment all proposals for the moving of the Japanese to another hotel have been cancelled, due to various objections as to cost and security arrangements at the proposed hotels."[11] Perhaps these were the reasons. However, a newspaper article may shed some light:

> The Homestead is known as an old summer hotel, well known and with an established clientele. It took the Japanese diplomats—400 of them—on the assurance by the government that there would be no Japanese there by March 1.... March 1 rolled around. The 400 were still there and 200 more were on their way in from other places where the[y] were being transported to the United States. The Homestead squawked to the government to keep its promise. "Find us a place for them," said the government. The Homestead was trying all up and down the coast and finally took part in working out a deal with Bon Air's owner, Maurice Puckett whose winter season is about over.... But the Bon Air did not press the matter when it was found that the community was objecting.[12]

Another newspaper article reads, "The Japs aren't coming. Telegrams informing Mayor Woodall ... to that effect came Thursday from Senators George and Russell and Rep. Paul Brown. The message states 'We are pleased to advise that order for removal of interned Japanese to Augusta has been cancelled. The Japanese will be kept at White Sulphur or placed in some other state.' ... So the Yellow Peril dissolves. Augusta is safe."[13]

The State Department began to search for a new hotel. Mr. Bannerman appeared somewhat desperate. His concern is indicated in the subject line he gives to a letter dated March 13, 1942, to Mr. Fitch: "Hotel accommodations near the Greenbrier Hotel at White Sulphur Springs

Four. Musical Chairs

to care for the expected overflow of Axis diplomats."[14] In another memo, he wonders if the military transports used to transport the South Americans could be kept moored off of Savannah or Charleston. He describes another possibility in a memo dated March 11, 1942:

> Mount Weather, Virginia was named as a place that possibly may be used to house the 330 Japanese ex-officials now detained at Hot Springs, Virginia.... The place in question is a weather bureau station, located on the top of Mount Weather Mountain.... There are a number of buildings which are controlled by the weather bureau, and which property is now up for sale.... The building[s] were erected in 1906 and have not been in use for a number of years ... do not have heat nor electricity ... at best they could not house more than 120 people.... Each building would require extensive repairs, complete furnishings, heating systems, installation of electricity and complete renovation for modern equipment ... these buildings are not at all suitable.[15]

Special Agent Bannerman continued his search. He notes that he surveyed the Mountain Lake Hotel in Virginia, the Pence Springs Hotel in West Virginia, and the Warm Springs Hotel in Warm Springs, Virginia. He recommends the Mountain Lake Inn, saying that "from the standpoint of location and facilities [it] is the best prospect to care for the large overflow of Axis aliens expected from South America."[16]

When the Music Stops

Although Bannerman suggested the Mountain Lake Lodge, two other agents visited it and took another view of its suitability. They write in a letter dated March 22, 1942, that the hotel is eighteen miles from the railroad station, at a height of 4,500 feet, and that "in the event of a snow storm, which is quite possible for at least another 5 weeks, the group could be isolated for a week or more for it would be impossible to get off the mountain, not to say a [thing] about bringing supplies to the hotel."[17] They report that the hotel has one phone, not all of the cottages have heat, many cottages have one bathroom reachable only through the porch, that there is no bell service, no valet, no storage space, no stores of any kind, "it is 8 miles to the nearest doctor and 18 miles to the nearest hospital,"[18] thirty-five miles to the nearest laundry, and state that "Practically all of the Italians are Catholics and the nearest Catholic Church is ... 55 miles away."[19]

Axis Diplomats in American Custody

On March 20, 1942, the State Department seems to have made the following decisions. It would lease The Mountain Lake Hotel that was previously rejected—perhaps they decided the threat from a blizzard has passed. The Italians and Hungarians at the Greenbrier would be housed there. A memo mentions that the owner of the Mountain Lake Hotel would see if "the cottages can be properly heated to avoid discomfort to the contemplated occupants."[20] The Japanese at the Homestead would be transferred to The Greenbrier, taking up the rooms now vacated. The Homestead would get its wish and would no longer be part of the detainee programs. However, the State Department, at the last minute, changed its mind.

The Grove Park Inn

On March 20, Special Agent Bannerman wrote to Mr. Fitch that a representative of the Grove Park Inn in Asheville, North Carolina, "called today and stated that Grove Park Inn is available to the State Department for exclusive occupancy on one week's notice. The hotel can care for 290 people at a rate of $8.00 a day per adult and $5.00 per day per child under nine years of age.... The hotel does not impose any time limit that the Department may have the use of the hotel. However their big season is the months of July and August and that he hoped his hotel would continue to be used into this period."[21]

The Grove Park Inn is another "grand hotel." A newspaper reports that the "Grove Park Inn has long been known as the 'finest resort hotel in the world' ... opened in 1913 ... is located on the side of Sunset Mountain.... In front is a green clad hill, and to the rear, or west, the golf links with the mountains in the distance. The inn is unique in construction, having been built of native stone and boulders many of which were sledded to the scene from various mountains sides in this area. Part of the structure is four stor[i]es in height and the red tile roof that covers the long building is a familiar sight from most points in the city. The hotel is surrounded by porches and terrace."[22]

The best known single feature of the hotel is the "big room ... a tremendous lobby 120 feet long and 80 feet wide in which 1000 persons can be entertained. Two huge fireplaces at each end burn 12-foot logs.

Four. Musical Chairs

Boulders and woodwork in the hotel are decorated with mottos and famous sayings.... Dining room and kitchen are in the wing toward the north. In the basement, in addition to baths, barber shops and offices, there is a large convention hall."[23]

On April 3, 1942, the *Asheville Times* had an article titled, "City buses are used to Carry 242 in group from special train."

> Two hundred forty-two Axis diplomats, their staffs and members of their families arrived here this morning and were interned at Grove Park Inn where they will remain the duration of the war or until an exchange can be made.... The group, made up of Italians, Bulgarians and Rumanians, was brought from White Sulphur Springs, WV on two special trains of 11 cars each.
> First of the two trains was backed onto a sidetrack beside the Southern Railway freight depot at 9:40 am and the second train arrived an hour later.... The passengers stepped from the Pullman coaches into waiting city street buses, and were taken directly to the inn. Seven buses were used to transport them and three trucks made two trips each to haul their baggage.... Federal officers, city police and railroad agents stood by as the transfer was made from train to bus and the diplomats will be kept isolated from the outside world at the inn.... A handful of spectators was on hand to witness their arrival, but officers kept the curious at a distance. Making of photographs was forbidden.[24]

The article went on to explain that the diplomats "were internees and not prisoners"[25] and that members of the group would draw their funds from frozen funds of their countries and pay their own hotel bills and other expenses. "Taxpayers of this country do not have to support them."[26]

As the Italians, Hungarians, and Bulgarians went from the Greenbrier to the Grove Park Inn, 330 Japanese moved from the Homestead to the Greenbrier. The Homestead was now empty. The Greenbrier had 521 Germans plus the newly arrived 330 Japanese.

The reception by the Germans of the Japanese was mixed. As a newspaper wrote:

> For 40 hours the 521 Germans had the Greenbrier all to themselves. Then came the yellow peril. From Hot Springs Va. where they also had been luxuriating in beneficial baths and solid comfort, 330 Japanese of various degrees of importance arrived to share the diplomatic Utopia with Aryan brethren. For all the blood brotherhood of Hitler and Hirohito, it soon became evident that if East and West were going to meet, it wasn't going to be as social equals. The Germans having had a noxious taste of Latin superiority, immediately began to look down their noses at the little brown so-and-sos who grinned and bowed and hissed with practice[d] politeness.[27]

Axis Diplomats in American Custody

The townspeople of White Sulphur Springs seemed to accept the arrival of the Japanese. However, Senator Kilgore of West Virginia seems to have complained, allegedly on the behest of his constituents, about the use of the hotel. Under Secretary of State Sumner Welles responded to the senator,

> You may assure your correspondent that the Japanese Officials have been and will continue under adequate surveillance and custody by agents of the Department of Justice, and that there is no reason to fear any untoward incident during the remainder of their stay in United States.... May I also be permitted to suggest that you inform your constituents that this Government is confident that the townspeople of White Sulphur Springs will realize that the temporary use of the Greenbrier Hotel is a war measure, and that their patriotic support will greatly assist the Government in the discharge of its international obligations.[28]

The Homestead, anticipating the departure of the Japanese, did not waste any time in trying to salvage its year. It sent out over 500 telegrams to its most frequent guests. They read: "The Japs are gone. Spring is here. When will we see you at the Homestead?"[29] In contrast, around this same time the Greenbrier sent out a note to its repeat customers that "the advent of Easter time—usually inaugurating our spring season at White Sulphur Springs—finds us rendering a service to our government, the termination of which is uncertain at this time."[30]

In his memoir about the Homestead, Ingalls writes:

> The Japanese left at 12:30 [on April 4, 1942,] and most of the population of Hot Springs was at the station to see the train pull out. With not the least urging in the world the personnel of the Homestead worked 24 hours removing guard houses, guard lights, partitions in the Homestead, and all physical evidence of the stay of the Japanese so that on Easter morning one could drive to the front door of the Homestead and walk into the lobby filled with flowers and see no signs that the Homestead had been [in] effect a prison for three months. Unfortunately only five guests took advantage of the opportunity.[31]

Rivals or Allies

When the Japanese heard that they were to go to the Greenbrier, an informant reports that Major Isai, the assistant military attaché, requested that "all Japanese refrain from entering into conversation with the Germans. He states that his reason for making this request was that they feared that the Germans may get information concerning the

Four. Musical Chairs

Japanese which might be of a confidential nature, and that [they] fear the Japanese secrets might be given to the Germans. It is being requested that all Japanese make no remarks or enter into any conversation with the Germans."[32] The *Times Herald* reporters, who were not the most reliable of sources, write about an incident after the Doolittle raids on Tokyo: "Wisecracks aplenty were shouted from the German end of the room, but the favorite gag was a long shrill whistle like that of a falling bomb, followed by a loud smack on the table. This was repeated again and again and never failed to produce loud guffaws—but not from the Japanese."[33]

Mr. Sibold writes:

> While the Germans, Italians, Hungarians and Bulgarians were here they all ate together in the dining room, and of course, made good use of the auditorium for movies at night. When the Japanese arrived on April 4, there had to be a little different arrangement because of their peculiar seating arrangement in the dining room, so we gave the Germans one end and the Japanese the other. The Japanese of course, were seated in a short circle from the center out and they sat according to rank: for instance the Ambassador sat at the center table—representing the "Rising Sun" and was surrounded by the other members and completely on the [outside] were the maids, butlers, etc.[34]

Mr. Morgan of the FBI writes:

> It is to be noted that since the arrival of the Japanese here at the Greenbrier Hotel where the Germans are being detained, the Germans seem to be taking a dictatorial attitude toward the Japanese in so far as to their rights here, the playground and other Japanese activities.... [The German Representative] has advised the Japanese pertaining to these matters and the Japanese are accepting these suggestions without any questions what so over. Senor Gortazar, the Spanish Ambassador here at the Greenbrier Hotel is very much disgusted with the dictatorial attitude the Germans have taken.[35]

Some Want to Stay in the United States

At the Greenbrier, the FBI has found an informant who periodically provided his impressions of the detainees. According to him, "it is reported that up to 50% of the present interne[e]s would, if given an opportunity, openly express a preference to remain in this country and that about 75%, in their hearts would like to remain here, but this latter 25% would not dare to so indicate their desires. The above data is based

Axis Diplomats in American Custody

on the fact that many of these people have been in this country for more than twenty years, and some have become Americanized and did not join up the Nazi Party until 1933 and after, and each one realizes that his political history will bear heavily on the life he will lead hereafter in Germany. They further realize that they will endure many sacrifices in the furtherance of the war effort."[36]

A few individuals at the Greenbrier approached the State Department and filled out formal applications to remain in the United States. There were sixteen Hungarians, three Germans, one German-Austrian, one Norwegian, and one Italian who requested to stay. Among them was Robert Minner, the man whose wife, with their two young sons, had decided not to stay at the Greenbrier. Another was the wife of a detained German newspaperman, who wrote:

> I, Elizabeth Sievernich ... state herewith my reasons why I myself and our two children want to remain in the U.S.A. although my husband is going to be, by mutual agreement between the German Government and the Government of the U.S.A. exchanged against accredited U.S. journalists who are at the present in Germany.... I was born in Cologne, German on March 12, 1899. My father migrated to the U.S.A. in the fall 1907 ... [with the family following in 1908]. The family came to the U.S.A. with the intention of making America their permanent home. Ever since the day of my arrival I have never been outside of the U.S.A. [She thought her father had completed his naturalization process, but he had died before completion. When she found out she took out her citizenship application on April 5, 1935, but the process had not been completed.] ... [My] two children are native born Americans.... For the following reasons I want to stay with my children in the U.S. Having myself lived in the U.S. since I am 8 years of age I consider America my homeland. All of the immediate members of family are living in the U.S.A. and intend to live in America for the rest of their natural lives. America is the homeland of my children by right of birth.... I can not take the responsibility up on my shoulders to have my children go to Germany, a country which they don't know nothing of. They are Americans and have a right to stay in America. I, as their mother apply to the proper U.S. authorities to permit me to stay with them in America, although I am not an American citizen yet.... Again I emphasis that neither my children nor I have ever been in Germany. We all are considering America our homeland. We want to stay here. I have never taking any part in any political controversy outside Americanism. I have always considered myself an American although until now I am not an American citizen.... Where my children want to stay, there I want to stay. They want to stay in America. So do I, their mother.[37]

Few at the Homestead asked to stay in the United States. One was Kyusuke Hoshide, the stool pigeon for Mr. Morgan, who wrote a confidential letter to State Department agent Poole:

Four. Musical Chairs

> Yearning for American civilization, I came to this country in 1914 after finishing Japanese High School. I entered Broadway Hash School in Seattle, Washington where I studied for two years. Here I took great interest in Christianity, and I was baptized in the Congregational Church in 1917. For three years I taught Sunday school at the Japanese Congregational Church....

(For economic reasons, he quit school to work in a Japanese export company for several years. He enrolled at Mayor College in Chicago in 1935. He transferred to De Paul University to study economics. In his third year he went to New York to continue his studying, where he took a temporary job as a clerk at the Japanese Embassy in New York. He left voluntarily at the end of November of 1941. He goes on to state that his wife graduated from a mission school in Japan but came to the United States in 1924. He indicates that he has no intention of going back to Japan. He continues...)

> My life in this country has been a very happy one.... I am full of appreciation and gratitude for the kindness shown me by the American people, and all these years I have aspired to contribute to the maintenance and promotion of American-Japanese friendship. I am confident that you will understand my sense of gratitude for the privileges and opportunities accorded to me by my "Second Native Country." In view of the above information I shall be deeply grateful if you will kindly present my case to the United States authorities for their consideration. I have complete confidence in the American spirit of fair play, and it is my sincere conviction that I have always been an asset to the organized social order, and as a member I wish to submit the following report: Having lived in this country so long [have never left the country since 1914], I really feel as though America were my own native country, and I would not only consider it an honor to remain in this country, but my duty to do everything I possibly could for the country. [He volunteers to work on a farm or to work in U.S. defense work] ... or do anything in my power if you will allow me to stay.[38]

Another woman at the Greenbrier, Annette Prior, a stenographer for the German Consulate in New York, was in love with an American soldier. She worried that her status as a detainee would harm his military career and confided in the informant that "the Germans here at the Greenbrier have made life miserable for her as they have implied that she is a traitor to Germany. She advises however that the young people believe she should remain in U.S. if that would be allowed her and that she should marry. The older folks think that marriage for her at this time is out of the picture."[39]

Five

Negotiations for Exchange

On December 19, 1941, the State Department, in a 2,500-word telegram, laid out the basic plan for the exchanges. Over the next three months, this plan would be clarified and slightly changed in response to various snags. Some of these snags were minor; others were deal-breakers. The Japanese requested very few changes. The Germans and Italians required a few modifications, as did the neutral Swiss and Portuguese. Larger disagreements were encountered with Britain and various South American countries. Moreover, the entire exchange almost collapsed because of opposition from, of all people, one of the U.S. diplomats held by the Germans in Bad Nauheim.

A memo dated December 19, 1942, for the attention of the German and Italian governments presented "the proposal of United States Government for the exchange of diplomatic, consular and other official personnel with their dependents, staff and personal effects."[1] The proposal was summarized in a later note from the State Department:

(1) General Proposal
(2) Permission to take all personal effects, subject to limitations on available space
(3) All diplomats exempt from all search
(4) Course and markings of vessels
(5) Transportation of American diplomats to Portuguese frontier
(6) Same facilities to be granted officials of other American Republics
(7) Portuguese Government to be requested to act as guarantor of exchange on Portuguese soil

Five. Negotiations for Exchange

(8) Press representatives, radio reporters, photographers to be included in exchange
(9) Inclusion of consular personnel and effects of other American Republics
(10) United States Government to guaranty safe conduct and obtain same from its associates. Germans and Italians to do likewise
(11) All assurances of safe conduct for the New York—Lisbon—New York voyage should be deposited with the Swiss to notify us when this done. The Swiss to be requested to act as guarantors to both parties of observance of arrangements
(12) Operational expenses to be divided on pro rata basis to be determined by the Swiss
(13) Personnel of the Red Cross shall be permitted to travel in either direction of the exchange vessel
(14) Representatives of Swiss Government to travel on exchange vessel as guarantor of execution of the agreement and as the power protecting interests of the governments whose personnel being exchanged
(15) Only Swiss representative has unrestricted use of radio. Passengers may not use it.[2]

A subsequent memo dated December 30, 1941, from the State Department clarifies who is included in the exchange. "List should include: diplomatic and consular officers, any other government officers, government clerks and custodial personnel of American nationality, and American unofficial nationals of the following categories only. Such properly accredited representatives of the American Red Cross Society and their staff, and properly accredited newspaper correspondents (including radio reporters and press photographers and their staffs).... [Of the above] ... members of the family [and] members of household staff."[3]

On December 30, 1941, the Swiss pointed out a snag. The proposal suggested that the Swiss Government was requested to act as the guarantor to both parties of the observance of the arrangement. Their memo states, "The Swiss government cannot undertake that responsibility."[4]

Axis Diplomats in American Custody

The Swiss only commit to communicate the receipt of safe conduct as proposed in the agreement. They also point out that the Swiss delegate on board the vessel agrees that only he shall be allowed to use the radio, but they suggest that in the event of an emergency, that the representative, in his discretion, allow other parties to use the radio. The United States agrees.

A second snag was also quickly remedied. The Italians, in a telegram dated January 2, 1942, disagreed with the limits on the quantity of personal effects that the United States had proposed, that is, the argument was about luggage. The United States, in its original proposal, wanted the limit to be that imposed by whatever vessel it could lease, as well as whatever limitations were in effect at whatever dock was involved. However, "the Italian government request the assurance that this limitation shall not be less than the three trunks and hand baggage."[5] This was the amount of luggage that the Italian government was allowing the American diplomatic personnel whom it was swapping. The United States in later telegrams agreed to this point.

On January 15, 1942, the Germans made their response to the proposals. They stated that they would agree to safe passage if the vessel did not enter the "zone of operations" around the British Islands and Iceland. They also proposed that additional people be authorized to be on the vessel, including "representatives of film companies, leading employees or representatives of companies [businesses], and leading employees of Chambers of Commerce ... [and also people in the countries] for study, teaching or other scientific reason including members of their families."[6]

The United States agreed to the German request, as long as it received a detailed list of all people to be exchanged in time for review and the ability to refuse to repatriate anyone who was a non-official member of the delegation, staff, or family. Such non-official people were to be examined on a case-by-case basis, as opposed to credentialed diplomats, of whom none were to be withheld. Germany agreed to this stipulation.

Some in the State Department warned against a too-broad interpretation of who was to be included in what was supposed to be an exchange of diplomats. Mr. Green of the State Department writes:

> All of the enemy governments, including Japan, in responding to the proposal of this Government for the exchange of officials ... have indicated their wish to make

Five. Negotiations for Exchange

the facilities of the exchange available on increasingly liberal terms to persons who are not officials.... It is hoped that after the exchange of the official parties is completed the opportunity for repatriation may be extended to non-official civilians.... [However] if you are agreeable we might accept in principle the suggestion of the enemy powers and agree to carry on the exchange vessels both to Europe and to the Far East as many non-officials found entitled to reparations—whether they desire that repatriation *or because their presence is unwelcome* [emphasis added by authors] as the space available after accommodation of officials will permit.[7]

Mr. Green's suggestion—that the exchanges could be a method of removing unwelcome enemy nationals—would change the scope of the exchanges, especially as it related to South and Central America. However, planning continued, with a mid–February memo from Mr. Long laying out what was expected:

If these negotiations are successful, a ship will sail on or about April 1 from New York—possibly from Baltimore or Norfolk—with approximately 900 passengers bound for Lisbon. This ship will then return to the United States from Lisbon with approximately 500 passengers. It will then proceed from an American port to Rio de Janeiro with approximately 900 passengers; at Rio it will pick up approximately 200 passengers and proceed to Lourenco Marques, where the entire number—approximately 1100—will be disembarked. At Lourenco Marques the ship will embark approximately 1100 passengers and will return to an American port.[8]

Almost all of these assumptions would prove incorrect. However, negotiations pressed on. The State Department had contacted Portugal to get its reaction to the proposal. The Portuguese pointed out a problem. It was impractical that the trains arriving from Rome and Berlin carrying the U.S. diplomats would arrive in Lisbon at the exact same time as the exchange vessel arrived from the east coast of the United States. The State Department amended its proposal to suggest that the boat arrive first, with the passengers to be held on board until the trains arrived. On March 31, 1942, the Portuguese agreed to this. They, in fact, had been in contact with the Germans and now reported a concession that the Germans have made to assist the Portuguese:

[I]n view of exceptional difficulties in arranging a simultaneous disembarkation German diplomats at Lisbon and entrance into Portuguese territory of trains with American groups German government has declared itself in agreement that American groups may cross Portuguese border as soon as trains reach frontier. Arrival of ship would then be awaited in Lisbon or in another place to be agreed upon. Portuguese Government has been asked to assume guarantee requested of it that no member of American group leave Portugal before all German groups have disembarked.[9]

Axis Diplomats in American Custody

British Request to Hold Some Back

As the State Department continued to work with Germany, Italy, and Portugal, a serious objection to the proposal was raised by the British. They worried that, in addition to "bona fide diplomats," other alien nationals could be returned to "the theater of war." They wrote, "In this last connection the British Government feels sure that the United States Government will agree that it would not be to the common interest to permit the return to Europe of individuals such as trained technicians, reserve officers, pilots, submarine specialists or espionage and sabotage agents.... The British authorities are in fact not prepared to facilitate the return of such persons."[10]

The British go on to express their hope that these people do not leave South America or Central America, or if they do that the United States keeps them in the United States. They make an example of one individual. "A particular case in point is that of one Konstantin von Massenbach, a former submarine commander, who has attached himself to the German diplomatic party from Venezuela, now on its way to the United States without having received a guarantee of safe conduct to Europe from the British authorities. Since the latter would be unable to give any such guarantees in respect of von Massenbach, it is hoped that the United States authorities will feel able to detain him in this country [i.e., the United States] for the duration of the war."[11]

Another memo from the British Embassy to the Department of State reads:

> The British Government agrees that it is desirable to prevent enemy nationals from being free to do as they wish in Latin America, particularly those who have been deliberately placed there by enemy governments for subversive purposes, and they are fully alive to the implications this whole question has for the security of the Western Hemisphere. Conversely, they anticipate that the United States Government will understand if the British Government should feel unable to grant safe conducts to such enemy nationals as there may be who because of their technical qualifications would be more likely to injure the common cause by being sent back to Europe than by being allowed to reside in Latin America.[12]

The British go on to suggest that they be given lists of nationals and be allowed to identify those who they feel should not be allowed back.

The perception of who would be a threat differed wildly. It was

Five. Negotiations for Exchange

not limited to military people. The criteria was whether the person could add to the enemy's war effort. Prohibited occupations included fishermen, seamen, newspaper editors, and publishers. A group of Peruvian tailors was deported from Peru because they allegedly had sewed uniforms for Japanese Embassy staff who were members of the Japanese Naval Reserve. The Intelligence Report, prepared by the Intelligence Division, Office of Chief of Naval Operations, Navy Department, describes the efforts taken regarding these tailors: "In connection with the secret investigation which was being carried out in Lima covering Japanese activities in the manufacture of uniforms ... nine Japanese were jailed ... and an order calling for their deportation was signed.... No further boats for deportation purposes were calling at Callao consequently ... it [was] recommended that the U. S. Government furnish air transportation."[13]

However, many of the diplomats were active military, were retired, or were reserve officers. Many of the individuals were experts in military matters, had extensive knowledge of industries, or had made studies of specific Latin American ports or airfields. Others had developed vast networks of friends and contacts. Some had done all three, such as Peter Riedel, the World War I ace and record-holding glider pilot, who counted friends in the highest levels of the U.S. aviation industry.

On the West Coast of the United States, under the infamous Executive Order 9066, the U.S. Border Patrol had started rounding up those of Japanese ancestry as a precautionary measure. Various U.S. agencies, including the Alien Enemy Control Unit of the Department of Justice, FBI, and Military and Naval Intelligence, identified approximately 2,000 of these individuals (out of 120,000 interned in camps in Arizona, Montana, and other remote locations) whom they felt should not be repatriated to Japan. "These objections are based on the contention of those agencies that ... those individuals concerned are either Japanese agents, Japanese sympathizers or have technical qualifications or associations of possible or probable value to the Japanese war effort."[14] In Hawaii, home to tens of thousands of ethnic Japanese, only a few thousand were taken to internment camps. A few of these camps were on the islands. Other Hawaiian Japanese were transported to the mainland.

However, if an alien national was not in one of these prohibited groups, he was now included under the broader scope of the exchange program. Originally, the people to be exchanged were limited to a precise group of accredited diplomats, staff, and families, with a few specific others such as credentialed news reporters. As these individuals were already credentialed when they entered the host country, both the host country and the home country were working off identical lists of people. Now, enemy nationals deemed undesirables were included in the exchange. The decision about who was undesirable was vague and determined by the host country. The host country would pick and choose, based on whatever internal reasons it came up with, those enemy nationals it wished to expel and labeled them as undesirable, and these individuals were included in the exchange program. What had started as a relatively straightforward collection of around 600 known diplomatic personnel in North, Central and South America, a process expected to take a few months and one trip to Lisbon and one trip to East Africa, had become a much more complicated program.

Some South American Countries Balk

Brazil, Paraguay, and Uruguay agreed to the concept of expelling the German, Italian, and Japanese diplomats from their countries. However, they wanted to make all the arrangements directly with the Axis powers. They also insisted that anyone whom they expelled embark from Rio de Janeiro instead of transiting through the United States.

Moreover, Argentina was not fully committed to the expulsion of Axis diplomats, or, more accurately, it agreed to the expulsion but seemed to want the United States to put them in charge of the entire program for South America. The State Department was highly sensitive that Argentina perceived itself as the first among equals of the South American countries but tried to mollify its need to stand out.

In the meantime, the Germans in South America were engaging in an intense lobbying campaign. In a memo dated March 2, 1942, the State Department wrote:

> From information which has reached the Department it has become clear that the Axis Governments are assuming an attitude which on the one hand is designed to

Five. Negotiations for Exchange

keep their officials for an indefinite period in some of the American Republics where their continued presence will be a source of danger from every standpoint and on the other hand derogates from the soverign right of the American Republics in question to determine the time and means of departure from their territory of representatives of governments with which they have broken relations.[15]

At this point, anyone working in the State Department had to be wondering what they had gotten into. They were simultaneously:

—calming England down about who was to be repatriated,
—making promises about lend-lease and trade concessions to dozens of South and Central American countries,
—stroking Argentina's ego about whether it was the premier South American nation,
—hitting just the right balance with Brazil, Uruguay, and Paraguay,
—convincing the neutral Portugal and Portuguese East Africa to allow entry of the exchange boats,
—arranging charter of one or possibly two exchange vessels,
—negotiating with Germany, Italy, Japan, and the other enemy countries about the specifics of the exchange,
—dealing with the approximately 800 diplomats currently at the hotels,
—trying to find another hotel, as the Homestead seemed unwilling to extend its lease and as the number of South Americans pending expulsion was getting bigger and bigger.

The State Department made a series of decisions which it may not have liked, but which were forced by circumstances. It backed off its demand that the Axis diplomats in Brazil, Paraguay, and Uruguay enter the United States first. Instead, these countries would arrange a ship to transport the German and Italian diplomats directly to Lisbon. The three countries also agreed to collect the Japanese diplomats and hold them in Rio de Janeiro. The exchange ship that the United States was using to transport the Japanese diplomats it held at the Homestead would make a stop in Rio, pick up these diplomats, then continue on its voyage to Lourenço Marques. The United States did not like its loss of control over these Axis diplomats, and it worried that not all of the Axis agents and provocateurs would be expelled. However, it agreed to the arrangement. A telegram to Spain dated March 6, 1942, reads:

Axis Diplomats in American Custody

> Please inform the Foreign Office (1) that the Brazilian Government is arranging for the direct repatriation from Brazil of European Axis officials now in Brazil and Paraguay; (2) that the Uruguay Government is arranging for the direct repatriation of European Axis nationals from Uruguay; (3) that European Axis officials in all of the other American Republics which have broken relations with the Axis are to be repatriated via the United States; (4) that the Argentine Government has recognized the impracticability of the repatriation via Argentina of Axis officials from the other American Republics.[16]

The United States' acquiescence may have been due to the delicate negotiations going on with Brazil concerning airfield rights in the northern part of the country. A more simple explanation is that the United States really had no cards to play. Germany was a longtime trading partner for these countries, had a huge commercial presence, and was ingrained in society, especially the high society that ran the counties. In the case of Argentina, both the United States and Germany had significant trade and long-standing relationships. The government of Argentina had to make a choice and decided to back America instead of Germany

The State Department took a harder line with Peru, Bolivia, and Colombia, likely due to the countries' proximity to the Panama Canal. The State Department felt that the German government was putting undue pressure on these governments to either refuse the American request for reparation of Axis diplomats or at least to delay any decision. The State Department would not allow the Germans to dictate policy in the Western Hemisphere. In a telegram to the Swiss dated March 12, 1942, it let the Germans know that the entire exchange program was in jeopardy, "[T]his Government must have a reply regarding [the exchange]. If the reply is not forthcoming the exchange will be unduly delayed and it will become necessary to remove the personnel now assembled at White Sulphur Springs to other quarters since they cannot be maintained indefinitely where they now are especially in view of the fact that this Government has no evidence whatever that the German Government intends to proceed to any exchange of official personnel."[17]

A separate telegram stated:

> The United States government has received reliable information that the German Government has instructed its official representatives in Bolivia not to leave that country to be repatriated through the United States unless compelled by

Five. Negotiations for Exchange

force and to threaten the Bolivian Government with reprisals if force is exercised.... Please ... inform German Government that there are no transportation facilities available for the repatriation of their officials except those provided by or with the consent of this Government; that the Argentine Government has indicated its clear refusal to receive the German officials pending their repatriation; and that the present attitude of the German Government indicates to the United States Government a probability that the German Government has no serious intention of proceeding to an exchange of official personnel.

You many continue that if this Government finds that the exchange of personnel is to be interminably delayed by new pretexts it cannot continue to maintain enemy personnel indefinitely at White Sulphur Springs which was taken over on the understanding that its use by this Government would be for a limited time. It will be necessary to seek other quarters for the personnel now detained at that resort and comparable quarters will not be available during the spring and summer seasons.[18]

On the same day, the U.S. State Department sent a telegram to the Bolivian ambassador that began:

The attitude now displayed by the German and Italian Governments constitutes positive confirmation that those two Governments are determined to use every method at their disposal to try to prevent the departure of their diplomatic and consular officials from the American Republics. If any proof had been required that these agents were destined for subversive activities of grave danger to the security of the American Republics and to the efficacy of our cooperative hemisphere defense plan, that proof is now clearly presented.

As I have stated before, the plans have been fully worked out for the transportation of all of these German and Italian officials by way of New York to Lisbon. The Argentine Government will not permit them to enter Argentina unless a previous safe conduct has been granted by the United States and British Governments for their passage from Buenos Aires to Europe and this safe conduct has not and will not be issued. Consequently, the only way in which these persons can return to their own country is under the terms of the plan formulated by the United States Government, of which the Bolivian Government is fully advised.

Naturally the United States Government cannot continue to send ships to remove these people. The ships designated for the purpose of removing Axis officials from the Pacific ports of South America are already under way and if the German and Italian Axis officials now in Bolivia reach Arica [a port in Northern Chile] by March 19 they will be put on board one of these vessels immediately thereafter.

It is clear that the continued presence in Bolivia of these officials would constitute a grave and continuing danger to the security of the state just as the continued presence of similar Axis officials in the United States, if prolonged, would constitute a danger to the security of this country. The threat of reprisal should not, in my opinion, outweigh the sovereign right of every one of the American Republics to take, for its own security, those measures which appear to it to be necessary and which are clearly recognized by every standard of international law.

Axis Diplomats in American Custody

I most earnest hope that the Minister will agree with my own belief that the step in question is of the highest importance as being in consonance with the spirit and the letter of the resolutions adopted at the Rio de Janeiro conference.

If these officials are not sent to Arica by March 19, there is no other prospect of their removal and their internment in Bolivia would, I am confident, be a source of danger to the security of the Bolivian state and source of continued disquiet to the Bolivian authorities.[19]

On March 21, 1942, the German government informed the Spanish mission that "German government desires to proceed as rapidly as possible to a proper exchange and that it has no intention to complicate or delay exchange agreement. Although Germany would prefer to have its diplomats return from Bolivia, Ecuador and Peru by port on east coast of South America, German Government agrees that they rejoin group in United States on express condition that every guarantee of security should be given to their passage to United States."[20]

Leave No One Behind

Originally a Swedish vessel called the *Kungsholm* was to be chartered for the exchange in Europe, and then the same vessel would be used for the exchange in East Africa. The ship was, in December of 1941, located in the Boston area. It could accommodate somewhere between 800 and 1,500 people, a range dependent on how many beds were squeezed into the first-class cabins and whether cots were placed in the ballrooms and sitting areas. However, during the time the negations were underway, the *Kungsholm* was chartered by the War Shipping Administration to become a troopship.

The State Department decided to charter two separate vessels and run a series of trips. This was due to the larger number of detainees now involved in the exchange, and larger ships were impossible to find. The vessel for the Lisbon exchange was the *Drottningholm*, and it could carry only around 1,200 passengers, about three hundred less than the *Kungsholm*. The Axis powers had been planning on the repatriation of 1,500 diplomats, staff, and families from both the United States and from the American republics. In the case of the Americans leaving from Berlin and Rome, the number was closer to a couple of hundred, with the remainder of the berths going to civilians fleeing Europe. The

Five. Negotiations for Exchange

Germans opposed a situation where some of their diplomatic group were left in the United States while all of the American diplomats were freed. They insisted that some of the American diplomats in Europe be held back until the second *Drottningholm* voyage. The State Department seemed to agree to this but met fierce opposition from, of all people, one of its own diplomats held at Bad Nauheim.

The State Department, through the Swiss, contacted Chargé d'Affaires Leland Morris, who was being held by the Germans at Bad Nauheim, informing him that he needed to select which of his group was to be left behind. He answered:

> It is a painful shock to me and surprise to me that there could be any question of departing from the principals laid down by the Department of exchanging official personnel first. I am sure that you will appreciate what it has meant to the Embassy's staff to have been held under strict police supervision day and night since the 14th of December last. They are in this position because they loyally stuck to their post and served the Government. In most instances civilians ha[d] repeated opportunity to get repatriated. If this proposal to include civilians on the first voyage must be insisted upon for reasons which do not appear clear to me I must request the Department to designate by names the members of the group who are to proceed and those who are to remain. I feel that this is a task which I cannot undertake myself to discriminate among the members of my group in a manner so vitally concerning their fate.... If a part of the group must remain I feel it is my duty and my wish to remain also to give them such comfort and assistance as may be in my power. Signed Morris.[21]

The State Department changed its mind. A telegram dated May 1, 1942, states, "In view of German insistence upon departure of all German officials on first voyage of Drottningholm arrangements are being made to place on board Drottningholm all German officials.... The original plan provided that all the German career officials be carried on the first voyage together with certain non-officials whom the Germans had requested. The non-career officials were to follow on next trip of vessel.... That is now discarded and all officials will be carried on first trip—career and non-career alike."[22]

Other Issues

Negotiations with the European Axis powers touched on other issues. The Germans insisted on a signed and notarized statement that any male age 16 to 45 that they sent back to the United States would swear not to bear arms against them. The United States agreed to this, on the condition that the Germans going back to Europe sign a similar document. The Germans wanted any exchange vessel after the first trip to originate from a port along the Gulf of Mexico, but the United States insisted that vessels be able to leave from ports anywhere on the east coast. The Germans acquiesced to this. There was some minor squabbling about the markings on the ship, the amount of baggage for each detainee, whether the baggage would be inspected, and how much money could be taken aboard. These issues were all worked out.

Japanese Negotiations

On December 13, 1941, the United States wrote to the Japanese with the basics of the proposed exchange:

> The proposal of this Government is that the Japanese diplomatic and consular personnel and their families will proceed on an appropriate passenger vessel provided by this Government to Lourenco Marques, that a similar vessel provided by the Japanese Government proceed simultaneously to Lourenco Marques with the American diplomatic and consular personnel and the members of their families from Japan and Japanese occupied territories, that the vessels exchange passengers and baggage at Lourenco Marques and return to their respective countries and that all the expenses of the Japanese mentioned above for travel and subsistence from their former posts of duty in the United States to Lourenco Marques will be borne by the United States Government.
>
> It is assumed of course in connection with all of the above that the Japanese Government will agree to accord similar treatment on a reciprocal basis to American nationals possessed of official status within the Japanese empire and in Japanese occupied territories while such American nationals remain there and in all that appertains to facilitating their departure and transit homeward.[23]

On December 26, 1941, the U.S. government presented a more detailed plan, which was essentially identical to the plan proposed to the German and Italian governments. The Japanese requested very few changes. One was that the vessels be marked as hospital ships, which they describe, "These ships have the following marks in common: Whole hull painted white, Red Cross emblem [on] upper part of hull supplied with electricity, Red Cross on port and starboard center of hull ... in accordance with (Geneva) Convention regulations. Chimney

Five. Negotiations for Exchange

bears Red Cross electrically outlined."[24] This was rejected by the United States. The United States wrote in a memo the Japanese, "The United States Government considers that misunderstanding might arise from designating as hospital ships under the Geneva Agreement of 1907 the vessels to be used for the purpose of the exchange and assumes that the Japanese Government will select another method of marking the vessels."[25] The Japanese agreed.

By May 1942, the State Department was cautiously optimistic about the Japanese exchange: "We do not anticipate any last-minute difficulties in connection with the Japanese exchange as long as the respective protecting powers continue to be convinced, as they apparently are at present, that the two Governments parties [sic] to the exchange are acting in good faith. The only possible complication which we foresee at this time is that which may arise when the treatment of the group of Japanese officials from Hawaii now being held incommunicado in Arizona becomes known to the Japanese Government."[26] The State Department had found a ship, the *Gripsholm*, and it readied for the long voyage to East Africa.

Six

Be Careful What You Wish For

A safe conduct is diplomatic jargon for a guarantee, as much as is possible in an active war zone, granted by a belligerent party that a specific vessel will not be attacked. The process of executing a safe conduct is complex. The vessel has to be clearly identifiable; the intended course, including specific way stations, speed, and times and dates of passage need to be established. Presumably the vessel will avoid travelling in a convoy, will not be escorted by any warships, and will not be armed. There are other restrictions dealing with the cargo, passengers, and avoiding radio contact. The country granting the safe conduct to the vessel agrees to notify its submarines, warships, airplanes, and shore batteries that the vessel is protected from hostile action, including stopping and boarding. The Swiss, in a telegram to the United States, wrote that the German government has agreed that "German forces will be instructed ... not to molest the ship on its voyage and to allow it to pass freely."[1]

A memorandum of conversation between the Undersecretary of State and the British ambassador explains the U.S. position regarding the American Republics:

> I said it should be obvious to the British Government that it was in the vital interest of the United States that Axis diplomatic and consular officials and also dangerous Axis agents of one kind or another should be removed from the other American Republics as quickly as possible. I said this was particularly the case in countries adjacent to the Panama Canal such as Colombia, Ecuador and Peru and almost equally important in other republics where we were obtaining large quantities of strategic materials the sources of which were exceptionally subject to sabotage. I said that it was impossible for me to admit that internment of these individuals by the countries involved was a satisfactory substitute for the request

Six. Be Careful What You Wish For

we had made.... I emphasized that it was a matter of primary concern to this Government to get these people out of the other American Republics and that in certain cases it would be impossible to get them out and to get our own nationals released from Axis-occupied countries in Europe unless we could give assurances that the Axis nationals would be permitted to proceed to Europe under safe conduct.[2]

The British told the Americans about "four Scadta [an airline in Colombia] pilots who left Colombia some months ago and returned to Germany by way of Japan [who] were shot down over London within a week after their arrival in Germany."[3] The Brits held their ground.

Although the British have granted safe-conduct to the S.S. Acadia and the S.S. Etolin, sent to bring Axis nationals from Peru, Bolivia, Ecuador and Colombia to the United States, they have refused to give any assurance regarding the further repatriation of these Axis nationals across the Atlantic. In fact, the British Minister at Quito informed his American colleague that the British Government reserved the right "to decline safe-conducts to persons of potential military value to the Axis." If this reluctance on the part of the British Government becomes apparent to the Spanish Government in charge of Axis interests along the South American West Coast, the Spanish Government will undoubtedly utilize this British attitude as a further excuse for delaying or blocking the efforts of this Government to remove Axis nationals from area and to bring them to the United States via the Acadia and the Etolin. Until the British give positive assurances that they will cooperate with the repatriation plans of the United States Government, it will be impossible to proceed with even the first step in this Government's plan for the repatriation of Axis nationals from South America.... The British Government desires the United States Government to intern rather than to repatriate any non-official Axis nationals whom the British may consider more dangerous in Europe than in the Western Hemisphere.[4]

Undersecretary of State Joseph Green writes, "If the British persist in this attitude, we shall be faced with insuperable difficulties in our endeavors to remove dangerous Axis nationals from the Western Hemisphere. It would seem essential to the success of the pending exchange negotiations that the British, without delay, agree to the principle that safe conducts must be granted for any Axis nationals or groups of Axis nationals whom any of the America Republics shall decide to transport to Europe or the Far East."[5]

Undersecretary Green sent a letter to the British Ambassador, Lord Halifax, which reiterates the position of the United States. "As a condition precedent to receiving in the United States these dangerous non-official enemy aliens, it has been necessary for us to agree that

Axis Diplomats in American Custody

they would be sent on to their home countries. You will realize that this Government cannot break faith with the American republics which have sent enemy aliens to the United States on these terms. Furthermore, other American republics which are willing to send enemy aliens to this country do not feel that they can do so unless we give assurances that the aliens will be sent home."[6] The Undersecretary of State, in unequivocal terms, stated that the United States had obligated itself to the transshipment of the non-officials associated with the diplomatic exchange program. Moreover, he indicated that this agreement to use the United States strictly as a way-station was a condition demanded by the various countries of South America. The Undersecretary goes on:

> In the opinion of this Government it would be far more detrimental to the war effort of the United Nations to have these dangerous enemy aliens in the Western Hemisphere than to have them sent to their home lands…. From Peru, Bolivia, Ecuador and Colombia there are being transported to this country not only the officials but a number of the enemy nationals there for onward transportation. A hesitancy has developed in these governments because of the limited nature of the British safe conduct across the Atlantic from the United States with the implication that the persons being transported to this country will be kept here indefinitely. We shall either have to forward them to Europe or return them to the countries where they came, for these are the conditions of our receiving them.[7]

The Undersecretary asks the Ambassador to "accede" to the safe-conduct request.

The FBI agents who had been dispatched in 1940 have worked with various South American countries to create lists of the Axis sympathizers, both official and non-official, to be expelled if war came. These republics have also explained to Berlin, Rome, and Tokyo that the exchanges are to occur. The warring parties have already agreed, in point eleven of the General Proposal, about safe conduct across the Atlantic. Yet somehow, no one bothered to bring the British on board. It is not known whether the State Department just assumed the British would not object, or alternatively, the State Department was playing a very close game and telling various parties what they wanted to hear with the idea that the United States could eventually prevail over any possible British objections.

The British escalated the dispute. The American Embassy in London heard a rumor that the Italians had reached an independent agreement with the British. Italian diplomats in Caracas or other Venezuela ports

Six. Be Careful What You Wish For

would thus avoid any transit through the United States. The British did not deny any such discussions with the Italians but merely stated that the Italians had changed their plans. The British then complained to the Americans that they might be willing "to grant safe conducts only for any genuine diplomatic or consular officials proceeding to the United States and not for any 'bogus' members of the party."[8] They gave an example of Piero Ferracutti, who was to be included in the official party from San Salvador, who, the British alleged, "is a qualified pilot who intends to join the Italian air force and was granted diplomatic status only on November 18, 1941."[9]

On February 13, 1942, Mr. Welles of the State Department called the British Ambassador, Viscount Halifax, to his office to discuss "the requests made by [the United States government] for safe conducts to be issued for the Axis diplomatic and consular officials and other dangerous Axis individuals in the United States and in the Western Hemisphere whom we did not desire to intern here and whom we did desire to deport on a ship chartered for that purpose."[10] In a memorandum prepared by the British Embassy, the English laid out a possible compromise position:

> [T]he United States authorities will wish to be able to secure the return from Europe of a certain number of their own nationals who are not members of American diplomatic or consular missions by exchanging them for a number of enemy nationals from the Western Hemisphere who are similarly neither diplomats nor consular officers.... In addition to bona fide members of diplomatic or consulate missions, the British authorities are prepared to facilitate the return to Europe of other enemy nationals who, though not entitled to diplomatic immunity, may be attached to such missions, if good reasons exist for believing that their return would be to the common interest.... In this last connection the British Government feels sure that the United States Government will agree that it would not be to the common interest to permit the return to Europe of individuals such as trained technicians, reserve officers, pilots, submarine specialist or espionage and sabotage agents. [It is] suggested that before any decisions are reached as to which of them are to be repatriated to Europe, discussions should be held between the United States security officers and the British security officers now stationed in this country.[11]

Negotiations continued, with the British proposing that lists be prepared of those whom the American Republics wished to include in the exchange, with the British holding some sort of veto power. A State Department official, in evaluating this proposal, writes:

Axis Diplomats in American Custody

> In submitting the lists to the British we were merely being honest with them. Our honesty of purpose seems to have been misconstrued by them as subservience.... To justify their examination of our lists, a certain number of persons must always be refused, but these refusals place us in an embarrassing position. We are forced to break our word and to renounce our solemn undertakings to certain South American Republics for we agreed to send these people to their native lands.... In the long run our refusal to honor our bond would probably inflict greater harm on the war effort of the United Nations than the return to German of twenty-eight assorted engineers, experts etc.... It seems unlikely that the return of any or all of these persons to Germany will in any way alter the course of the war. Any aid which these persons may render can have but the most infinitesimal effect on the final outcomes.... Their aid cannot even approach the proverbial drop in the bucket.... It should be remembered that such a setback to American prestige in Latin America would not displease the British who have long resented American ascendancy in that part of the world.[12]

The British requested another meeting with the undersecretary, as, "Mr. Welles had expressed appreciation of the British point of view but had found it somewhat too inflexible and that he had agreed with Lord Halifax that a redefinition of the British attitude might be discussed."[13] However, positions did not change. The British stated that "the policy of this government [i.e., the British] might be expressed most bluntly as being that on account of lack of shipping there would be no such repatriation."[14]

More meetings occurred and more letters were traded, but neither side budged. Secretary of State Green reached his limit. He wrote:

> I do not believe that the necessary modification of the British viewpoint can be obtained by a further communication to the British Embassy and I suggest that we do one of two things: Either wait until we are ready to ask for a safe conduct and then ask the British Government through our Embassy at London for a blanket safe conduct for the vessel and all that we place on it or to inform Lord Halifax that this Government cannot agree that the British Government shall have the power to veto the arrangements we are making for the exchange of our people abroad, for the national defense, for the security of the Western Hemisphere and for the common interest.[15]

For a period of time, the State Department ignored the threat from the British to withhold shipping privilege due to their objection to the broad sweep of the exchange program, perhaps thinking that they can bully their ally. A memo dated February 25, 1942, from the State Department acknowledged the receipt of the British Embassy's aide-memoire but stated, "These negotiations are already so far advanced that only certain technical details remain to be settled."¹⁶ In mid–March, both sides flinched. The United States agreed to allow the British to look at the lists of those to be repatriated, and they are allowed to note those individuals whom they find objectionable. The United States did not commit to honoring these objections, but agreed to review these individuals on a case-by-case basis.

Although the United States, from a policy perspective, may have been correct, the British may have had a better sense of the Nazi character. The United States required each male between the ages of 16 and 45 to sign a pledge not to bear arms. In November 1942, a letter was sent from Germany to Argentina. The letter mentioned a Mr. Keidel, who was sent from Bolivia to Germany under the diplomatic program. The letter was somehow intercepted by United States authorities and examined. The examiner notes, "Previous Records ... show that Keidel had reached Germany, from Bolivia and enrolled in the Naval Artillery in Germany, together with a group of other repatriated Germans."¹⁷ There was a handwritten note, perhaps from Mr. Fitch, which stated, "A pledge is never worth more than the signature on it. I have noted his name for court martial if caught."¹⁸

Many South American Countries Purge Undesirables

Within a few weeks of the start of the war, many South American countries had already delivered Axis diplomats to the United States. Some came by plane, others in regularly scheduled passenger service; one group actually came on a banana boat. A large contingent of Latin Americans arrived aboard the *Santa Lucia*, which docked at New York on January 21, 1942. The group was composed of 42 German officials, 56 German nationals, 8 Italian officials, and 5 Italian nationals, a total of 111 people expelled from Colombia.

As more Axis officials arrived, they were transported to the Greenbrier or the Homestead. As non-official Axis arrived, some were taken to these hotels. The disposition of the other nationals, however, caused problems. A memo dated February 16, 1942, from Mr. Bannerman recounts a discussion he had with Lt. Yudelson of the War Department:

Axis Diplomats in American Custody

> Lt. Yudelson called the Special Division and took up with the Internees Section the question of the special status of deportees from Colombia of Italian and German nationality now in the hands of the War Department. He stated that there [has] been delivered to the Provost Marshal General a letter in English addressed to the Swiss Minister, by the deportees from Colombia who were sent to the United States on the Santa Lucia and are now confined at Camp Upton. In this letter the group complains that it is not being accorded the special treatment promised to it by the Spanish Ambassador in charge of German and Italian Interests in Colombia. It is complained that, among other thing[s], the men and women have been separated, the men being confined at Camp Upton and the women and children at Ellis Island.
>
> ... [Lt. Yudelson] stated that the War Department has no official knowledge that any special treatment is to be given to the group of Germans and Italians deported from Colombia and that it had no facilities for confining these persons together by family groups. He added that the War Department knew that aliens from Colombia are to be "held for repatriation" but that it would be glad to have an official statement from the Department of State regarding the general subject of alien deportees from Latin America indicating the status of the deportees from each country and the special treatment, if any to be given to each group of these.[19]

It appears that the State Department had been prepared for a limited number of such non-officials. Instead, the State Department, in broadening the scope of who could be repatriated out of the American republics, had opened the floodgates.

What began as a controlled, closely monitored deportation program to detain potentially dangerous diplomatic and consular officials of Axis nations and Axis businessmen grew to include enemy aliens who were teachers, small businessmen, tailors, and barbers—mostly people of Japanese ancestry. Over two-thirds of 2,300 of the Latin American internees deported to the United States were Japanese nationals and their families; over eighty percent came from Peru. About half the Japanese internees were family members, including Nisei, who asked to join their husbands and fathers in camps pending deportation to Japan; family members were classified as "voluntary internees."[20]

This problem was spotted very early on by Tannenberg, the German representative at the Greenbrier. He was concerned that the first group of Axis personnel kicked out of South America, the group that came in immediately after the war started, included individuals he did not feel fit into the correct profile. In a memo dated January 30, 1942, to Assistant Director Ladd, Special Agent Lawler conveyed a complaint from Tannenberg: "[He] then reported that the group from Bogota had

Six. Be Careful What You Wish For

arrived, but that whereas the group originally consisted of 130 persons, only a part of them namely those immediately connected with the Embassy and Consulates, had been allowed to come to the White Sulphur Springs for transfer to Europe. Tannenberg stated that in the original group there were 75 German nationals who had been assured both by the Colombian Government and the American Ambassador that they would be exchanged. Nevertheless these 75 were separated from the remainder of the group at New York (where they had arrived from South America then culled out by American authorities and quartered in another camp)...."[21]

Despite these early indications that the program might result in too many enemy nationals and in enemy nationals who might have been harmless, the State Department doubled down. It sent a representative, Mr. Ara Warren, to prod the South American countries to expel all potential Axis sympathizers. The State Department lobbied the War Department to free up vessels for ferrying service. When only two ships were made available, and each could only be committed for one trip, Mr. Warren warned the South Americans not to miss this only opportunity. Several South American countries begin to turn the tables on the State Department:

> Peru quickly recognized the Pearl Harbor attack as a windfall opportunity to rid itself of its Japanese population and seize their property. [Peru wasted little time in severing diplomatic relations with Japan and] the Peruvian government immediately followed this action by freezing accounts and holding of Axis citizens and then swiftly passed legislation declaring cancellation of all land leases to Japanese, Germans and Italians. Concomitantly, the United States' assault on West Coast Japanese Americans only facilitated similar Peruvian actions against its Japanese colony despite lack of any evidence linking Japanese to espionage or other subversive activities.[22]

The *Acadia* was a military transport controlled by the Wartime Shipping Commission. The first voyage of the *Acadia* was completed on April 25, 1942, when the boat landed at New Orleans with 491 Germans, 69 Italians, and 94 Japanese. The vessel had made four calls at South American ports, picking up Germans, Italians, and Japanese from Bolivia, Peru, Ecuador, and Colombia. Passengers included 158 German officials, 52 Italian officials, 63 Japanese officials, 333 German nationals, 17 Italian nationals and 31 Japanese nationals. These individuals were sent to either the Greenbrier or the Homestead, with some of the nationals

Axis Diplomats in American Custody

being sent to internment camps that were being set up by the Immigration and Naturalization Service. These camps were originally set up to house the Japanese Americans from the West Coast and a relatively small number of Italian and Germans who resided in the United States and whom the State Department or the FBI deemed suspicious.

The *Etolin* made the next voyage to South America. It docked at San Francisco on May 17, 1942, with 493 passengers from Ecuador, Colombia, and Venezuela. The vessel did not carry any officials. There were 328 German nationals, 14 Italian nationals, and 151 Japanese nationals aboard. These people were sent to Immigration and Naturalization camps. Mr. Warren brags, "Our efforts to prevail upon the Ecuadoran Government to expel dangerous Axis nationals have been long and arduous and at times appeared to be in vain. I feel however, that we can already claim considerable success, as a total of 42 of the 48 nationals departing on the ETOLIN (a U.S. military transport) were included on our list of dangerous nationals ... the only dangerous nationals who will be permitted to remain are those married to Ecuadoran women ... [who promise] to abstain from any political activity."[23]

Just how dangerous were the individuals included on the lists prepared by the State Department is unclear. One of the South Americans caught up in the expulsion program was Dirk Albers. He was expelled from Montevideo, Argentina. He was born in Germany, had no military experience, and had no technical qualifications. He was listed as a wool buyer but at the time of his deportation was not employed. He belonged to the German Club, German Sports League, and the German Mutual Aid Society:

> On numerous occasions Albers has been reported to this office as an officer of the German Army, as a member of the German secret service, and as the leader of a sabotage group. It has been alleged that Albers is an alumnus of the Helldorf-Bohle school of sabotage in Hamburg, Germany. He numbers among his acquaintances numerous Germans who have been reported as agents of the Nazis. It was also reported that little is known of his background in the German colony: Albers is inactive in the affairs of the German community and he has never associated himself with any of the official groups in the city although he is listed as a contributor to the German Winter Help.[24]

Arturo Albrecht was from Misiones Montevideo, Uruguay. He was born in Germany. He worked at the docks as a porter and had no military background or technical skills.

Six. Be Careful What You Wish For

He has admitted to officers of the embassy that he was a member of the Nazi Party, a member of the German Work Front, and a one time contributor to the German Winter Help Fund and stated that he voted on board the German ship Petagonia in 1938 for Hitler. Albrecht advises in an interview with officers of this Embassy, that he made three trips to German[y] since first coming to Uruguay, the last journey being in 1927. On each occasion he traveled on German vessels, being signed on in the capacity of a cook. He admitted that he had received two years of compulsory military training in the German Infantry in 1910 and 1912. It is noted that the Uruguayan police have been cognizant of Albrecht's activities and according to reports they have carefully watched his activities for two years. It is believed that the subject is an individual who if properly directed by the Germans would undoubtedly be capable of performing many valuable services for them through his contacts in and about the port of Montevideo and even though subject is not believed capable of performing duties on his own initiative it is believed that his continued residence in Uruguay constitutes a potential threat to the Allied war effort.[25]

A memo titled "Regarding activities of the United States Government in removing from the various other American Republics dangerous subversive aliens," the U.S.'s overriding policy is spelled out:

> The United States Government has since the outbreak of war received the hearty cooperation of the other American Republics in the question of the expulsion of aliens of enemy nationality and other dangerous aliens who were apparently serving Axis interests within their territory. The United States Government has provided facilities to bring to this country approximately 3,000 such aliens of whom roughly 2,000 will have been repatriated when the Gripsholm departs on its second voyage. In addition, approximately 750 enemy aliens have been repatriated direct on neutral vessels from Venezuela, Brazil, Paraguay and Uruguay.
>
> The program of this Government and of the other American Republics associated with it has already resulted in the elimination or virtual elimination of Japanese colonies in several countries such as Panama, Costa Rica, El Salvador, and Ecuador. It is believed to have broken up to a great extent the local German organizations in many Central American countries and in Peru. For example, of the 14 particularly dangerous Germans listed in a report of June 16, 1940, as being the head officials of the Nazi party in all the Central American Republics, 9 were deported to the United States, of whom 4 were repatriated, and 5 are still held here. There is no information to indicate that any of the remaining 5 persons listed in the report are yet in Central American and it is believed that they returned home before we entered the war.
>
> The cooperation which we received from the other American Republics varies in terms of the local laws, the national policy of each country, and other circumstances peculiar to the case of each individual Republic and not in terms of willingness to cooperate in the interest of Hemisphere defense. For example, the belligerent nations of Central America and the Caribbean islands have in general been willing to send us subversive aliens without placing any limitation on our disposition of them. In other words, we could repatriate them, we could intern

them or we could hold them in escrow for bargaining purposes. Peru, though not a belligerent country, has been content to expel subversive aliens and turn them over to us, their enemy, without requiring of us a firm promise to repatriate them. On the other hand, Venezuela has been unwilling to discuss the possibility of turning aliens over to us for repatriation or for internment; and Colombia, Ecuador and Mexico have insisted on the most explicit guarantees from us before turning over to us any aliens for repatriation. The attitude of these latter governments is based on internal reasons which probably have ample justification in terms of the local situation.

... Our experience in this matter and general observation of Axis methods leads us to the conclusion that all German nationals without exception, all Japanese nationals, a small proportion of Italian nationals and more individuals than might be expected among the political and racial refugees from Central Europe are all dangerous and should be removed from their present sphere of activity as rapidly as possible.

... It is desirable that the repatriation of inherently harmless Axis nationals may be used to the greatest possible extent in obtaining the repatriation from Axis territory of nationals of the other American Republics whose presence in enemy territory gives the enemy a certain amount of bargaining power.[26]

This memo reveals a possibly more sinister motive behind the States Department's decision to permit the most widespread acceptance of South American Axis nationals—the United States needed hostages to exchange for American nationals held in Axis countries.

Be Careful What You Wish For

If six weeks before, the State Department had been worried that too few Axis nationals would be expelled from South America, it now faced the opposite problem The *Acadia* was forced to make a second voyage, picking up passengers from Ecuador, Colombia, and Venezuela, a total of 477 German nationals, 7 Italian nationals, and 3 Japanese nationals. The only diplomats it picked up were five Japanese officials from Venezuela. Soon afterwards, a ship called the *Shawanee* was pressed into ferry service. It arrived in New Orleans in late June. It carried 107 German nationals from Peru, 341 Japanese nationals from Peru, 10 Italian nationals from Peru, and also 68 German nationals from Bolivia. There were no diplomats, no correspondents, nor any type of Axis officials on board.

Within the United States, as early as the spring of 1942, some in

Six. Be Careful What You Wish For

the government were raising concerns not over the policy per se but its magnitude. A memo dated April 13, 1942, from Mr. Green to Mr. Ladd notes that:

> The situation in regard to the repatriation of officials and non-official European Axis Nationals from the Western Hemisphere is as follows.... There are 716 European Axis officials or persons entitled to official treatment at White Sulphur Springs and at Asheville; there are circa 250 persons of a similar category on the Acadia (the troopship sent to pick up detainees): a total of circa 966 persons. All of these must be repatriated. In respect to the non-officials we are formally obligated to repatriate the circa 700 persons traveling on the Etolin (another troopship), the circa 250 on the Acadia and the 230 Italian nationals on a list yet to be prepared by Prince Colonna. There are circa 140 persons still to come from Venezuela and according to Mr. Ara Warren there are circa 1,500 additional person whom we are apparently obligated to bring to the United States from the West coast of South America and to repatriate. In addition there are circa 400 Axis nationals who have already been brought to the United States from Central America and the Caribbean Area. This is a grand total of circa 4,208 persons to be repatriated (not including an indeterminate number of European Axis nationals in the United States.) Apart from our commitment to the other American Republics, the German Government has indicated its wish that all of the German nationals in the above categories be repatriated. In addition we have offered to repatriate all German nationals from this country who wish to return to Germany but have not yet received a reply from the German Government.[27]

Mr. Green was so concerned about the number of South American detainees coming to the United States that he wrote,

> In view of our commitment to repatriate (1) the balance of the Axis nationals brought to this country on Etolin (2) the non-official German national[s] in this country who wish to return home and (3) the voluntary Axis repatriates from the other American Republics (with particular reference to Bolivia, Peru and Ecuador) the situation has now changed radically and a third trip of the Drottningholm appears inevitable. In fact, because of the success of Mr. Ava Warren's mission and the number of Axis voluntary exiles to be repatriated from Bolivia, Peru and Ecuador, it is assumed that a fourth and fifth trip of the Drottningholm will be necessary.[28]

Three Weeks of Bedlam

The State Department realized that it was facing an immediate logistical problem. Mr. Bannerman wrote to Mr. Fitch on April 16, 1942:

> The 500 Axis officials and non-officials will arrive at New Orleans on April 24th. Of this group 355 persons will depart on the SS Drottningholm on the first

Axis Diplomats in American Custody

exchange, while the remaining 145 persons (Japanese and Germans) will be lodged at the Greenbrier Hotel. At the present moment the Drottningholm has not left Sweden and possibly will not leave for 48 hours, which means that a[t] minimum ... the Drottningholm cannot sail from New York until May 1. There are two days of train travel between New Orleans and New York which means that there will be five days between April 24th and May 1st that this party of 500 will have to be provided with lodging.... It is quite impossible to keep them on the train during this period as train facilities are inadequate and uncomfortable, therefore a hotel properly equipped with rooms, dining and laundry facilities must be provided.... The 145 destined to the Greenbrier hotel cannot be accommodated there until the German career officers already there are moved out to the Drottningholm. The Greenbrier now has 831 occupants and apparently no more can be accommodated....[29]

Mr. Bannerman continues, "Informal inquiries, without revealing the source have been made of the Gibson hotel at Cincinnati. [This hotel has] 1000 rooms, is completely equipped to handle a large group for a few days and has all the necessary facilities available without causing extra expenses, delay or inconvenience."[30]

Negotiations started almost immediately. An April 17 letter from Mr. Davis, general manager of the hotel, states: "Regarding the housing of a diplomatic group ... April 25 through April 30 ... we agree to provide accommodations on floors segregated from the rest of the hotel. In addition, the Roof Garden will also be placed at the disposal of this group for the purpose of lounge and meal service. Both sleeping floors, dining hall and laundry and any other facilities used by this group will be absolutely private and not utilized by any other persons...."[31]

A price of $8.50 per person (adult), $5 per child, and $5 per government employee was given. Mr. Sumner Wells, acting secretary of state, replied to Mr. Davis in a short note which includes the sentence, "From April 25 and for not less than four days we propose rates American plan of $7.50 per adult per day.... Please wire immediately whether this offer is acceptable."[32]

The *Acadia* arrived in New Orleans with nearly 700 passengers. Two hundred were sent to the internment camps. "The 500 persons rounded up in South and Central America consisted of 99 diplomatic officials and 401 non-officials. However, the entire group of 500 was accorded diplomatic treatment."[33] This group consisted of seventy Italian officials, twenty-four German career officials, thirty-eight German non-career officials, 283 German non-officials with families, and

Six. Be Careful What You Wish For

eighty-five Japanese officers. Because of the delay with the *Drottningholm*, they were transported by rail to the Gibson.

Little was reported in the press when the diplomatic parties arrived. Only a seventy-five word article from the Associated Press described "500 Axis diplomats and consular officials, en route to Europe or Japan which had broken off relations with their government ... had landed at New Orleans and were transported by rail to Cincinnati where they will remain for a few days...."[34] as they transited to their home countries. The hotel was located in the heart of the city, and they were isolated on the top four floors of the ten-story structure, with regular guests using the lower floors.

The Gibson had a large dining hall, a roof garden, cocktail lounge and laundry. The detainees were allowed to visit the stores in the hotel at pre-arranged times. Historian Robert Ernest Miller writes:

> For nearly a month in the late spring of 1942, more than six hundred Axis diplomats, consular officials and their families lodged in the top four floors of the Hotel Gibson. This surreal internment was part of a larger international exchange between Axis diplomats still residing in Allied nations in the Western Hemisphere and American and Latin American diplomatic personnel who shared a similar plight in Axis-controlled Europe. Hotel staff extended every possible courtesy to the enemy aliens. The Hotel Gibson brought hair stylists and barbers on site to service its guests. Foods that had seemingly been in short supply in downtown restaurants such as coffee, bacon and fruit juices were readily available to the Axis guests. Stenographers who were fluent in German were summoned to the hotel to write letters for some of the detainees. During the detention at the Hotel Gibson, one female Japanese envoy who was pregnant was taken to Jewish hospital, where she gave birth to her baby.[35]

In a meeting held April 28, 1942, the German internees asked that facilities be provided "to spend several hours in the open air for exercise privileges."[36] The request was denied by Mr. Bannerman of the State Department, who explained "In view of the fact the stay at the Gibson Hotel will only be for a few days and the problem of guarding the people for this exercise privilege would be too great to be properly handled, it is decided that such exercise privileges cannot be granted...."[37]

The *Drottningholm* continued to be delayed, and the five hundred passengers, including nearly 80 children, spent nearly five weeks in the hotel, well over the minimum of four days Acting Secretary Welles had promised or the "few days" Mr. Bannerman predicted. Another request, made about a week after the arrival at the Gibson, this time from one of the Border Patrol agents, asked that the detainees be allowed to use a nearby park for occasional outings. The agent as already secured the cooperation of Cincinnati police to provide guard duty. This was also declined.

Eventually the Axis personnel left the Gibson. Three hundred and sixty-six went to Jersey City and the first exchange vessel. The other 144 were sent to the Greenbrier, room having become available, as this was the number of guests at the Greenbrier who were simultaneously sent to New York to board the *Drottningholm*. Conditions were toughest on the children.

A State Department memo notes, "Every one of [the children] were inoculated at the hotel against ... whooping cough and those children who were ill were quarantined in the hotel. Permission of the health authorities at Cincinnati was obtained to move them out of the city under quarantine conditions on the train. All the children suffering from whooping cough or measles were sent direct to the Greenbrier Hotel and a special quarantine ward was set up for them and they did not ... go directly to New York."[38]

Seven

The Actual Exchange

An *Asheville Citizen* article dated May 7, 1942, reads:

> Two hundred twenty-one of the Axis diplomatic and consular group which has been interned at Grove Park Inn since April 3 left by special trains yesterday afternoon for Jersey City, New Jersey where they will embark this morning to return to their Homelands—Italy, Hungary and Bulgaria—under an exchange plan. Among those departing were the two ranking diplomats who have been at Grove Park Inn, Don Ascanio Colonna, Italian ambassador to the United States and Dimitri Naoumoff, minister from Bulgaria to this country. No ranking diplomat from Hungary was in the party which has been interned here.... In the departing group were wives and children as well as diplomatic and consular agents. There was a considerable number of servants, also.... The party left aboard two special trains. The first, carrying the higher officials and most of their staff members, with their families, pulled out of the Southern Railway yards at 4 o'clock, and the second train with minor staff members and servants aboard, departed about 45 minutes later.... It is understood that another group of Axis diplomatic and consular internees will be sent here from internment at Cincinnati to replace those who left yesterday....[1]

At the Greenbrier, on May 5, 1942, in the Virginia room, Adolph Blum, a butler from Washington, D.C., and Miss Fiedel Bugersiter, a maid from Washington, D.C., were married by Father Pipp, a Catholic priest from the White Sulphur Springs area. The next day, "in the lobby of the hotel during the departure of the group, the Japanese Diplomatic Corp detained here were all in attendance, extending farewell greetings to the departing Germans. A Japanese patriotic march "Aikoku Shinkokyoky" was sung by the Japanese group and also three cheers in Japanese were given as the departing group left the lobby of the hotel. Dr. Hans Thomsen, former German Chargé d'Affaires, being one of the last Germans to leave extended a short greeting to the Japanese in attendance as he left the hotel, concluding his short speech which was in German with "Heil Hitler" with arm outstretched."[2]

Axis Diplomats in American Custody

At White Sulphur Springs, the Associated Press reported:

> In quiet and orderly fashion, some 400 German diplomats, newspapermen, their wives and sleepy-eyed children filed out of the stately old Greenbrier hotel last midnight to board three special trains for Jersey City and the long voyage home. Many of them visibly repressed their excitement while casting farewell glances at the mountain resort where they had been interned since last December, awaiting exchange for Americans held in enemy countries.... West Virginia state troopers assisted federal officials in charge of the internees at White Sulphur Springs in moving the internees from the hotel to the railway station a half mile away. Baggage had been loaded beforehand—and those who saw it paid particular attention to the fact that there seemed to be no more luggage leaving than had arrived in the first place. A close check of the buying by the aliens in the hotel's shops, an authoritative source said, disclosed that they bought in reasonable amounts and there was no hoarding. There had been reports in the village of White Sulphur Springs that the internees were buying great quantities of such articles as were available to carry home.... Behind them they left a small contingent of Germans and all of the several hundred Japanese aliens who were brought to White Sulphur Springs from Hot Springs, Va.[3]

The two groups converged in Jersey City. Some spent the night at the Pennsylvania Hotel, and all were at the dock the next day to board the ship *Drottningholm*. The group consisted of 226 Italians, Bulgarian, and Hungarians from the Grove Park Inn; 426 Germans from the Greenbrier, seventy Italians from Hotel Gibson (from South America), ninety-nine Germans from Hotel Gibson (also from South America), and 164 other Germans and Italians, for a total of 985 passengers.

The passenger list for the first *Drottningholm* read:

German Officials from the United States	174
German Officials from Cuba	15
German Officials from Guatemala	43
German Officials from Mexico	43
German Officials from Dutch Guiana	2
German Officials from Dominican Republic	8
German Officials from Colombia	45
German Officials from Panama	25
German Officials from Nicaragua	6
German Officials from Costa Rica	5
German Officials from Venezuela	42
German Officials from Haiti	5
German Officials from Ecuador	36
German Officials from Peru	83
German Officials from Bolivia	18

Seven. The Actual Exchange

German Newspaper Correspondents from Mexico	5
German Newspaper Correspondents from United States	20
German Newspaper Correspondents from Colombia	5
German Nationals from United States	21
Italian Officials from United States	94
Italian Officials from Panama	19
Italian Officials from Guatemala	77
Italian Officials from Nicaragua	6
Italian Officials from Colombia	10
Italian Officials from Venezuela	16
Italian Officials from El Salvador	5
Italian Officials from Costa Rico	3
Italian Officials from Cuba	5
Italian Officials from Dominican Republic	5
Italian Officials from Mexico	3
Italian Officials from Ecuador	16
Italian Officials from Peru	29
Italian Officials from Bolivia	24
Italian Newspaper Correspondents From United States	15
Italian Nationals from United States	44
Italians Nationals from Colombia	3
Bulgarian Officials from United States	10
Hungarian Officials from United States	34
Hungarian Nationals from United States	4

The *Drottningholm* left Jersey City on May 7, 1942. It passed uneventfully across the Atlantic. As it traveled, the U.S. diplomats in Bad Nauheim were assembled. They went by train to Lisbon, timed to coincide with the *Drottningholm*'s arrival.

The Gibson Is Closed

At White Sulphur Springs, for few days, the Japanese had the run of the Greenbrier. An agent reported that there were 64 Germans and 405 Japanese and stated, "Had to sit on the yellow bellies when the Germans left. They wanted the space in the hotel vacated by the Germans and in addition an extra 133 rooms.... During the conferences I really got an insight on the Japs—their inferiority complex in wanting what the Germans had whether they were any better rooms or not.... On the surface of course they are Axis partners but underneath they have little or no regard for each other.... I hope we soon kick the s—— out of the so-and so's and I want to a have had a hand in it...."[4]

Another agent reported, "After the departure of the German Diplomatic Corps from the Greenbrier Hotel ... that the Japanese headed by Morito Horishima, former Japanese Consul General in New York City came to Mr. George O'Brien, Assistant Manager of the Greenbrier Hotel and Mr. E.P. Poole, Special Agent of the State Department, relative to making different arrangements concerning their rooms. They were very desirous of obtaining a suite formerly occupied by Dr. Hans Thomsen (which was now occupied by Mr. Gramms, who now represented the remaining Germans at the hotel) for Mr. Saburo Kurusu, Official Envoy of Japan to the United States, who (was at the Greenbrier).... (The request was refused and the Japanese) became very indignant, stating that they felt they were being discriminated against, since Gramms is a German 'nobody' and that their positions as well as Mr. Kurusu's entitle them to have this room from Gramms and that Gramms should be changed. It was apparent from the information furnished the writer ... that the Japanese here have little use for the Germans and feel that they are superior to the Germans and should be entitled to accommodations better than those furnished the Germans...."[5]

In Cincinnati, the remaining South American detainees spent another week at the Gibson. On May 14, 1942, they were loaded into one of two trains. Train number one departed Cincinnati at 9:00 am. It contained 218 passengers, 63 Japanese and 155 German non-officials and families. This train went to Asheville. Train number two left the same day, but not until 10 pm. It carried 117 German non-officials and traveled to White Sulphur Springs. By midnight on May 14, 1942, the Gibson's role in the diplomatic exchange program was over.

Second Acadia Arrival

Around mid–May 1942, the military transport *Acadia* arrived in New Orleans from a second voyage along the west coast of South

Seven. The Actual Exchange

America. It carried eight Japanese and fifty Germans who were sent to the Grove Park Inn and 342 Germans who were sent to the Greenbrier. The Asheville Citizen reported:

> German nationals and Japanese officials, on their way home from South America, arrived in Asheville yesterday and were interned at the Grove Park Inn.... The Germans, mostly blond and blue-eyed, smiled occasionally but the almond-eyed Japanese were grim-visaged, looking neither to right nor left.... Two little Japanese girls did break through their reserve however, snickering as they pointed to a small sign on the back of one of the police department motorcycles. It read: To Hell With Japan, K.O. Tokyo; A small German girl, blond curls hanging other shoulders, carried a doll tenderly on one shoulder and had a teddy bear tucked under one arm.[6]

On May 28, 1942, an additional forty-five Japanese and Italians from Mexico arrived at the Grove Park Inn, bringing the hotel's total to just over 300.

Drottningholm Returns from Lisbon

The *Drottningholm* safely returned with its load of U.S. diplomats as well as European refugees. It carried 147 American officials from Germany, Italy, Rumania, Hungary, France, Portugal, and Switzerland. There were nine newspaper correspondent from Italy, thirteen from Germany, and one from Rumania. There were 414 American nationals from various countries in Europe. There were 86 aliens who accompanied the American nationals, typically spouses and children. The *Drottningholm* also carried 166 South American officials and 72 South American nationals

Second Drottningholm to Lisbon

The vessel left New York Harbor on June 14, 1942. Four hundred and seventy-two Germans and two Italians arrived from the Greenbrier. One hundred sixty Germans and 10 Italians arrived from the Grove Park Inn. Various other European Axis nationals, who had been on their own recognizance, held in detention on Ellis Island, or were held at assorted other internment camps, went on board.

Axis Diplomats in American Custody

The passenger list included very few officials—13 German officials from Bolivia and 2 German officials from the United States and one Rumanian official. These officials did not travel on the first *Drottningholm* due to illness, and their absence was known by the German government. The remaining passengers were all nationals and were predominately from Latin America. They included:

German Nationals from Peru	133
German Nationals from Ecuador	274
German Nationals from Bolivia	30
German Nationals from Colombia	316
German Nationals from Mexico	20
German Nationals from United States	16
Italian Nationals from Bolivia	13
Italian Nationals from Costa Rica	2
Italian Nationals from Colombia	7
Hungarian Nationals from United States	10
Bulgarian Nationals from United States	7

A contingent of thirty-five Germans was returned from New York to White Sulphur Springs. It is unclear who these individuals were. They may have been people prohibited from boarding the *Drottningholm*, although, up until this point, all clearance had been processed prior to any alien leaving the hotels. They may have been people who at the last moment decided they wanted to stay in the U.S. Most likely, they were extras sent to board the *Drottningholm* in case, for some reason, more berths became available, if, for example, a first-class cabin was converted to a third-class allowing more people to squeeze in.

Some Are Paroled

In Asheville, during May and June, a few of the detainees were paroled. An article in the *Asheville Citizen* speaks of how some individuals were simply released into the community:

> Some of the group departing yesterday were released on interim paroles.... Hearings were conducted last week and early this week at the hotel for a number of members of the diplomatic corps who requested permission to remain in this country.... In cases where it was found after the hearing that the aliens in question obviously were not dangerous and would in fact aid the United Nations war effort, recommendations were made to the attorney general that they be granted interim

Seven. The Actual Exchange

paroles. These recommendations were concurred in by the attorney general.... Nine men in the group were registered yesterday by Mrs. Cecelia McConnell of draft Board No 1 under the selective service training act. There was one Italian and one Austrian included in the group and the remainder gave their native countries as Czechoslovakia and Hungary.[7]

One of the persons not granted parole was Robert Minner. This was the newspaperman whose wife came to the Greenbrier with their two children and elected not to enter the hotel grounds as, if she did so, she and the children would not be allowed to stay in America. Mr. Minner was sent back to the Grove Park Inn and would subsequently be sent on the *Drottningholm* back to Germany.

Luckier was Margrete Sjogreen. She was Norwegian by birth and had been a nurse for an Italian diplomat stationed in San Salvador. The *Asheville Citizen* reports: "An attractive, petite blond, the first thing one notice[d] about her was her sparkling blue eyes, her obvious sincerity ... her natural blond hair that was almost white."[8] She had traveled from San Salvadore to Guatemala, then to White Sulphur Springs and then to the Grove Park Inn. She explained that she was to stay in San Salvador for two years, but the month before she was to leave, the Germans occupied Norway and she had nowhere to go. She did not want to go to Germany, a place where she knew no one, and had petitioned the State Department to stay with an aunt in Minneapolis, a request that was granted, the newspaper reported, then went on, "Miss Sjogreen could not keep away from the subject of the children in this war, however, and the conversation soon turned to them. 'It's so terrible for them,' she said. 'I can't help being sorry for all of them. When something like this happens to them so early in life, they never forget it. Their never get over it. It does something to them. I hope that those who were here are not bombed. War is hell,' she said quietly, with emphasis on the word is."[9]

The First Japanese Exchange

The Japanese at the Triangle T Ranch left Dragoon on June 8, 1942. An agent writes:

> On the train trip from Arizona to New York, the Hawaiian group of Japanese were restricted to their cars and were not allowed to mix with the other Japanese on

Axis Diplomats in American Custody

the train. Upon arrival at New York, the Hawaiian group was taken off the train separately and into the Pennsylvania Hotel and lodged in a wing of the hotel which was cut off from all communication with the other Japanese there. A special dining room was arranged and this group, at no time, had any contact with other Japanese who were to be repatriated on the GRIPSHOLM. [Once the sailing time was set] the Hawaiian group was brought from the hotel and placed aboard the GRIPSHOLM not more than four hours prior to the departure of the ship. At all times this group was kept under strict surveillance and their questions as to the whereabouts of other Japanese officials were not answered.... The treatment was to [keep] them from having any contact with any group whatsoever regardless of who they might be ... to insure that the information regarding the attack on Pearl Harbor and known to the Japanese Hawaiian group could, in no way, get out through any contacts this group might have, thus delaying any information they might be able to take back until the very last minute.[10]

At the Greenbrier, *The White Sulphur Springs Sentinel* wrote, "With the same calm and dispatch which have marked other comings and goings from the Greenbrier hotel here in the last six months, Japanese internees departed for the seaboard on June 10."[11] The Japanese also left the Grove Park Inn, leaving it empty of diplomat exchange personnel for the first time since April and it returned to normal commercial operations. Around the country, Japanese enemy aliens were transferred from internment camps. On June 18, 1942, the *Gripsholm* sailed with twenty-three Japanese from the Triangle T, ninety-four from Asheville, 407 from White Sulphur Springs, and 424 from the internment camps or who had been free on their own recognizance.

The vessel departed from New York on June 18, 1942. Like the *Drottningholm*, the ship had a large sign painted on the sides identifying the vessel as "Diplomatic." It sailed with lights lit so that U-boat captains could easily identify it. The vessel arrived two weeks later in Rio de Janeiro. It moored out in the harbor, not at a dock, with Brazilian military with machine guns patrolling the nearby piers. An additional 417 Japanese passengers, including diplomats and officials from the Japanese embassies in Brazil, Uruguay, and Paraguay, were ferried to the vessel.

The Serpa Pinto

In a memo dated March 6, 1942, it is observed that:

Mr. Tannenberg expressed considerable concern over ... the opinion that the Drottningholm is somewhat smaller [than the original boat expected] ... and is of

Seven. The Actual Exchange

insufficient capacity to adequately accommodate the number anticipated after arrival of additional groups from South America. [The suggestion to utilize a Portuguese boat was being made] to facilitate the diplomatic exchange rather than cause further prolonged negotiations.... These suggestions are in effect that those German and Italian nationals who have only a temporary diplomatic status, that is, those who are to be exchanged as private individuals, those who have accompanied diplomatic groups here from Central and South American countries and those who are only temporary employees of the various embassies and consulates, should be repatriated as rapidly as possible by utilizing Portuguese steamers plying between the United States and Lisbon, provided the same guarantees and securities could be obtained for those vessels as for the diplomatic transport. Mr. Tannenberg stated that about 250 to 300 such persons could be named and that such proposed repatriation of them would reduce discussions regarding diplomatic exchange to the original limitations.[12]

The use of the *Serpa Pinto* provided a relief valve to allow the gross numbers of those being repatriated to Europe to come close to the 1,500 originally anticipated in the earliest negotiations, when the *Kungsholm* was slated as the mercy ship. Because this figure was reached and as the ship sailed very close in time to the first voyage of the *Drottningholm*, the Germans apparently accepted that the exchange terms had been satisfied. They did not hold back American diplomats in Europe as they had once threatened until a second voyage of the *Drottningholm* but instead treated the *Serpa Pinto* sailing as justification to release all of the American diplomats at Bad Nauheim.

The Gripsholm *Arrives in Africa*

The *Gripsholm* arrived in Lourenço Marques, Portuguese East Africa, on July 22, 1942. Two vessels which had earlier left the Orient arrived at about the same time. The *Asama Maru* arrived in Lourenço Marques on July 24, 1942, carrying approximately 800 civilians from Japan, Southeast Asia, and the Philippines. She was accompanied by the Italian vessel *Conte Verde*, with about 600 passengers from Shanghai.

The *Gripsholm* left Lourenço Marques on July 28, 1942, transited back around the tip of Africa, then crossed the south Atlantic and entered the dangerous water off the east coast of the U.S., its floodlights blazing and hoping that any German U-boats would recognize it as an exchange ship.

Greenbrier Closes

The Greenbrier still had one hundred and twenty-three Germans and Italians. The hotel was desperate to return to normal operations as it was losing the summer season and as the number of remaining detainees was so low. Management asked for relief from the State Department. The State Department approached the Grove Park Inn, which had been free of detainees for only a few weeks, to see if it was interested in hosting them. They agreed. A headline in the *White Sulphur Springs Sentinel* reads: "Last of the Axis Internees Leave Here…. The Greenbrier Hotel Completes First Wartime Service, Now Open to Public…. Last of Germans are Removed Wednesday by Special Train."[13] The article notes that "some 100 odd Germans, who have been interned here for the last several months, were escorted [to the depot] where they boarded a special train to be taken to Asheville, NC."[14]

An article in the *Asheville Citizen* reads, "Officials of the State Department here maintained the usual secrecy concerning the movement of a new group to the hotel, which had not been occupied by aliens about three weeks…. As has been the case with several groups, there were many children in the crowd and they manifested more interest in what was transpiring than did the adults. The entire crowd, however, seemed to be in good spirit and many of them were laughing and talking among themselves. There was not so much the appearance of self-consciousness as has been the case with some of the others."[15]

On July 11, 1942, the last large group of South Americans was moved to the Grove Park. This was a group of ninety-nine Germans from Mexico. On July 15, 1942, the *Drottningholm* made a third voyage. One hundred thirty nine Germans from Asheville were included in this trip; the other passengers were from internment camps all over the country or were German or Italian nationals of unofficial status who desired to return to the homeland.

The Gripsholm *Arrives Back in New York*

The *Gripsholm* arrived in New York on August 25, 1942. Ambassador Joseph C. Grew publicly complained about the treatment he and

Seven. The Actual Exchange

the other diplomats held by the Japanese received. One of the detainees, Robert Bellaire, a United Press correspondent, said that detainees were denied food, were not allowed to exercise, were not given new clothes as old ones wore out, and that the Japanese delayed the delivery of medicines for the sick. The first line of a newspaper article published in August 1942 reads, "American diplomats in Tokyo were treated with a savagery unparalleled in the history of civilized nations."[16]

New York Times correspondent Otto D. Tolischue was jailed in Tokyo with six other American newsmen and a Canadian newswoman named Phyllis Argal. Tolischue reports:

> ... we were held in solitary confinement under severe conditions of hardship for six months under charges of espionage and violation of the National Defense act. Miss Argal was tied up and handcuffed when she was arrested and was repeatedly slapped until her face was cut. CBS Representative W. L. Wills was slapped during the whole examination period lasting more than three months. He was forced to squat for hours in Japanese fashion with the result that he still is suffering an injury to his left knee. Jasper N. Nellinger was slapped, kicked on the shins and forced to stand for hours with his hands above his head.
>
> To force a confession the police threatened me with firing squads ... in Korea, three American missionaries were among 22 captives thrown into a verminous prison so small that some had to stand while others slept on the floor. The Japanese forced water down their throats until they were nearly drowned, beat them with rubber hose and belting.... Men taken prisoner in Hong Kong reported that the invaders raped Chinese, Eurasian and white women, including three British nurses. Afterwards the Japs bayoneted and burned the nurses....[17]

These images of the maltreatment of U.S diplomats and citizens while held by the Japanese would temper the public's view towards the next groups of Axis diplomats to arrive in the United States.

The *Gripsholm* sailed again to exchange Japanese for Americans, but no diplomats were involved in this exchange. The voyage took place in late August, with Japanese civilians and American civilians trading places in India. A newspaper article reports, "There has been no talk as yet of an exchange of war prisoners. Difficulties in this connection include the fact that the United States holds few Japanese prisoners of war. Furthermore, the Japanese attitude toward their own soldiers who fall into enemy hands is that they should not have allowed themselves to be taken."[18]

No additional exchanges were made with the Japanese, although there were thousands of Allied nationals trapped in the Orient. There were several reasons for this. Historian Arthur E. Barbeur suggests that "Japan rebuffed overtures for further exchange because the Allies lacked prisoners of sufficient stature."[19] Other possible reasons may include that the treatment of Ambassador Grew and the other detainees had left a bad taste in the mouths of many. In addition, as Mr. Bannerman writes to Mr. Fitch:

> It is the general opinion that the Japanese exchange is definitely off. There has been no exchange of notes cancelling the exchange but as a result of the following it cannot be seen how the exchange can be completed.... The Japanese have admitted executing some of the American Army fliers captured in Doolittle's raid on Japan without compliance to any of the terms of the Geneva Convention. The Department sent a note to Japan, reported to be the strongest one we have ever sent and stating that all Japanese who were in any way connected with the trial which sentenced these fliers to death, would be rounded up and given the extreme penalty for their actions. It also stated that any future acts by the Japanese would be dealt with in the same manner.... At least two months have elapsed since our last inquiry to the Japanese about the exchange and there has been no answer, so it can practically be written off the record that any further exchanges with the Japanese will occur.[20]

In Asheville, over a hundred detainees from South America were still at the Grove Park Inn. Hotel management had, over the last few months, been approached by both the army and navy for use of the hotel as a convalescent center. The army dropped out on hearing that the hotel had taken on more detainees. The navy responded differently, by offering more money. In a series of carefully drafted letters, the hotel's management seems to have been playing the navy against the Special War Problems Division. As a result, the State Department began to search for another hotel.

Eight

End Games

At this time, in China, Japan, and others areas of the Orient, the State Department estimated that between 7,500 and 15,000 United States nationals were being held by the Japanese. The United States felt that it needed a similar number of Japanese nationals to allow negotiations for an exchange to occur.

On the West Coast, particularly around Los Angeles and San Diego, almost all ethnic Japanese were rounded up and placed in internment camps. However, in Hawaii, perhaps because Japanese made up over a third of the population, a different approach was taken. Specific individuals were targeted. These people were Buddhist priests, radio personalities, teachers at Japanese schools, what would today be called community activists and organizers, and other leaders of Japanese social and business groups. Approximately 500 Issei and 100 Nisei men were placed in camps in Hawaii, or taken to camps in the United States by March 1942. Issei are Japanese who are born in Japan and later move to the United States. Nisei are the children of Issei who are born in the United States. Soon afterward, the wives and children of these men were asked if they would "volunteer" to join their husbands. Over one thousand accepted and were soon sent to camps on the mainland, although, for a time, the families were not all at the same camp.

In the summer of 1942, another sailing of the *Gripsholm* was anticipated. However, this time the ship would not trade diplomats or other officials and semi-officials but instead would exchange ordinary citizens. A girl named Ella Tomita was one of those to be exchanged. She was thirteen at the time and living on the island of Oahu. She writes:

> I would like to tell you about myself first. I was born in Laupahoehoe on the Big Island. My Dad was the Buddhist Minister in charge of the Buddhist Temple. He

was also the Principal of the Japanese School.... Being in a leadership role, he also acted as a coordinator, interpreter and resource person for the community. He not only preached and taught reading and writing but he helped his temple members keep in contact with their relatives in Japan by writing letters for them and reading to his members correspondence received from their relatives in Japan.

[On December 7, 1941] soon after we reached home, possibly about 9:00 pm, we heard a loud knock at the front door. Two policemen were at the door and said that they came to get "Sensei" by FBI orders. They did not say why my dad and the other ministers were arrested. The two police officers were nice but only said that it may be a few days....

About a week or so later we heard that our fathers were taken to the Kilauea Military Camp which is located in the Volcano area, which is very cold in December. We therefore sent some clothing and toiletries. After that we never heard from our fathers nor were notified as to their whereabouts....

In late summer, my mother received an official government notice saying that she and all children under 18 must pack some clothing and be sent to the mainland. We had no choice. Three older brothers and a sister remained in Honolulu.... Again, there was no explanation or reason given to us. We were under the jurisdiction of the Department of Immigration and Naturalization Services. Others who were relocated were under the jurisdiction of the Department of War. We were taken to one of the back rooms at the Honolulu Immigration Station. We all had to be fingerprinted then given a long ID number to hold in front of us to have a mug-shot taken. The officials only then told us that our fathers were sent somewhere on the mainland. They further informed us that we were headed to New York where there was an exchange ship we were to board. Then and only then we would be able to see our Dads. We were to be expatriated in the Singapore area via the S.S. Gripsholm which was to leave the port in New York.[1]

However, plans for the *Gripsholm* went awry. A letter dated August 27, 1942, from Mr. Bannerman to Mr. Fitch has the subject line "Arrival of Hawaiian Japanese at Grove Park Inn." It reads:

Colonel Tate of the War Relocation Authority has informed me that 133 Japanese, consisting of 37 women and 96 children, left San Francisco by train at 4 p.m. on August 26. They will arrive at Asheville North Carolina via the Southern Railroad at 7:45 pm on August 30.... The Japanese should be informed that they are permitted to take three suitcases as stateroom baggage on the Gripsholm and all remaining baggage must go as hold baggage.... It is believed that many of these Japanese have husbands who are interned in the United State in Army or Immigration camps. We will make an effort to have these husbands released so that they may accompany these Japanese back to Japan. It should be told however that we are making an effort and we cannot promise that such will be accomplished.... The sailing date of the Gripsholm has not as yet been determined.[2]

In her narrative, Miss Tomita suggests a reason for the change in plans. "We docked in San Francisco two weeks later on August 26,

Eight. End Games

1942. We were immediately herded onto a train with all shades down. We traveled along the northern route of the United States. The Pullman train made a stop in Chicago where we were told that since the war activity in the Singapore area had heightened we would have to be diverted to North Carolina. Upon arrival there we were bussed to the Grove Park Inn in Asheville, North Carolina."[3]

An Asheville newspaper article describes the arrival of the Hawaiians: "One hundred thirty Japanese women and children arrived here at 7:45 last night after a long trip from Hawaii and were interned at the Grove Park Inn, pending completion of arrangements for their exchange with Americans now in Japanese held territories.... The number of children included was unusually large and there were no men. There were some boys in the 18 to 19-year-old age group."[4] The Hawaiian Japanese settled in with the one hundred or so Peruvian Japanese already at the hotel. There were an additional eighty or so Germans, also primarily from Latin America.

A letter from Fitch to Keeley reads: "With reference to the present passenger list for MS GRIPSHOLM my records show 1356 at the moment available to go,"[5] and he provides a list by region including 137 available at North Carolina. Another document is titled "List of Japanese Nationals From Hawaii now detained at Asheville"[6] and provides the names of these Hawaiian Japanese and which of the Hawaiian islands they come from.

Montreat

The navy still wanted the Grove Park Inn, and the State Department was concerned about the continued costs of leasing the hotel. The State Department was unsure whether the detainees would be kept at the inn for the duration of the war, whether they would be repatriated at some future date, or whether they would be eventually turned over to the Immigration and Naturalization Service for detention. "The decision to place these aliens in a hotel after leaving the Greenbrier was apparently based on the fact that by our commitments to the Colombian government we guaranteed to accord official treatment to certain Colombian Germans. With the Grove Park Inn we also have immediately available facilities to care for any diplomatic Axis aliens or other officials who must accorded hotel treatment and may from time to time be brought from South America or other points."[7] Nevertheless, the promise to keep these detainees did not necessary mean that they be kept at a swank hotel.

Renegotiation of the Grove Park Inn contract seemed out of the question. The State Department was paying $26,560 for 131 guests and 30 immigration guards per month. The navy was offering $28,073 per month for 100 patients.

The State Department began to investigate alternate locations. The Robert E. Lee Hall in Black Mountain, NC, lacked heat. The Manor, which was located a half mile from the Grove Park Inn, was "sort of a ramshackle affair.... It is decidedly quite a come-down from the Grove Park."[8] The Fairview Sanatorium, on the outskirts of Asheville, was also considered but was deemed too small and had security issue. In a letter describing the possibility of moving the detainees to a hotel at nearby Lake Lure, NC, an agent writes, "It should also be noted that under the proposed Lake Lure living set up, the scale of living of these Axis Nationals will be considerably reduced to such an extent that no one could successfully level criticism at the Department and claim that we are keeping these Nationals in luxury. We anticipate difficulty in leaving the State of North Carolina with these aliens at the present time as there are five cases of scarlet fever and three cases of pneumonia."[9] The State Department ultimately decided against Lake Lure, in part because it would require too many guards to adequately provide surveillance and because the cost was too high.

The State Department settled on the Montreat Assembly Inn, about twenty miles from Asheville. This was a retreat center run by the Presbyterian Church of the United States. The rate was $2.80 per alien per day, regardless of age, and $3.80 per day per guard or State Department representative. This was approximately half the cost that had been charged at the Grove Park. However, maid service was not included except for the Americans, and food was to be served cafeteria style.

On October 26, 1942, the internees at the Grove Park Inn were put on six buses and driven the twenty miles to the Assembly Inn. A newspaper noted the large percentage of women and children among the Japanese group.

Eight. End Games

A note from the State Department reads: "One of the Japanese children from Hawaii who are being held at Asheville is now at a critical state of illness. It will be noted that this illness occurred the day before the Asheville group was moved [to] its new quarters. Furthermore ... the child was recovering from scarlet fever but that her family did not heed medical advice regarding her diet with the result that she became ill once more. Mr. Bannerman has been requested should the illness become more serious or should the girl die from it to take due precautions to obtain evidence that the Department has no responsibility in the matter."[10] The child subsequently recovered.

The start of the detention period at Montreat was not smooth. An agent writes:

> It is very hard to do business with our hosts, The Mountain Retreat Association. They are out to get every dime they can. Instead of hiring extra help to serve the food, they bring over several teachers from the adjoining school to do the job. I have been complaining ever since I arrived. There was absolutely no heat in my room, every room was filthy, the food we were served was exactly the same as that served the aliens ... the dishes ... were not washed properly, our waiter was a bus boy who also tended the furnace during meals and served us with very sooty hands. Maid service for the Americans consisted of having one's bed made up and nothing more. These are just a few of my complaints.... However all have been remedied.[11]

Soon after the detainees arrived, a representative of the Swiss legation visited the facility. Among his findings were:

> ... larger portions of food for detainees, more green vegetables for detainees, enlargement of hotel ice box facility as the present space is insufficient to care for the food now being handled. Arrangement ... for hotel staff to clean the lobby and halls each day and provide for collection of trash within the hotel twice a day, repair of leak in hotel hot water boiler. Arrangement to provide washing tubs or rent washing machines for detainees to do their own laundry and provide space and lines for drying. This will prevent the washing being done in the hotel room bath tubs.[12]

The Swiss delegate notified the State Department that he became sick with dysentery after visiting Montreat. He also notes in his report that twenty-five of the Germans had also become sick. In a formal report rebutting the Swiss delegate's report, a State Department agent notes that the Japanese had eaten the same food and not complained. In a less formal note to his boss, he writes, "Off the record, I want you to know that the Swiss representative who visited here started the last evening of their visit with scotch highballs, had a great quantity of beer with various Germans after dinner, and concluded the evening with a party in their room where a rum concoction flowed very freely. Stomachs sometimes resent such treatment.... With the exception of an occasional steak, we Americans eat the same food as the aliens, and none of us has had any ill effects to date.... Of course this is no Grove Park Inn, but when you consider the food that American detainees are getting in Germany and Japan I don't think the people here are faring too badly."[13]

Two hundred and sixty-four individuals, including 152 children, were housed from October 29, 1942, to April 30, 1943. There were approximately 130 Japanese women and children from Latin America and Hawaii and approximately the same number of German men, women, and children from Latin American, as well as one State Department representative, an Interior Department representative, and Immigration and Naturalization Service guards. A constant issue was winter clothing, as the detainees from Hawaii of course had no winter garments and the Peruvian Japanese had been limited in what baggage they could pack. The ministry does not appear to have helped deal with threadbare clothing and deteriorating shoes, and they lacked any kind of coats or gloves or hats for the approaching winter. The agent on the scene made an appeal to the State Department for $1000 for use at the local department store. Mr. Bannerman writes, "Mr. Franklin of SD (State Department) called and stated that the Department has received protest form the Spanish Embassy and the National Board of the Y.W.C.A. about the lack of clothing allowed the Japanese at Montreat. This of course is no reflection on our efforts but is the result of Army regulations which did not permit the Japanese to take sufficient clothes with them when they left Hawaii.... It is my opinion that the Japanese are largely interested in heavy clothing for winter wear and are not so much concerned about the amount allowed them but do want winter clothing which at the moment they cannot purchase as they have no money."[14]

If food and clothing were not offered, the Assembly Inn did offer spiritual ministry. "It was an interesting time to witness to these Axis diplomats. Into each of the hotel rooms had been placed New Testaments in both the German language and the Japanese languages.

Eight. End Games

Further, church groups visited at Christmas and handed out presents to all the children. Christmas carols were sung at the retreat center, with many joining in the familiar carols. One simply doesn't know what seed of the gospel were being planted by the Holy Spirit during this time."[15]

Sometime in January 1943, the Japanese made a request for ten Buddha statues. The request was refused on the grounds that such statues were not available in the United States. The Japanese changed the request to ten "copies of the Buddhist Bible and of the Buddhist Gathas (hymn book)." This request was passed up the chain of command, with a handwritten note from Federick Lyon, one of the agents at the hotel, commenting, "Aboard the returning Gripsholm was an American who with two others had been put in the Bridge House at Shanghai. They had requested a copy of the Bible—their request was categorically denied. Can't see why we should send to Hawaii to get 'em—and help these Japs."[16] Another agent adds his own note: "These tricky snakes may be able to get more than religious inspiration out of these books. I certainly can't see why we should send to Hawaii to get them...."[17]

The Diplomatic Exchange Program Changes

Ella Tomita, the young girl from Hawaii, continues her narrative:

Upon our arrival we were then bussed to Grove Park Inn in Asheville, North Carolina. We stayed in Asheville about a month, where I became very close friends with a German girl who was already at Grove Park Inn with her parents. She came from Bolivia and others from Peru.... We stayed at Montreat until April 1943. In April we were sent to the Crystal City, Texas Internment Camp. We were one of the first ones to enter that family camp which our fathers helped to build. Our fathers went through a lot of hardship too. We finally got to meet our fathers in May 1943 when we reached Crystal City. It took two years to see him. During those two years they were sent to various camps throughout the United States. My dad was sent to Fort Sill, Oklahoma and Camp Livingston, Louisiana, to name a few. We were considered "prisoners of war." Mail was censored. We found out later that some never reached us.... We returned after Europe's war ceased."[18]

Another detainee at the Montreat was Mary Mantel. She writes of her time there:

My father's name was Herbert Erich Mantel. He was a diesel mechanic, born in Hamburg, Germany on August 17, 1898. He traveled to Darranquilla, Colombia in

Axis Diplomats in American Custody

the 1920s. I think. He was Chief Engineer on a riverboat on the Magdalena River at first, and later he managed the German Club in Puerto Colombia. He married my mother, Clara Eugeni Struss, a native Colombian of German and Spanish descent. She was born in Ocana.

I was born in 1935. In 1942 we moved from Puerto Colombia to Barranquilla, when my parents bought a house there. I remember one day getting on a school bus to go to the German school. When I got home I found out that my father, along with many others, had been arrested.

Life turned upside down for me that very day. I was uprooted from my home, my grandparents and my uncles and aunts ... my mother's parent and siblings. We were very close, they all helped raise me from baby on, until we were taken away from them....

We were taken to Buenaventura, and in May of 1942, we were sent to the U.S. along with other families, on the SS Acadia. The ship sailed from Buenaventura on the Colombian west coast, through the Panama Canal to New Orleans LA. I remember crying on the ship because the men could not go outside during the passage, and I didn't want to leave my father's side.

In New Orleans we were put on Pullman trains and taken to the Greenbrier Hotel in White Sulphur Springs, West Virginia. That was on May 19, 1942. Because we were with a group of diplomats, we were treated very well. (My mother's aunt, Annie Struss, was married to Otto Kugelmann, one of the diplomats. They were exchanged with American diplomats right away.)

I remember we were treated like guests. I especially remember my first taste of cornflakes for breakfast. That made a great impression on me. (I can still taste them.) There were lots of other good meals.

We children played all over the hotel. I remember finding some money in one of the couches and running to tell my parent. I remember roller-skating and one time jumping from an inside balcony and breaking my right arm. I still skated with my right arm in a cast. Another memory was my dad taking me to the river in front of the hotel to put a little sailboat in the water. It sailed away to where we could not get it.

On July 9, we were moved to the Grove Park Inn, in Asheville, North Carolina. Shortly after this we were taken to the Assembly Inn in Montreat, North Carolina.[19]

As the third year of the war dragged on, the State Department assessed its diplomatic exchange program. There were no U.S. diplomats left overseas, but there were remaining U.S. nationals both in the European and the Pacific theaters. There was little hope for any exchange in the Far East. Europe, however, was another matter, with mercy ships, including the *Drottningholm* and *Gripsholm*, still making the trans-Atlantic voyage.

However, the diplomatic exchange was over. A Department of State memo dated March 23, 1943, with the subject "Transfer of

Eight. End Games

Montreat detainees to the Immigration Service" reads, "Arrangements have been concluded between the Department and the Immigration Service for the transfer of the Germans and Japanese at Montreat from the custody of the State Department to the Immigration Service. The detainees will be taken to Crystal City, Texas, with certain single persons probably being sent to Camps Kennedy and Seagoville."[20]

All the individuals at the Assembly Inn at Montreat left on April 30, 1943. After that there seems to be no real tracking of what happened to the internees. When the war ended, a few of the South American detainees in the internment camps made it back to their South America homelands, a few returned to Japan or to German or Italy; most seemed to melt into American society.

Comments by Hotel Management at the End of the Program

At the Triangle T, in a summary letter to Mr. Fitch, Mr. Baily wrote, "It is my belief that the stay of the Japanese at the ranch has been successful from our standpoint and that they leave here contented with the conditions under which they have lived for the past three and one half months and in first rate physical condition."[21] He wrote a subsequent letter, urging the quick settlement of the final billing, as, "Mr. Huntington, one of the proprietors of the ranch ... is intending to leave immediately for service in the Army...."[22]

General Manager Sibold of the Greenbrier wrote, "Hotels can serve as well as any other line of business in American defense. We were requested to take the diplomats of Germany, Italy, Bulgaria and Hungary and house them until such time as the government could arrange transportation and the exchange of these diplomats for our own in the same countries. We accepted that job promptly. We have 100 percent cooperation on the part of our staff in that we are rendering a service by the hotel profession to the government in a time of stress and emergency. We have endeavored to do a good job in order that at the conclusion we, as representatives of the hotel business, will be considered as having done the job in an acceptable manner and I believe that, by so doing we have rendered a service to the profession and have placed in the hands of the government evidence that the hotel business is an integral part of the American enterprise system ready, willing and able to serve promptly and efficiently in times of emergency as well as in times of peace."[23]

Mr. Ingalls of the Homestead writes,

> It is difficult to convey an idea of the strain under which the management of the Homestead was placed during approximately the three months the Japanese were with us. It is never easy to be a prison guard and none the easier when you feel that the person guarded is an enemy of your country. Such a guard is almost as closely confined and his movements as limited as the prisoner himself. In spite of knowing the conditions under which these people were here and recognition that many of them were of high type, the alien faces and the alien conversation which was overheard at every turn was irritating to a degree. No case that the management knows of occurred where anyone broke under the strain but there were close cases. One waiter reported such an occasion. It was the day after the fall of Singapore and by coincidence the day when the sugar shortage became apparent. That day we removed the full sugar bowls from the table and passed the sugar. As the waiter poured the coffee the Japanese whom he was serving first scrutinized the table, then looked up at him saying, "Ho! We take Singapore, you take sugar bowl." This waiter said, "I sure wanted to pour the hot coffee down his neck."[24]

Mr. Ingalls sent a note to his regular guests: "By the time spring returns to our valley, all traces of alien visitation will be gone."[25]

At Montreat, the State Department and the owners of the Assembly Inn bickered over the bill. The Assembly Inn had, in addition to the regular lease payment, added on an additional approximately $7,000 for damages. The State Department insisted on an inventory of the damaged items, and a long series of memos and meetings began regarding what was damages caused by the guests, which should be an add-on charge, and what was normal wear and tear, which were to be covered under the lease payment. The State Department believed a figure of around $679 was appropriate. Agent Briggs believed that the figure should be closer to $2000, as he felt that the Assembly Inn management was planning on having the Department pay for many improvements and upgrades to the hotel. The squabbling became very detailed: "Dr. Anderson claimed that the side walls were all badly marked up with pencils and crayons and scratches and that to eliminate these marks it was necessary to paint the entire wall. I informed Dr. Anderson that the walls were rather dirty when we originally arrived

Eight. End Games

at the hotel and there is no question but that our responsibility in this matter is limited and that he could expect only a small percentage payment of the total sum."[26] They argued about missing silverware, with Dr. Anderson insisting the guests had stolen spoons as souvenirs and Mr. Bannerman saying that the items were simply lost over the course of the many months of occupation and hundreds of meals and that as such any losses are part of any hotel's normal operations. More argument ensued over linens, window screens, shrubbery, the varnish on the floors. Mr. Fitch wrote, "I share the view that Hotel management is endeavoring to hold us up.... The statement presented is unconscionable.... The Association has undoubtedly made money out of the Government contract and have found us easy marks from whom they hope again to have a pound of flesh. Remember—the flesh is rationed!"[27]

Mr. Bannerman, in a summary of the overall program, mentions that "five exchange vessels were handled by this office MS GRIPSHOLM, SS SERPA PINTO and three voyages of the MS DROTTNINGHOLM with all the ships sailing from New York. In total 3,974 Germans, Japanese, Italian, Hungarians, and Bulgarians were placed aboard these vessels for repatriation to their respective countries."[28] He says that each piece of luggage was handled an average of at least five times, and that at least 56,000 pieces of luggage were handled. There were eighty-four separate train movements for a total of 67,979 miles. The total number of State Department agents involved was 141. The duties involved "police protection, supervision of the guarding en route, baggage transfer, space assignment on the trains, supervision of meals, train schedules, illness of passengers and providing of doctors, censoring of communications, securing of hotels, adjustment of rates ... all arrangements involving other Government departments, providing Immigration guards for all movement, direction of all baggage transfers, arranging and assembling from all over the country of Axis officials for repatriation...."[29]

Bannerman concludes: "Despite the number of persons handled and the many problems involved, not one complaint has been made by the Axis officials on their treatment at the hands of the Special Agents. This is a remarkable in itself in view of the hundreds of Axis diplomatic officials involved, who were ever alert to the slightest infringement of the exchange agreement as regards the treatment of diplomatic personnel."[30]

The Diplomatic Exchange Winds Down

The Diplomatic Exchange program continued on, in a new form, until 1944. It morphed into a program dealing with Axis nationals and not diplomats. A September 2, 1942, memo to Mr. Fitch from Bannerman states that "the main efforts of the State Department will be concentrated on removing the dangerous Axis aliens from the South American zone to the United States where we can then exercise full control over their actions. This means that for some period of time to come there will be a constant movement of aliens from South America and there will be an increased concentration of Axis aliens in American internment camps."[31]

Although the exchange of diplomats and officials had concluded, some South American countries continued to send more enemy aliens into the United States. The conditions of their voyages from South America were not always good. A State Department official relates:

> The USAT FREDERICK JOHNSON arrived at New Orleans, Louisiana October 21, 1944, with 132 enemy aliens from Latin America and 67 repatriated seamen. The enemy aliens consisting of men, women and children were brought to this country for internment and exchange purposes.... I was informed that certain conditions aboard the vessel were unsatisfactory....
> ... the ship ... is entirely unsuited for the transportation of alien women and children ... the ship is perfectly suited for the transportation of alien single males ... not a single item was added to the ship which would normally be deemed necessary for the handling of a large groups of women and small children. The purpose of the voyage was apparently overlooked by the authorities at Panama.
> ... The alien women and children were quartered in the lower after hold. This consisted of a room about fifty feet by forty feet with bunks in tiers of four. There were no portholes that could be opened although the ventilation system was very good. The bunks consisted of piping covered by canvas which would fold up against the supporting pipes when not in use. The bunks, perfectly flat without supporting edges, were sufficient for adults in good health but were dangerous for small children. Any baby or child rolling off such a bunk would fall three feet or more to a steep deck with a good chance of a serious injury. There were no beds or bunks as would be found in a stateroom on the entire ship for use by children consequently the children had to be watched at all times to prevent injury. The only exit from this hold consisted of a single companionway about five feet wide

Eight. End Games

which opened into the hold occupied by the men.... In the event of an emergency it is doubtful that the women and children would have been able to negotiate these companionways to the upper decks in a matter of minutes.

There were an ample number of bunks for all aliens concerned but Germans, Japanese and Italians were of course all crowded together.... There was only one latrine on the entire ship for use by the 132 aliens. This latrine was located in the after part of the ship and the only entrance was through the men's quarters. Hours had to be arranged whereby the men and women divided use of the latrine. This was extremely unsatisfactory from every standpoint as can well be imagined. The constant use of this one latrine by 132 persons of different nationalities necessitated for sanitary reasons that it be thoroughly cleaned three times a day. About 45 minutes were required for each cleaning of the latrine which further restricted the time that it was available for use by the group. It should be noted that the women and children had to pass through the men's quarters to reach the latrine.

Drinking water was available to the entire ship from 7:00 AM to 9:00 PM after which it was cut off. There was no fresh water during the entire voyage for bathing or washing purposes.

There was not one single chair, bench or stool for the aliens to sit upon until the ship reached Salinas.... Prior to Salinas, the men, women and children either sat in their bunks or on the deck ... there was not one single table on the entire ship for use by the aliens for any purpose. This meant that there was no central mess hall which necessitated that the aliens eat their food in their quarters without benefit of chairs or tables. This condition was somewhat remedied by Lts. Cottrell and Casey who arranged to have some planking from hatch covers sawed into the proper lengths to cover about ten bunks in the men's quarter. These impromptu tables were too low to stand up to and too high to use while sitting on the deck.

The food for the aliens was prepared in the crew mess and then brought down to the men's quarters where the aliens ate. The odor of the latrine was ever present. The aliens ate from military mess kits which were the only items available aboard ship. This added considerably to the difficulties of the women and children eating in the hold....

Under such conditions Lts. Cottrell and Case insisted that the aliens spend all possible time on the open deck. This would have relieved the problem somewhat but the deck available to the aliens was only six feet wide and 90 feet long. Without chairs or benches to sit on ... and with persons constantly walking back and forth along this deck it was not very comfortable or satisfactory to say the least.

... When the FREDERICK JOHNSON arrived at Panama, the authorities placed aboard sixty-seven repatriated seamen who had just come from the Pacific area. On board ship were forty-two Japanese aliens. The situation immediately became extremely serious and the Military Escort Guard, faced with a situation not of their making, had to post a twenty-four hour armed guard to prevent the seamen from violence against the Japanese aliens.... In the past there have been a number of complaints to the Swiss and Spanish by aliens on conditions aboard the USAT CUBA which brought previous groups of enemy aliens to New Orleans. Actually the USAT CUBA is a luxury liner compared to the USAT FREDERICK JOHNSON....[32]

Axis Diplomats in American Custody

No one reason can explain why the United States allowed enemy nationals from South America to continue to be sent to the United States. There were no more diplomats to exchange. The threat of sabotage or the like in South America seemed less plausible every day, especially as the individuals being transported had more and more innocuous backgrounds. Perhaps the United States felt compelled under the original exchange agreements reached just after the war started. It is also possible that the State Department was anticipating exchanges for American nationals or POWs.

Nine

Vichy French at the Hotel Hershey

"Germany invaded and defeated France in the spring of 1940. A large portion of southwestern France was left unoccupied by the conquering army. A new French government, sympathetic to the Nazi regime, was established in the town of Vichy. As part of political protocol, the Vichy government sent Gaston Henri-Haye to Washington, D.C. to serve as the French ambassador to the United States."[1] Some questions were raised as to whether the United States should recognize the government of Nazi-occupied France, but acceptance was quickly granted, and the United States had a legation in France including Chargé d'Affaires S. Pinkney Tuck.

On November 7, 1942, the United States launched "Operation Torch," the invasion of French North Africa. On November 11, 1942, the Germans, fearing they would be outflanked in the south and not trusting the French, occupied the remaining portion of the country, although they allowed the Vichy French to, at least in appearance, rule part of the country. The American diplomats were taken by the Vichy French to a hotel at Lourdes, a city which they still controlled. The group was increased by American news correspondents and also by Red Cross volunteers who were in Southern France.

In Washington, the State Department listed 245 people as belonging to the Vichy French legation, scattered around consulates in Chicago, New York, and several other cities, but with most in Washington. The number included 130 officers and staff; the remaining 115 were dependents. The Secretary of State quickly decided that "the Vichy government no longer exists and therefore [it] is not capable of representation by a third power such as the Swiss government."² The State Department viewed Henri-Haye as an ex-ambassador and his people as quasi-enemy nationals. Henri-Haye disputed this, insisting that he represented French interests in America and that he and his people were entitled to privileged status. One State Department official expressed the opinion that Henri-Haye thought of himself not as a detainee but as a guest of the State Department. The State Department decided to give him and his legation favorable treatment, not because of diplomatic protocol, but as leverage, hoping that Henri-Haye could be used as a bargaining chip to help spring the American detainees held by the Vichy government at Lourdes.

In the United States, the number of die-hard Vichy French within the French legation is difficult to estimate. A memo prepared by Assistant Secretary of State Long for President Roosevelt notes, "A number of the French were known to be Allied sympathizers and seem to be willing and able effectively to serve the Allied cause. Accordingly it was not necessary nor desirable to subject them to confinement."³ Others within the State Department, however, believed that there were "other French personnel of doubtful or unknown attachment to the Allied cause. It comprises persons who, like the ex-Ambassador, desire to return to France, and those who do not wish to return and whose disposition must be decided upon following examination of their cases with respect to their political sentiment and activities."⁴ The Secretary decided that all of the French should be housed in an appropriate location "regardless of their future intentions or present action in resigning their official positions. The Department will consider each case in due time and render a decision.... This policy will apply in every case regardless of the statements of the individual."⁵

Why Hotel Hershey

The State Department decided that Henri-Haye and his staff would soon leave the French embassy in Washington, and, following the model used at the start of the war with the German and Japanese legations, they began to look for a first-class resort to house them. The State Department considered approximately a dozen hotels, mostly in

Nine. Vichy French at the Hotel Hershey

North and South Carolina. Newspapers across the country published stories of the arrest of the pro–Nazi ambassador and his staff and speculated on where they would end up.

Joseph Gassler, general manager for the Hershey Hotel, sent a letter to Cordell Hull, Secretary of State, on November 12, 1942, offering the hotel's services. "I have the honor to advise you that Hotel Hershey has placed its facilities at your service.... I shall be very happy to have these people as our guests and assure you, my dear Secretary, that we will do our utmost, in every respect, to give the high standard of service which the famous Hotel Hershey knows how to give."[6]

Mr. Gassler's letter also included details about the specific conditions of the arrangements. Tariff for adults was set at $7.50 per day per person, children (0–12 years old) $4.00 per person, and guards $4.00 per person. Incidental expenses incurred were to be billed to the State Department at cost, and gratuities were also to be paid by State Department funding.

The hotel was chosen to sequester the Vichy French government representatives for several reasons. The hotel was cooperative, the quality of accommodations was quite high, and the hotel was in a secluded and defensible location near Harrisburg, Pennsylvania. Moreover, it was a first-class establishment. In a newspaper article, the Hershey is described: "The 175-room Hershey Hotel formerly was a favorite stopping place for the well-to-do. The 10-year-old sandstone hotel is entirely surrounded by gardens. One garden is devoted to roses, another boasts every kind of flower grown in Pennsylvania and a third is an exact replica of the famous Versailles garden in France."[7] Included in the group at Hershey were many individuals who presumably were used to high society. A list prepared by the Border Patrol refers to "His Excellency Gaston Henri-Haye, the ambassador: Major General Auguste Bonvite (military attaché), Madame Bonvite, Major Bruno Deru Assistant Military Attache, Vicontess Daru, Count Christien de Nicolay—attache."[8]

The Ambassador and Entourage

The Vichy French arrived at the Hershey on November 17, 1942. No press were present. The State Department "does not want any newspaper photographers or pressmen on the hotel grounds ... does not want any photographs taken of the French officials.... In fact as little publicity as possible attendant on this move is the department's policy."[9]

Life at the hotel was quite comfortable for the internees. The *New York Times* reported that "the guests would have access to the adjacent Hotel grounds and that the government would provide movie picture shows and games rooms. Senior staff also enjoyed the Hotel's golf courses. In spite of home front wartime rationing, the Hotel continued to serve a variety of foods, and fresh flowers were delivered twice a week. The wine cellar was also open to the internees, although all liquor bills were paid by guests."[10] According to Erika Dreifus, the French had access to one and a half acres just behind the hotel and two adjacent acres between 9:00 a.m. and 5:15 p.m., the large porch stretching across the hotel's front was open from 9:00 a.m. to 9:00 p.m., "[and] golf [was] permitted to one foursome in the morning and one foursome in the afternoon on the nine hole course immediately adjacent to the hotel."[11] Indoor activities included ping pong, chess, and poker.

The reaction from the town was muted. Many were unaware that the hotel was being used as a detention site. Bill Cagnoli was a busboy at the hotel during this time. He remembers, "There was a fence put around the Hotel Hershey. I had to have a Secret Service pass to get in to work, and all the French were interned up there, that were of the Vichy Government. The federal government would send me my check and my tips for being a bellhop or busboy, you know. These people would eat, live, and dine in that hotel and do whatever they want. The only thing they had to pay themselves was whatever they drank, as far as alcoholic beverages were concerned."[12]

In a long letter to his boss, Special Agent Seward told about the antics of a Mrs. Catherine Waterbury Gordon, who came to the hotel on February 11, 1943:

> After the then recent death of her husband, in order to join her mother and stepfather, Mr. Charles Brousees.... Very soon after their arrival, Mrs. Gordon and her stepfather segregated themselves from the French group, including her mother, and their intimate relationship became apparent to everyone.... This relationship has reached the stage where the general opinion of everyone in the hotel is that Mrs. Gordon is her stepfather's mistress.... This situation has become somewhat acute and recently there occurred a scene in the dining room between Mrs. Gordon,

Nine. Vichy French at the Hotel Hershey

her mother and Mr. Brousees.... This intimacy between Mrs. Gordon and her stepfather has greatly upset Mrs. Brousees. She is now left almost entirely alone by her family, which aggravates her present condition, is despondent, frequently bursts into tears, and has recently stated she would prefer living alone than in the hotel with conditions such as they are. She is beginning to realize that this is commonly known throughout the hotel and she is steadily becoming more emotionally upset.[13]

In another memo, the French are described as:

... behaving like spoiled children at present and are behaving with utter disregard to the rules and regulations governing their boundary limits. They have used abusive and profane language to the guards, have deliberately crossed the restricted boundaries in the presence of the guards and have dared the guards to take any measures against them. They have destroyed hotel property and have destroyed the signs put up by the guards indicating the boundary areas.... It is the general opinion of Mr. Lyons and others that we will have to use severe restrictions upon the French unless they mend their ways and, in my opinion this [is] necessary, otherwise the Hershey situation will soon be entirely out of hand....[14]

Another memo complains about the destruction of property:

With respect to the damage and "willful destruction" of property by the French detainees, as distinguished from normal maintenance and needful repair, I am obliged to report that it is considerable. Several expensive rugs and carpets were burned, wine-stained or otherwise damaged almost beyond repair: lamps were dented or broken, desks and tables were hacked, dented, scratched and stained to such an extent that re-surfacing and refinishing is required: and many of the rooms had to be completely redecorated because of grease stains, deep scratches, writings and other wall marking.[15]

Of particular notice were the two boys in the Imbault-Huart family:

The boys have been caught throwing lighted matches between the cushions of chairs, chalking walls and have been in every nook and corner of the Hotel in which they had no business.... Mrs. Imbault-Huart [complains to the agent] that her sons are not getting sufficient air and exercise, but she does not make any attempt to send them outside where there is plenty of room to play. Consequently they are inside most of the time getting into mischief.... The general attitude of the Imbault-Huart [family] appears to be one of resentment and non-cooperation, and the definite refusal to make the best of the situation in which they are placed.[16]

The ambassador's constant companion was a large Dalmatian. They would often go walking in the Versailles-style rose garden. He also liked to take the dog to the dining room, where the dog would eat

Axis Diplomats in American Custody

at his side. Since their arrival at the hotel, some of the French had hoarded food, with the ambassador being perhaps the worst offender. The agent in charge at the hotel writes, "I didn't see any particular harm in it ... until about a month ago when the food situation became acute and rationing was introduced to the American people ... information came to me that the Ambassador had had about twelve boxes made to pack his food in ... [the agent then lists the foodstuffs] ... 6 Virginia hams, 100 lbs. salt, 100 lbs. sugar, 300 pieces soap ... 12 (3 lb. cans) Krisco [sic], 1500 individual Bouillon cubes, 12 gals dressing and cooking oil, 8 lbs. beef tongue in glass jars, 48 cans of Spam, quite of bit of chocolate candy, 100 lbs. of dog food."[17]

Some of the staff reached their limits. A memo to Mr. Fitch states, "The agent tracked down one of the French boys who traveled on skis beyond the recreation area. Later it was found that a large swastika was drawn on the snow at the back of the hotel. One of the French boys, age 16, was in the habit of entering an elevator raising his hand and arm saying Heil Hitler. He ceased to do this after being hit by the elevator operator."[18]

One of the French wrote to a friend:

> "It's been a long, cold hard winter ... and we've sadly needed your merry laugher in this blankety-blank gilded cage. If I ever do get out of this mad-house.... I suppose, only someone like myself, who loved America, and who considered it, after all these years, as home, can feel as embittered and so darn mad about all this ridiculous situation, as I do....
>
> With the passing of winter, many of our restrictions were lifted. From having a small space, of about 500 yards, and a large verandah, to walk around and around and around in all winter, we now are permitted the [run] of practically the whole estate [for walks]. The gardens and park, though I hate to admit it!—are perfectly beautiful. But beautiful things, and Spring and Summer don't help much, and our hearts are filled with nostalgia and homesickness—and the sense of injustice is so acute at times, as to be almost unbearable....
>
> We have a Victory garden—which is a great success! We tore and clawed at that thar' land like caged up lions (it was an old corral) and it looks wonderful now, landscaped, and the harvest is in full bloom. It really saved our sanity. Our first reapings were "radishes." When we feel particularly "blue" we go and sit under a tree, with a bunch of them in our hot little hands, and munch! Such fun!
>
> Robert has not been well for months, he gets wild fits of crying and homesickness for "school" and his friend, which upsets me greatly. You wouldn't think a child so young would mind all this.... There is no schooling for them. We are cut off from all contact with the outside world. We manage to get a few books. No movies. We are allowed to go, by turn, in fours, once a week to the Village to do a little shopping accompanied by a guard—which we find humiliating...."[19]

Nine. Vichy French at the Hotel Hershey

Fall from Grace

The internees took advantage of the freedoms they enjoyed, often ignoring boundaries on the grounds and abusing shopping and medical excursions to downtown Hershey, Palmyra, and Harrisburg. Unnecessary and fictitious doctor appointments were scheduled to enable illegal town visits. As the internment wore on, the prisoners grew restless. Vandalism to the hotel increased and certain internees had trouble controlling displays of pro–Nazi sentiment. Moreover, during the several months of internment, most of the officials declared their allegiance to the Free French Government and were allowed to leave the Hotel and seek political asylum in the United States.[20]

The United States tolerated this misbehavior in part because it was still negotiating with what remained of the Vichy French government in France, trying to exchange the Vichy diplomats held at the Hershey for the American diplomats held by the Vichy French in Lourdes. However, in Europe, the German government began to have doubts about the sustainability of the Vichy government. In late summer the Nazis took the American diplomats from the Vichy French deep into Germany to a hotel in the town of Baden-Baden. The U.S. State Department was furious at the Vichy French, feeling that they did not stand up for the Americans, who had diplomatic immunity and were under the protection of the French. The State Department realized that the value of the Vichy French diplomats to the Germans was minimal, and Ambassador Henri-Haye's stay at the luxurious Hershey was viewed as an unnecessary extravagance.

The State Department had always allowed the French detainees, as long as they could convince them that they never supported the Vichy government and never supported the Nazis, to petition the Immigration and Naturalization Service, where they are almost always promptly paroled, given a status as "temporary visitor," and allowed to pursue employment.

A newspaper report states, "A number of those (sent to Hershey) have been released after offering their services to the United Nations military effort."[21] Others went to Washington to help the French Military Mission, headed by General Berthouard. The State Department made clear, however, that release from the Hershey was not connected with joining the Free French movement. However, the State Department lobbied the War Department to provide passage to those French from the Hershey who wished a return to North Africa. Some of the French at the hotel went to New York, others to Georgia and California. The State Department provided transportation to those wishing to return to their former place of residence in the United States. The former French consulate from San Diego and his wife, for example, took a first-class train compartment and traveled with forty-two pieces of luggage.

The State Department pushed the French to either take parole or to be prepared to be moved to a smaller hotel. Most took parole, and of the initial group of 245 French detainees, only a group of sixteen remained in the palatial hotel. These sixteen were the same group which had been together since their removal from the Washington embassy and included the troublesome Imbault-Huart boys.

Lesser Accommodations

In the fall of 1943, the State Department decided it was time to move the French to a less costly hotel. The Lake Lure Inn in western North Carolina was considered, but the Shenvalee Hotel in New Market, Virginia, about forty miles from the Greenbrier and Homestead, was selected. The Shenvalee Hotel "is a small hotel ... and contains twenty-three rooms and fourteen baths. The hotel grounds cover 200 acres and contains a 9-hole golf course in excellent condition and a tennis court."[22] A letter from Mr. Fitch dated September 16, 1943, reads, "when Henri-Haye, upon being advised ... that his group would be transferred from the Hershey Hotel to the Shenvalee Hotel ... [he] immediately rushed downstairs to the hotel desk to consult the hotel guide. Upon seeing the hotel listed he stated it a wonder his group was not place in a $1.75 room hotel."[23] The Hershey at this time charged $20/night for regular visitors.

> That same night the French group had an outside dinner and of course discussed the hotel situation. Mrs. Tanquerey urged the Ambassador to strongly protest the move and finally the Ambassador told the group that he would refuse to enter the hotel on his own will and that he would have to be carried in. The French have

Nine. Vichy French at the Hotel Hershey

made up their minds not to like the new accommodations at the Shenvalee Hotel and we should be prepared for a strong protest because of change in the quality of accommodations.... In order that the American group held at Baden-Baden will not be subject to any reprisals because of the change of hotels for the French officials.... I wish to again state that the Shenvalee hotel is not on par with accommodations at Hershey.... The food served will be plain and good ... the furnishings of the hotel are plain and simple, nothing luxurious, but they are clean and neat. The hotel is being completely cleaned and rearranged to suit the needs of the French group.... The French group has been living in considerable finer style ... [this move] represents a large reduction in costs of maintenance. It is also a reduction in the quality of accommodations. There are several estates that could accommodate the French group but these are furnished with costly items of furniture and in view of the willful destruction of property by the French at Hershey such estates have been rejected for consideration as the Department would probably have a large damage bill on its hands.... The transfer from the Hershey Hotel has been set for September 27th ... [the Shenvalee hotel] will be comfortable and pleasant but such qualities will not compensate the French who will feel that their honor has been offended.[24]

The uproar caused the State Department to reconsider the Shenvalee. It looked for another lodging, and on September 25, 1943, the French diplomats were sent to the Three Hills Estate at Warm Springs, Va. It was owned by the Homestead Hotel and was

located six miles from Hot Springs, Virginia and is situated on the side of a mountain on an estate comprising 65 acres. There is ample room space to care for the detainees and three well equipped cottages of five rooms each for the housing of the Immigration guards. The estate is well furnished and is extremely comfortable. It has been in operation up to the present time as a quiet resort for a restricted clientele. We are arranging for the Homestead Hotel to operate Three Hills on our behalf, thus guaranteeing a high standard of food and service and avoiding the many problem of obtaining supplies and services.[25]

However, the French were displeased. A letter dated October 30, 1943, from Fitch to Brandt includes a remark that "the proposed transfer of the French officials from the Three Hills estate at Warm Springs, Virginia, which [has] been found inadequate for their needs and desires...."[26] Another note was written just after the arrival of the French at the Three Hills and states that the French are "waiting developments on their protests."[27] Another memo says that "After arriving at Three Hills, Warm Springs, Virginia, Ambassador Henri-Haye refused to allow any baggage to be taken to their rooms or any of their heavy luggage to be put in storage."[28]

No exact explanation is given for the dissatisfaction of the French.

Axis Diplomats in American Custody

It may have been that another hotel, the Cascades Inn, was the original destination for the remaining French. There is a series of letters and memos concerning the up-fitting of the hotel, especially for work done regarding the heating of the building, so possibly the hotel was not ready. Another possibility is that, with winter coming, heating the huge manor home of the Three Hills Estate was too costly. Another explanation could be that, with all of the valuable antiques and expensive furnishings, the State Department was worried about the French inflicting damages as they did at the Hershey. Most likely, however, is that the French threw a temper tantrum and got their way.

They were moved to the Cascades. This was a hotel near the Homestead and was, in fact, owned and operated by the Homestead.

> There are about four acres of fairly flat land immediately surrounding the Inn. About 200 feet west of the Inn this land slopes abruptly into a small ravine. The property comprises 12 acres in all and is not fenced in which gives the impression that the property is much more extensive than it is. In addition to the Inn there are a number of summer cottages (... now empty) on the grounds. The ground is covered with grass, well-kept and shaded by large oak trees. On the slope toward the ravine is a small pavilion housing a medicinal spring and a small pool, filled with water from the spring, whose temperature remains at approximately 74 degrees. This pool, although small, is said to be suitable for bathing.... The Inn ... is used as an over-flow for the Homestead Hotel which is four miles away.... There are 14 bedrooms on the second floor, everyone of which has either a private or communicating bath.... To make use of the Inn for the purpose envisaged, considerable improvements (mostly of cleaning and refurbishing) are needed. Mr. Slosson, the manager of the hotel, agreed to undertake this by moving to the Inn suitable furniture and furnishings which he thought could be released from the Homestead Hotel after November 1.... The food is good. The manager said that he would provide an adequate staff to serve the guests.... In conclusion it may be said that whereas the Inn may not meet all the requirements a former ambassador may deem necessary to his well-being it is reported to offer a number of advantages over the Three Hills establishment.... The Inn reflects a certain measure of the Homestead atmosphere to which he will undoubtedly be susceptible. Among the registered guests figures an extensive number of prominent people, including well-known representatives of the foreign mission at Washington, the professions, and industrial and banking interests.... Mr. Henri-Haye regardless of everything that may be done to make the Inn a comfortable place for his sojourn will probably find sufficient fault with the place to demand greater liberty for himself and his entourage as a compensation.[29]

Ten

Diplomats Captured in North Africa During the War

As the Allies began to achieve military success, they recaptured territory once held by the Axis forces. On several occasions they captured Axis soldiers and in several instances captured Axis diplomats. There were a total of twenty-four Germans and thirteen Italians, officials, dependents, and employees, captured in French North Africa. Six of the Italians had "left Tunis five days before the surrender of the German-Italian Army in Tunisia and went to Cape Bon. On Cape Bon they hoped to get a plane to take them to Italy but every plane sent for the purpose was shot down by the American Airforce. One official actually got in a plane but this plane was shot down five miles off the coast and he was saved by a passing trawler."[1] They were referred to as the German and Italian Armistice Commission. The War Department and the State Department could not agree whether the group consisted of diplomats or military personnel. If the latter, of course they were to be treated as prisoners of war. If the former, then they had to be given safekeeping, immunity, and safe passage. The State Department prevailed, not so much due to the nature of who the captured people were, but because they could be used for "bargaining and exchange purposes." In a note to Mr. Fitch dated February 11, 1943, Mr. Bannerman writes:

> In the matter of exchanging the American diplomatic officials held at Baden-Baden [i.e., the group formerly at Lourdes] the German government has insisted on the return of the military personnel of the German and Italian Armistice Commission which was captured in North Africa. Some of these military officers are

now in this country and others are enroute here.... At the moment the War Department in whose custody these military officers are now held is claiming that such officers should be held for a prisoner of war exchange.... One of the conditions upon which the War Department will release these military officers for diplomatic exchange purpose is that the State Department accept entire custody and responsibility for this group which numbers about 250 persons....[2]

The War Department agreed to let the State Department handle the matter. At first the plan was to move the French from the Hershey Hotel to the Lake Lure Inn and to move the Armistice Committee to the Hershey. However, in a letter dated February 20, 1943, Mr. Fitch writes:

> The list of the diplomatic official members of the German and Italian Armistice Commission who are to arrive at New York within a few days for the purpose of detention and exchange [is attached]. This group of officials will be held under detention at the Ingleside Inn, Staunton, Virginia, pending arrangement for exchange of American officials held at Baden-Baden Germany.... The German government has accorded all the Americans at Baden-Baden an official status and free from searches. On the basis of reciprocal treatment the Bureau of Customs has been requested to grant free entry to this entire group. In like manner, a similar request has been made to the Federal Bureau of Investigation, the Office of Naval Intelligence and the Military Intelligence Service.[3]

Ingleside Hotel

The State Department, worried about the treatment of its personnel held at Baden-Baden, scrupulously examined the Ingleside Inn. In a February 19, 1943, letter from Mr. Fitch, he evaluates the Ingleside, stating:

> I am noting the facilities offered by the Ingleside Inn ... so that a comparison may be drawn as to the treatment the Armistice Commission will receive.[4] [Mr. Fitch goes on] ... the rooms are fairly spacious.... The hotel has no objections to dogs, cats or other Axis pets ... the hotel service will be very good.... Heating will be more than adequate and hotel will be comfortable.... Detainees (will be) permitted to exercise on the hotel grounds.... There is an eighteen hole golf course and arrangements can be made for the detainees to play golf.... Food served detainees will be equivalent to that American public is receiving and is very well prepared and served. [The] hotel is noted for its cuisine. If the detainees desire, hard liquor can be purchased for them at their expense, however there is a bar in the hotel which serves light wines and beer.... The Ingleside Inn also has an outside swimming pool and tennis courts.[5]

Ten. Diplomats Captured in North Africa During the War

He goes on to note that shopping is available and medical care is nearby, including a local physician, who will be on call at any time.

From an article dated March 3, 1943, the United Press writes, "The State Department announced today that former German and Italian consuls general at Algiers, who were captured in the North African invasion, have been brought to the United States and are being held pending exchange for American diplomats whom the German seized in France and took to Germany."[6]

A State Department memo refers to "one member of the Italian group, Alessandro Cultrera, Royal Cancelliere, [who] was repatriated to Italy on the first voyage of the *Drottningholm*. He was formerly stationed in Lima Peru, and was brought to this country on the SS *Acadia* and arrived at New Orleans. From there he went to the Gibson Hotel at Cincinnati and was sent directly to Jersey City on May 7th to return to Italy via the *Drottningholm*. He had three months leave and was sent to Algiers on September 1st and was captured by American troops on November 8th."[7]

The people of Staunton pushed back very hard against housing the Germans and Italians in their town. After they arrived, the townspeople complained about the perceived privileges afforded the Axis diplomats at the Ingleside. A State Department agent writes to his boss:

> Relative to our conversation, concerning the attitude of the people of Staunton toward the detainees at the Ingleside Hotel, it must be stated that they are not accepted in a favorable light. The natives feel that the detainees are given entirely too much freedom and are not treated according to the standards prescribed for prisoners of war. I at times have tried to relay to some individuals the fact that our group is not within the same category as prisoners of war, and because of international agreements are being treated on a basis parallel with those which are being accorded American citizens who are now under detention in Germany. This explanation has met with no intelligent understanding because the provincialism of this town is deeply imbedded in the minds of the natives and they cannot justifiably accept anything that does not harmonize with their already established beliefs. Throughout the numerous trips to town of our group, they have always been treated with courtesy by the local merchants and their [sic] is no concrete reason for criticizing their attitude, exclusive of basing my conclusion on several indiscreet remarks that I have heard. Several articles written in the local newspaper have been an incentive to guiding the natives in drawing up unfavorable beliefs of the group at the Ingleside. It is believe that no remedy can be offered as a means in attempting to change this biased attitude, simply because, as I have

Axis Diplomats in American Custody

already stated, the provincialism of the Old South is still very much in evidence in Staunton....[8]

A letter dated August 18, 1943, from an agent perhaps explains the hostile attitude of the townspeople:

> There is no question but that there is some resentment against the detainees which is only natural in view of the general attitude towards Axis prisoners and the fact that the hospital at Staunton has now received over one thousand cases of wounded American soldiers.... Whenever a group of detainees goes outside of the hotel ground they are accompanied by one Immigration Inspector and civilian guards depending the number of detainees. On the walking trips through the surrounding country and shopping visits in town, the entire group is in civilian clothes and the townspeople are unable to tell when there are guards with the group or whether they are all detainees. This accounts for many of our complaints that the detainees are being allowed to move around town and through the surrounding country unescorted and without guard.[9]

A women in town actually wrote to Mr. Hoover:

> My Dear Mr. Hoover.... I am writing concerning the prisoners at "Ingleside" just out of town. As I understand it they are supposed to come into town under guard for "necessary shopping only." Since they are being served three excellent meals daily, is it necessary that they come into our grocery stores and buy food: We are rationed to three pairs of shoes a year. They come in and bought $1,000 worth of shoes from one of our shoe stores. They are buying yards and yards of material from our dry good store, none of which could possibly called "necessary." They come to town constantly and are very disagreeable to the people who have to serve them. Do you know why they cannot be restrained a little more? Certainly they should not have to buy our food, especially under the present food conditions.... I hope I have not taken a liberty, but it does get a little under my skin to see the way these people are pampered by our government, and I do think it very bad that they are allowed to buy our food. There are many people here who agree with me on this matter (signed) (Miss) Eloise Waldrop.[10]

A situation involving the American flag illustrates the fine line the FBI and State Department walked. Traditionally, a flag had been flown in the lobby area. However, it was removed when the Axis diplomats arrived. A letter from Mr. Bannerman explains: "Reference is made ... concerning inquiry by the local reporter at Staunton on the display of two American flags. Inquiry on this matter has come from a Senator and a Congressman from Virginia and has been answered by the Special Division to the effect that on a reciprocal basis we have avoided displaying a flag at the Ingleside as we prefer not to subject our people at Baden-Baden to salute or bow to a Nazi flag or a photograph of Hitler

Ten. Diplomats Captured in North Africa During the War

each time they pass through the lobby of that hotel.... It is requested however that an American flag be displayed on the outside of the Hotel."[11]

However, a different story was presented to a local reporter by the representative of the State Department. Special Agent Madden writes in a separate letter:

> If you [Mr. Fitch] recall, upon your arrival here at the hotel, with the detainees, on the night of the 28th of February, we had two large American flags on display, over the fireplaces, in the opposite ends of the lobby. After discussing with you the ethics relative to the display of these flags, you more or less advised that it would be more appropriate to remove these flags some late night when no one could see this removal. This was done and no comments of any kind were made.... Today, Mr. Catlett ... a reporter for the Staunton Evening paper [telephoned and discussed the flag. Contrary to what he had heard, I told him that] we had removed the flags but that it was done, not by any one's request but because of the fact that they had collected entirely too much dust and grime and had to be properly cleaned.[12]

The local paper, under its dateline of April 15, 1943, printed the following article: "Ingleside Flag Down for Cleaning.... A report current Wednesday that an American flag in the Ingleside Hotel had been taken down because it offended the sensibilities of the German and Italian diplomats quartered there was denied by a representative of the State Department.... This representative ... said that the flag had been taken down to be cleaned and for no other reason."[13]

Madden writes in another letter:

> Once again another article has appeared it the local paper pertinent to the display of the American flag at the Ingleside Hotel.... The local editor, through his representative ... was informed by me, under advice from Mr. R.L. Bannerman, as of April 23, 1943, that all further articles regarding the internal operations of the Ingleside Hotel would have to come to him as releases from the Press Representative of the Department of State. His past actions prove that he refuses to be guided by any instructions from the Department of State and will use his own deductions concerning the printing of material that affects the Ingleside. His articles, I believe, are acting as subterfuges, to create dissension and discordance in the minds of the Stautonians, not only against the detainees who are stationed here but also against the Department of State.[14]

In the summer of 1943, the Allied Army successfully took Italy and the country capitulated. At the Ingleside, where the Germans and Italians of the Armistice Committee resided, tensions rose. Mr. Fitch writes in a September 22, 1943, letter, "We are proposing to move the

Italian official group out of the Ingleside Hotel and house them in the Shenvalee Hotel. This is occasioned by recent developments in Italy which has caused a certain amount of tension to develop between the German and Italian groups at the Ingleside Hotel."[15]

A Sense of Foreboding

The State Department was in a difficult spot. As the German losses in Europe mounted, the State Department began to fear the worst. Although given a low probability of success, the United States contacted the German authorities and floated the idea of an exchange of the Ingleside diplomats for the Allied group in Lourdes.

Time passed and the Germans did not respond. When they finally did contact the Swiss, they presented a list of conditions and demands that the United States had no interest in pursuing. On the battlefield, the Allied noose around Germany was tightening, and the State Department felt a sense of foreboding about how desperate the Germans might become, a feeling of doom so strong that the Secretary of State wrote a letter to President Roosevelt:

> As you are aware we have been negotiating with the Germans for the better part of a year in our effort to obtain the liberation of the diplomatic officers of this Government, our other citizens who have been assimilated into official groups such as newspapermen and relief workers and the officials of the other American republics who were all seized [by] the Germans on French territory. The total number of such individuals is 266. We received in June a communication from the German Government demanding in exchange for these few individuals some thousand of Germans in this country and in other countries of this hemisphere. As I have informed you, we refused the German proposal.[16]

He goes on to state that he is fearful that the diplomats may be held as hostages to be exchanged for German officers who are worried about being tried for war crimes, and he fears that they may be used as shields to prevent attack on these high officers.

In a memo recounting a phone conversation, the assistant secretary of state reports that the president sent a letter to the secretary of war. In the memo, General Strong states that some of the members of the captured group of Germans from North Africa were military and that they were considered prisoners of war. General Strong could not

Ten. Diplomats Captured in North Africa During the War

view their exchange without having serious doubts of the repercussions upon the best interest both from the military point of view and from the intelligence point of view. He felt that their return to Germany would cause a loss of thousands of lives.

Nevertheless, the U.S. government acceded to the German request. The secretary of state wrote to the Swiss charge:

> In return for the release for repatriation of the American official groups at Baden-Baden and Galesburg ... totaling about 270 people ... the United States government will release for repatriation the 25 German officials from Algeria now at Ingleside, the 17 members of the French official group at Hershey who wish to return to France and all the German nationals from the other American republics who were brought to the United States before July 1942, with a view to repatriation with the exception of 201 individuals who have communicated to the United States Government their unwillingness to be repatriated and 37 individuals who are not available for repatriation (due to security concerns, or health reasons).[17]

At this point, something occurred in Germany. The Germans ceased to communicate. The last German response was from July 28, 1943. The State Department wrote to the Swiss delegation on November 16, 1943, asking them if they knew the situation. They responded, "Naturally the Department wishes to do everything possible to expedite this exchange, but as each concession in the past has resulted in further German exactions, the department fears that even a show of anxiety on its part regarding the slowness of the German reply might be interpreted by the Germans as an indication that if they hold out we will eventually meet even more disproportionate demands. The Department would accordingly be grateful for any suggestions that you can give it concerning what it might do to hasten matters."[18] The Swiss indicated that, according to their confidential sources, "all exchange proposals require final approval of Von Ribbentrop and Hitler and they believe this may have delayed matters."[19]

Shenvalee Hotel

The surrender of fascist Italy to Allied Forces in 1943 severed its uneasy alliance with its Axis partner Germany. U.S. State Department officials in charge of civilian enemy internment thought it prudent to separate the German and Italian internees held at the Ingleside Hotel near Staunton. On October 4, 1943, nineteen Italians—some of whom were high-ranking diplomats—were transferred from the Ingleside Hotel to the Shenvalee resort hotel on the outskirts of New Market. The group traveled by bus from Staunton, accompanied by several State Department officials in charge of the transfer procedures.

"The hotel contains 23 rooms and 14 baths…. There is a fair sized lobby, a large dining room and a large recreation room in the basement. The furnishings are clean and neat but simple. The hotel is not elaborate but is comfortable. It is noted for its meals in the usual plain southern style. The grounds surrounding the hotel are open and level…."[20]

The entire property was posted off limits. A guard contingent of nine New Market men, assisted by a guard dog, worked eight-hour shifts. "The idea was to keep them in healthy condition and as happy as possible until they could be returned their country after the war."[21] Like the Ingleside, the Shenvalee Hotel and its surrounding golf course were closed to the public, but the internees were free to roam the extent of the hotel grounds. Their dubious status—neither free men allied with the United States nor prisoners of war—allowed them privileges equally dubious in application. They were allowed trips under surveillance into the village of New Market and a recreation program that included mountain hikes, tennis, and golf—all designed to keep them occupied and to maintain their health. Italian internees were not required to perform work, although today some witnesses recall Italians voluntarily working on nearby farms.

At the Shenvalee, the Italians demanded a letter from the Virginia alcoholic beverage control board to permit the entire group to purchase beverages, as the hotel did not have the appropriate permits. They complained about dry cleaning. One member wished to stay in the United States but only if he was given a job to help the Swiss delegation. Enrico Bombieri, the former Italian minister to Tunis, wanted to be sent back to Europe, but he demanded that he be sent by plane and not by boat. Others in the party wanted to be sent to Buenos Aires or to North Africa.

As time passed, the value of the Italians to be used in some kind of exchange with the Axis Powers diminished. The Italians threatened a hunger strike, as State Department agent Madden writes, "in recognizable protest over the fact that neither the Swiss nor the Department

Ten. Diplomats Captured in North Africa During the War

of State had granted them any concrete evidence, since their separation from the Germans on October 4, 1943, that either one of the above Departments were materially interested in their status."[22] Making matters worse for the Italians, the Legation of Switzerland cut off the monetary stipend of about $12 per month that many of them had been receiving. Although the sum was small, it was all that most of the Italians had for spending money for cigarettes or the movies. The State Department continued to provide lodging, meals, laundry, and some clothing. Moreover, the Immigration Service was facing budgetary issues in part due to the expense of running the large internment camps at Crystal City, Texas, and other locations.

Near the end of 1943, a scandal erupted. A desk clerk named Mrs. Frank O'Roark was spotted passing letters with Luigi Bosinco, an Italian detainee:

> Information gathered from her was to the effect that upon the initial entrance of the detainees to the Shenvalee Hotel, Luigi Bosinco struck up an over the desk conversation with her and from this informal introduction, he began to secretly relay letters of admiration to her. She in due turn began answering them and until their detection this cross correspondence continued. Mrs. O'Roark has outwardly proclaimed her love for Luigi Bosinco, to the end whereby she would be willing to leave her family and her home and run away with him. Realizing the futility of this condition and attempting to spare her all possibilities of scandal in her place of residence, New Market Virginia, a corporate of 600 people, she was given the opportunity of establishing an alibi for resigning. On December 24, 1943 Mrs. O'Roark was advised that her services would be dispensed with on December 28, 1943 and that at that time, her cause for resignation would be relayed to the Hotel manager, so as he might officially permit her to go and would not become too suspicious because of her voluntary withdrawal. It is to be noted that her father is the incumbent police chief of New Market and is a most respected citizen the community. For this reason and because of her marital status, that is the mother of a young child, it was evident that all precautions be taken to safeguard any gossip that might be injurious to either her immediate family or to her parents. This attachment between Mrs. O'Roark and Luigi Bosinco is the property of the Italian group but it is believed that its existence is unknown to any of the employees with whom she has worked or with whom she must once again take up community residence.
>
> Today, December 28, 1943, Mrs. O'Roark stated that she could not possibly establish an acceptable reason for leaving, hence it became obligatory to have her officially discharge for accepting letters on two separate occasions from a detainee and failing to notify the State Department Representative. She was advised that her secret would be guarded and that her future was within her own making.[23]

Axis Diplomats in American Custody

In May 1944 the only successful escape in any of the various exchange programs occurred. The escapee was Luigi Bosinco, the same individual who had attracted the attention of the desk clerk months earlier. He was last seen at 8:30 p.m. and reported missing by the Italians at around 10:30. He left with no money. His hat, overcoat, and other property were still in his room. By midnight, a thorough search of the hotel had been completed, the local and state police notified, and bus service shut down. However, no general alarm was given and the authorities were instructed not to tell anyone where Bosinco had come from. Mr. Madden, in his report, writes:

> It seems that he [Bosinco] gained his escape through the rear of the recreation area, plodded through the fields and scaled two or three fences which eventually brought him out on the main highway. Once he reached Route #11, the main artery into Washington, D.C. he proceeded north and continued walking until he came into the community of Mount Jackson, Virginia, a small corporate which lies approximately eight miles north of the Shenvalee Hotel. It must have been around midnight when Bosinco arrived in Mount Jackson, and he immediately started a campaign to raise money for himself and to solicit a room for the night.... Evidence shows that he presented himself at a home where he possibly saw two women seated in the front room and after having them answer his constant ringing of the doorbell he, in exceptionally poor English, solicited lodging from them but they refused his request. Once the women had returned to their parlor and noticed that Bosinco was still loitering about their premises and because their husbands were away at the time, they telephoned another prominent citizen of Mount Jackson to come to their home immediately. This citizen was rather late in arriving at the home of these women and because of this Bosinco had disappeared. It is difficult to predict the possible repercussions that might have resulted if Bosinco had been discovered by this alerted individual. Since Bosinco's return to the Shenvalee Hotel he has shown himself to be most depressed and despondent, consequently, our guard system has been alerted to watch him carefully, believing that he is a threat to once again attempt to escape.[24]

Bosinco explained that he was attempting to get to Washington to plead his case for parole to Mr. Franklin C. Gowen, a person who worked in the State Department and who had recently visited the Shenvalee, where he met with Bosinco among others. Bosinco was restricted to the hotel for three weeks, a light punishment perhaps due in part to the feeling that the group was soon to be exchanged. It is not known if Mrs. O'Roark played any part in Bosinco's escape.

When the Italian government under Mussolini collapsed, "the Italian group asked a number of questions regarding their status in view

Ten. Diplomats Captured in North Africa During the War

of the capitulation of the Italian Government. They were most anxious to know whether they were to be repatriated or released from detention in this country. Their general attitude was that they were no longer to be regarded as enemies of this country."[25] In another memorandum concerning a meeting of Minister Bombieri and Consul General Arrivabene, "both officials speaking on behalf of their respective groups stated that as before their loyalty is to the Government of the King of Italy. Their actions in the past have been controlled by this factor as they had serve their King under any type of Government he chose, implying that their service in the Fascist Government was occasioned by their loyalty to the King and not because of Fascist leanings.... They plainly indicated that they are no longer to be regarded as enemies but are in fact now our Allies.... Consul General Arrivabene [is of the opinion that] there is no possibility of exchange as his Government is now functioning with the Allied High Command."[26]

Since early summer, the State Department had been considering parole of the Italians:

> Any form of parole on a more lenient basis will practically require the removal of the group from New Market to some other locality because there is nothing in New Market or the surrounding territory that interests the Italian group and if permitted to travel the entire group will automatically leave this area. New Market is a true southern community and any infringement by the Italian group on the customs and habits of the community will result in serious repercussions. If the Italians are to be given more freedom of action it is suggested that they be transferred to New York where they will readily be absorbed by the city and their existence will not be a constant source of interest as is the case at New Market.[27]

However, the State Department took no action, and the Italians stayed stuck in New Market.

The Italians were allowed to go to town on their own recognizance. However, they were not allowed in town on Saturday, as this was the day the town filled up with outsiders from the nearby farms. Usually, the internees went to the movies:

> About 9 pm Wednesday, October 4, Mr. Ceccotti, one of the Italian detainees who was returning to the hotel was attacked by a group of young men at Walden's corner. Mr. Ceccotti was knocked to the ground and then an attempt was made to kick him which he resisted by kicking one of the assailants and at the same time calling for help. Mr. Manfredi, another of the detainees, was also returning to the hotel and was within one hundred feet of the location where Mr. Ceccotti was attacked. Mr. Manfredi came to his assistance and the group dispersed but

immediately returned and one of them engaged Mr. Manfredi in exchange of blows. When Mr. Ceccotti arose to his feet the entire group of young men ran away.[28]

The police were notified and the four young men were quickly apprehended. To avoid publicity, the complaint was filed not by Mr. Ceccotti or by the State Department, but by the chief of police. The four boys pleaded guilty, were fined, and were given 30 days jail time, which was suspended for one year pending good behavior. Mr. Ceccotti was examined by a doctor, and his injuries were slight.

The Italians stayed in New Market. In November, the new Italian government agreed to the repatriation of the seventeen Italians. One of the original internees, Minister Enrico Bombieri had been repatriated in July. The group left the Shenvalee Hotel at 7:20 in the morning of December 5, 1944, with 4,700 pounds of baggage. They travelled by train to Camp Patrick Henry in Virginia, a staging area for personnel going abroad. "The eighteen Italians were provided with helmets, gas masks, musette bags, sea-sick pills, medical kits, goggles, anti-gas powders and various other items. At the Shenvalee Hotel prior to departure to the staging area, Consul General Arrivabene indicated that he viewed his arrival in Italy with some apprehension and hoped that he would remain in U.S. military custody for a short while after arrival.... In general, the Italian group was not very happy about leaving.... They all realized that conditions in Italy were not good, and that the pleasant life they led as detainees, minus cares and worry, was forever gone."[29]

Exchange of Vichy French and Germans

Agreement was reached. Two hundred and seventy-one Allied personnel held at Baden-Baden and Godesberg would be exchanged in Portugal for 26 German officials at Ingleside and 687 Germans nationals, and those members of the French official group at Cascades Inn who wished to return.

An article dated February 16, 1944, in the *Daily Illini* reads:

The Swedish motor ship Gripsholm left New York today for Lisbon to carry out an exchange of American and Axis war internees, the State Department announced today.... Among the passengers on the Swedish liner, the department

Ten. Diplomats Captured in North Africa During the War

said, were 18 former Vichy French diplomats, 26 German consulate officers and their families who were seized in the North African invasion, and a German consul officer and his wife taken in Italy.... She will bring back American diplomats and others trapped when the Germans overran the formerly unoccupied zone of France. In the group, the department disclosed, will be approximately 156 relief workers, and newspaper correspondents....[30]

Eleven

Japanese Captured in Europe Near the End of the War

As Allied forces prevailed in Europe, 132 Japanese diplomats fled Berlin. Some went to Sweden, where they were captured. Others tried to enter Switzerland, where they were refused entry. The "status" of these individuals is not exactly clear. When captured, a report titled "Japanese Intelligence Report" was issued by Supreme Headquarters, Allied Expeditionary Forces, Office of the Assistant Chief of Staff, G-2. The subject line reads "Germany, Japanese Nationals Overrun by Allied Forces." A section reads, "With few exceptions, the passports were marked or stamped 'Diplomatic' even though the individuals did not carry [an official stamp] issued by the German Foreign Office and it was obvious that an attempt had been made to cloak the entire group with the protecting cover of diplomatic immunity."[1]

A State Department Official writes, "Diplomatic and consular officers of enemy Power accredited to another enemy Power and captured in the field in course of hostilities may be made POWs and are not entitled to claim as right customary diplomatic or consular privileges and immunities.... (However, the State Department continues, although it recognizes the military's authority to treat these Japanese as POWs, to conduct interrogations and searches, and to hold them under military control, it hopes that the military actually treats them as diplomats. The State Department hopes to...) protect American and United Nations citizens now held by Japs and use Jap diplomatic and consular officers to extent possible for psychological warfare.... That the group constitutes trump cards for new exchange negotiations for United Nations

Eleven. Japanese Captured in Europe Near the End of the War

Nationals including sick and wounded POWS...."[2] Although no U.S. diplomats were in Japan, it was hoped that these diplomats could be exchanged for American nationals who had not been able to get out of Japan or perhaps for prisoners of war held by the Japanese in Japan.

The group included the Japanese ambassador to Germany, General Hiroshi Oshima. It included three lieutenant colonels, a rear admiral, a colonel, a naval captain, a naval commander, and a major in the engineering corps. The group also included technical advisors as well as family members, cooks, chauffeurs, maids, businessmen, and reporters. The group was initially held at Bad Gastein, Germany. A small number of other Japanese diplomats captured in Italy who were held at Mantecatina were added to the group. The group was then moved to Le Havre, where they at first lived in tents as they awaited transportation. The State Department eventually had them moved to a hotel, where they awaited an available ship to the United States.

Not Welcome

Back home, the State Department researched various hotels to house the Japanese. The Sedgefield Inn near Greensboro, NC, the Mid-Pines in Southern Pines, NC, the Kirkwood Hotel and the Court Inn, both in Camden, SC, and other hotels were considered, but the State Department selected the Bedford Springs Hotel. This hotel had been evaluated by the State Department back in February 1942 as they searched for a location to place the Japanese who were leaving the Homestead, but had been rejected because "the hotel is very old, lacks the necessary facilities, has few bathrooms and is definitely reported to be not a first-class hotel."[3] Nevertheless in 1945 it was selected, perhaps, as one newspaper quoted a State Department official as saying, "because it was the only suitable unoccupied major hotel near Washington."[4] Another newspaper report states, "It was admitted that an earlier plan to locate the Japs in a southern state was abandoned because of local sentiment of an adverse nature and desire of the State Department to avoid any sign of hostile attitude which might be used by the Japanese government as an excuse for reprisal in treating American citizens now in Jap custody."[5]

Axis Diplomats in American Custody

The hotel had been taken over by the navy at the start of the war, and over 7000 sailors received radio operator instruction there. The final class had graduated in December 1944. It was vacant, although new owners had plans to renovate it and open it for summer lodging. However, they agreed to lease it to the State Department if the government would guarantee at least four months' occupancy. The fee was $3.00/day for each detainee and $1.50/day for each American stationed there.

The resort was less than three hours from Washington, DC. The resort was founded in 1796 and had been visited by eleven presidents. It had an antebellum architecture, was built of native stone, and had its origins, like many of the big resorts of the time, back in the 19th century as a place for curative baths and waters.

The local population vehemently opposed the use of the hotel. It may be because the war had been dragging on for years, casualties had hit every community, and the Japanese, as news about Bataan and the island fighting got out, were especially disliked. It could have been because the legation included what many perceived as military people and not diplomats. Whatever the reason, the town reaction was overwhelmingly negative. At a State Department meeting with Representative Tibbott, the representative pointed out:

> The Department had overlooked the peculiar nature of the population in the manufacturing center of Johnstown and in the mining areas of Cambria County. He stated that the situation in that area was always difficult whenever the laboring population, which is particularly receptive to propaganda, is stirred up. That they had not readily forgotten the difficulties that they had had some years ago when there was a strike, that another strike had just been averted this week and that owing to propaganda statements which have been circulated he believed it very possible that a serious strike affecting war production was the least of the evils than might result from having the Japanese accommodated at Bedford Springs. He pointed out that one union had already passed a resolution to desist from buying war bonds if the Japanese are accommodated at Bedford Springs. [Mr. Tibbott expressed] his personal view that the Japanese should be placed in a [Civilian Conservation Camp] in northern Pennsylvania.... The congressman stated that if he was not given satisfaction on this subject he intended to take the matter to the floor of the House and that if there were any repercussions in his local area through failure of the Department to listen to his warnings, he would hold the Department strictly accountable.[6]

In an editorial in the *Johnstown Tribune*:

Eleven. Japanese Captured in Europe Near the End of the War

The old hotel with its newer luxurious annex has been favored as a summer resort by well-to-do Americans for many years. It will resemble a prison during the occupancy of the Japanese only in that guards will be employed to prevent wandering off the premises. We would be the last to recommend the ill-treating of any prisoners of war, whether they were from diplomatic or military ranks. That would not be the American way. On the other hand, to house them and dine them as though they were welcome guests come to spend a pleasant vacation seems to us to be piling it on a bit thick. Any one of the Army barracks not now needed by the armed forces would have been good enough for these prisoners of war and would have saved the American taxpayers a considerable sum of money. The Japanese war lords have shown no such consideration for American and British citizens who have fallen into their clutches.... And what about those American prisoners of war who are being used for bayonet practice by the Japs and the thousands of American civilians thrown into filthy concentration camps and put on a starvation diet by the Sons of the Rising Sun?[7]

A letter to the editor in the *Johnston Tribune* of July 7, 1945, expressed the sentiments of many in town:

[To] Editor of the Tribune—At the regular monthly meeting of the Veterans of World War 2 a wide discussion was held on the recent move by our State Department officials to house the Jap diplomats and their families at the beautiful Bedford Springs hotel. During the discussion several members voiced views of some of our boys who have been prisoners of war and wounded in both theaters of action. One serviceman who had been a POW in a German concentration camp for 17 months stated that there is an overcrowded condition at the camp where he was sent to convalesce in one of the bordering states of Pennsylvania. Because both hospitals in Pennsylvania were filled to capacity he could not be sent to his home state. The fact that the Bedford Springs Hotel would provide an excellent rest camp and convalescing center for some of the boys who are now in hospitals and rest camps outside our own state, the serviceman feels bitter because the Japs are given the seclusion and luxury of the hotel while they must remain in the overcrowded camps outside Pennsylvania. This serviceman considers the recent move by our State Department officials as a poor showing of their appreciation of the sacrifices and hardships endured by him while fighting for his country....

This opinion is shared by the majority of servicemen returning in this area. A wounded serviceman who has recently been returned from hospitals in Belgium and Paris reveals the facts of the over-crowded conditions in a hospital on the East Coast where he was hospitalized on return to this country. He stated that in his ward there were 59 patients for the 39 available beds. A furlough plan by the hospital officials was necessary to relieve the overcrowded conditions. He also felt that in fighting for his country he is more entitled to the beauty and comforts of the Bedford Springs Hotel than the Japs of Pearl Harbor fame.... The people [of the adjacent counties] should have the use of the resort for their returning liberated and wounded sons before continuing the bitter fight against the barbarous Japs.

We are sure that the opinion of our sons and brothers who are now fighting the

Axis Diplomats in American Custody

treacherous murdering Japs in the hot malaria and vermin-infested jungles of the many island fronts in the Pacific is that they are being stabbed in the back by the officials that are responsible for the luxury and comfort they are providing for our worst enemy.

What about our own boys who are now being held prisoners in the filthy Jap camps and are dying from malaria, dysentery and malnutrition? Were these boys given any thought when the outrageous concessions were granted to the Jap diplomats and their families? Were they not the same Japs who helped plot and destroy our Navy and installations at Pearl Harbor which caused the death of many of our brave boys who died for a better and safer world to live in? If so, why treat them as visiting dignitaries and provide them with one of the finest health resorts in Pennsylvania?   We hope that this outrage is corrected before too many of our boys who are fighting in the South Pacific hear of it and suffer a serious morale setback. Signed T.J. Jordan Commander, Johnstown, July 7, 1945.[8]

For decades, the townspeople had availed themselves of the curative waters from the natural spring near the hotel. The water ran through a pipe to the road, and, for security reasons, the State Department cordoned off the area. At the same time, a local paper ran a story with the headline: "Says Japs Used U.S. Prisoners of War for Bayonet Practice. Korean Deserter Adds He Saw Massacre of 154 Yanks, Britons."[9] Conditions in the area became so tense that a state department official felt compelled to ask who had legal authority. He writes, "The question has been raised as to who will have jurisdiction in case of trouble at the Hotel, such as one of the local citizens being apprehended by a Department guard in attempting to injure one of the detainees. Should the case be referred to the local courts, State Court [or] to the U.S. Commissioner.... It is requested that an opinion be given on this question as the local sentiment is not favorable to the detention of the Japanese in the locality."[10]

The government allowed extra piping to be added from the spring, giving the locals access to the water. A local judge and the postmaster worked tirelessly to put down rumors. The State Department held meeting with the veterans of foreign wars, a local of the steelworker's union, and other groups to explain their positions. State Department officials put out notices that the Japanese ambassador would not have use of the golf course and would not have access to liquor. The Bedford food supply would not be imposed upon to feed these prisoners. Food would be supplied by Washington, DC. A newspaper article stated, "The famed hotel resort would be used merely as a place of internment

Eleven. Japanese Captured in Europe Near the End of the War

with the service reduced to an absolute minimum and devoid of any special privileges."[11] Another article quoted John E. Puerifoy of the State Department: "These diplomats will be treated as prisoners, not as guests.... They will have the same ration points for food as Americans have."[12]

The newspaper article quoted a State Department spokesman as saying, "The Japanese are holding some 12,000 to 40,000 U.S. citizens as prisoners.... These Japs from the German Balkans are 'blue chips of the war to us.' We hope to exchange them for many of these prisoners."[13] Per a newspaper article, a townsperson was quoted as saying, "But they must be treated right as we hoped to exchange them for Americans ... perhaps even for General Wainwright himself. (Lt. Gen. Jonathan Wainwright had commanded U.S. forces in Philippines and had been captured when that country fell early in the war.) These sources did not suggest how many Japanese Wainwright was worth."[14]

Preparations began for the arrival of the detainees. A six-foot-tall wooden fence was erected around the exercise space. Guard houses were put up. A memo dated June 20, 1945, from the State Department begins. "In accordance with previous discussions concerning the detention of the Japanese Diplomatic Group at the Bedford Springs Hotel, Bedford, Pennsylvania, arrangements have been completed and work has begun on the installation of microphones in twenty rooms to be occupied by various Japanese officials."[15] The memo goes on to list the officials, who include the Japanese ambassador, reporters, and various military attaches.

The Stay

The first group of thirty-three diplomats arrived in Bedford in mid–July, including Oshima, the Japanese ambassador to Germany. He was soon joined by 147 Japanese and eleven diplomats from Thailand. The group included thirty-four women and thirty-seven children. They had arrived earlier on the *Santa Rosa* troopship, which carried 5,000 U.S. troops returning from the war. Oshima's group went by train, not in luxurious sleepers, but in coach cars, for an eighteen-hour trip to

Axis Diplomats in American Custody

Bedford. They were met, according to a press report, by a crowd of several hundred people. There "was no demonstration, just a few hoots and jeers at the start being stopped by warning from police."[16]

Small groups of other Japanese diplomats arrived until approximately 180 were held at the hotel. The Thai group, because the United States was not at war with Thailand, was released to the Immigration Service. The Japanese settled into days of reading and walking a small paddock.

A memo from Mr. Fitch describes activities of the wife of a Japanese diplomat. The husband was not at the hotel:

> In compliance with the telephone request of Special Agent Hall, a discreet investigation was conducted relevant to the activities of Mrs. Irmgard Yamamoto, one of the detainees now residing at the Bedford Springs Hotel, Bedford Pennsylvania. It appears from the occasions of common gossip among the hotel employees, that the subject has been discovered in rather indiscreet situations on several occasions. It is a practice of Mrs. Yamamoto to entertain two and three men at a time, in her room behind locked door, tacitly giving rise in discrediting speculations. She also has created the habit of spending a great part of her time in the rooms of male detainees living in other buildings outside of her immediate wing. In one instance she was found lying on the top of a bed fully clothed with two Japanese male companions who were also dressed. Immediately upon the entrance of the chamber maid into this particular room and situation, the subject jumped from her reclining position as did her male companions and attempted to comb her disheveled hair.
> One of the amiable male companions was seen to enter an adjoining room and adjust his trousers which had been unbuttoned. Although nothing of a concrete nature can or will be avowed ... pertinent to her seemingly indiscretion, circumstances tend to show that she is not conducting herself as would be expected of a person in her standing.[17]

As was the case at the Homestead with the Japanese, factions developed between the military and the diplomats, but unlike the Homestead, the diplomatic group, and not the military, wanted to control the group:

> Since their initial arrival it has been and continues to be the so-called Embassy group that is the controlling and deciding factor for all points of issue in the Japanese group as a whole. This method of decision is beginning to be met with antagonism by the other groups such as the Military and Civilian, who claim that they do not have proper representation, on the controlling committees established by the Japanese Ambassador.... The policies of the group are decided by a small committee, all of whom are former representatives of the Japanese Embassy at Berlin, and who believe that they are still the active powers behind the conduct

Eleven. Japanese Captured in Europe Near the End of the War

and policies of all individuals concerned. On several occasions the Embassy committee has failed to respect the problems and conflicts of the non-diplomatic members and have been interested only in their own ... welfare. This condition has given rise to widespread dissension in the other groups and might be the cause behind a possible internal revolt.[18]

A few days later, in another memorandum, Mr. Madden, the State Department's representative on scene, writes:

As you know, there are non-diplomatic groups here who have been unwillingly forced to recognize the potency of General Oshima. It has been possible, through hidden contacts, [to take] the pulse and thoughts of the group as a whole.... The internal control of the Japanese actions at this hotel are being rigidly supervised and directed by Ambassador Oshima who still believes his authority to be all-powerful. The semblance of dictatorship might or might not be within the limits of his position but it is noteworthy to advise you his latest directive. General Oshima informed his "aides" that "any member of the Japanese group who is seen talking to the enemy [apparently the Department of State's representative] is to be condemned and their actions will be subject of a written report at the home office upon their return to Tokyo."[19]

Arthur Barbeur writes, "By the middle of October, the Department of State had decided that there was no reason to detain the Japanese any longer in the United States."[20] The departure date was tied to the availability of a suitable passenger ship and to the expiration of the four-month contract with the hotel. Several of the Japanese asked not to be sent to Japan, but instead to be sent to Europe or to remain in the United States. All were denied except for Mrs. Yamamoto, who was allowed to go to Germany. She was a native German. Barbeur continues, "At the same time, the State Department asked American authorities in Europe not to send any more Japanese to the United States. Instead, they suggested that the British be requested to take responsibility for repatriating those still in Europe."[21]

A newspaper reports the departure of the Japanese:

A special seven coach B & O train left Cumberland shortly after 4 o'clock yesterday afternoon carrying [members] of the Japanese consular staff and their families on the leg of their trip back to war-shattered Japan. The group, all captured in Germany, [included] the former Japanese Ambassador to Germany Oshima, his wife and girl.... Almost as soon as the buses [from the hotel] pulled to a stop, a crowd began to gather around the special train, on a siding below Williams street but there were no demonstration, not even a "boo." ... Several of the Rising Sun partly shielded their faces with their hands as flashlight bulbs from the cameras of news photographers went off. The majority however ignored the crowd, boarding

Axis Diplomats in American Custody

the train as though there was nothing unusual about the situation.... There was nothing elaborate about the day coaches in which were consigned, most of them looking like second-rate carriers but as one guard was heard to remark "The accommodations are a damn sight better than those the Japs afforded the Yanks on the march from Bataan."[22]

Conclusion

In writing this story, we found it is difficult to imagine the entire country all in agreement about anything. Today we see inaction in the face of mounting world tensions. Sixty years ago the State Department Special War Problems Division, the FBI, and the Bureau of Naturalization and Immigration, newspaper publishers, local governments, hotel management, and townspeople could work together.

One of the things we found impressive was that the government actually functioned. We were astonished that the plan for the original exchange of diplomats was put together by a small group of officials in less than a month and that the entire first exchange was completed in about six months, without any major incidents.

We are amazed that the townspeople in White Sulfur Springs, Hot Springs, and Asheville were supportive of the program. Perhaps this was due to the fact that the war had just started. Later, we would see the hostility by the townspeople of Staunton and Bedford towards the diplomats captured in Europe. Their feelings reflected the months of rationing and shortages and the toll of injuries and casualties to the local boys. But the initial group was treated with great respect and professionalism. Years later, in a private correspondence, a hotel manager writes, "At all times the Japanese diplomats, their wives and children, were treated as any other Homestead guests."[1] It is still amazing to us that, as far as we can find out, no one at the Greenbrier, Homestead, or Grove Park Inn ever "spit in the soup."

There does not seem to be an accepted term for the detainment or internment of the diplomats. However, when Ambassador Oshima was captured in German near the end of the war, he and his entourage were held in Bad Gastein, a location populated by "a mere handful of

Conclusion

American soldiers in the area and of several thousand Wehrmacht and Luftwaffe officers and men, many of whom were still armed."² The military's inclination was to treat him as a prisoner of war, but the State Department asked them to instead treat him as if he were a diplomat. The military acceded, granting to Oshima freedom from interrogation and imprisonment. The military told the State Department they would provide Oshima with this favored status, which they referred to as "honorable custody."³

In the archives at the Greenbrier Hotel is a photograph taken near the beginning of the war of the Japanese diplomats from Washington. They look haughty and arrogant. Another photograph, taken in 1945 at the hotel in Bedford, is of those Japanese diplomats who had been captured late in the war as they tried to escape the collapsing Germany. They are stoop-shoulders, hands held behind them or hung listlessly, an attitude of defeat, humiliation, and disbelief.

As mentioned in the first chapter, an article in the *White Sulfur Springs Sentinel* of December 12, 1941, states that a "Gala New Year is Planned at Resort" and says that the celebration will provide "the right kind of adieu to 1941 and the welcoming salute to a new and is to be hoped, a better new year."⁴ The celebration was cancelled. For six months the hotel did its patriotic duty. However, as soon as the diplomats left, the town carried on, and the July 24, 1942, edition of the newspaper carried an advertisement for a dance at the Greenbrier, the proceeds to benefit the Red Cross and USO.⁵

Ernest Angle, the sailor from a small town about twenty miles away from the Greenbrier, died in the Pearl Harbor attack. Four years later, at Bedford, the State Department faced a strange dilemma. They had been holding a group of one hundred and thirty Japanese who had been part of that country's diplomatic mission to Berlin. They were a mix of military and government officials. An editorial in a local paper is quoted at length below:

> I am told that those important Japanese [the group at Bedford] whom I consider war criminals have diplomatic status and may be immune from a war trial....
> [These 130 people, including wives and children] have become wards of our government at $3 a day and 50 ration points per person a month. Gen. Jonathan M. Wainwright and 110 high ranking U.S. army and navy officers were imprisoned, stripped and humiliated, slapped, beaten and kicked. However, our department of state selected a resort hotel where these arch-Axis plotters have newspapers,

Conclusion

magazines, outdoor shuffleboard, card games, ping-pong tables, organized children's sports, 400 pounds of ice a day and expert American medical attention.... These Japanese military diplomats should be in a jail or military prison.... We should abide by international agreements on the treatment of military prisoners and diplomats but we should go no further. One concluded after a visit to Bedford Springs that General Oshima and his military staff should be transferred to the equivalent of a Nuremberg jail rather than rest in big porch chairs beneath the high white colonial pillars of one of America's older health resorts. They were masters of starvation, disease, sadism and wholesale indecencies when the Axis wars were going their way. Our State Department peace at any price diplomats cling apparently to the hope that resort surroundings will pay off in Jap good-will and friendship.... We must assume a sterner attitude and realize that diplomatic protocol need not provide sanctuary to double-crossing militarists who seek protection under any law....[6]

This article was published in October. The war was over. The atomic bombs had been dropped on Hiroshima on August 6 and on Nagasaki on August 9. The Japanese had agreed to unconditional surrender on August 15. The surrender document was signed on September 2, 1945, which became known as V-J Day.

On V-J Day in Bedford, the townspeople celebrated by taking what the local paper calls a "Victory Parade Around Japs' Hotel," consisting of "an hour long parade of more than 1,000 celebrating Americans circling in autos around Bedford Springs hotel...."[7]

The surrender ceremony in Japan took place on the USS *Missouri*. This vessel was built during the war and reported for duty with the 3rd fleet at Pearl Harbor on Christmas Eve, 1944. Its firepower was used at Iwo Jima and at Okinawa. Now, on September 2, 1945, it was in Tokyo Bay as the emperor of Japan formally surrendered his country.

At this point, the State Department faced a choice. To many in the country, the entire diplomatic exchange program had been about reciprocity, that is, to trade diplomats for diplomats. With victory, however, the United States now had all the cards. There were no U.S. diplomats held by the Japanese. Any American military prisoners of war that had been held by the Japanese were being released to U.S. troops.

The State Department was under great pressure to classify the Japanese at Bedford Springs as war criminals or to treat them as military officers. Either way they could have handed them over to the War Department to be brought in front of military tribunals. Alternatively the State Department could continue to act as it had for the last four

Conclusion

years and provide the legation with the immunity and safe passage dictated by diplomatic protocol.

A year and a half earlier, when the war was still in question, a baby was born to a German couple interned at the Ingleside Hotel. The State Department arranged for a christening, and the ceremony included piano and violin duets and singing by a choral group of German men and women:

> Consul General Pfeiffer spoke to the participants in three languages, German, Italian and English. The context of his talk in English can be summed up in the following: To you Bettina [looking at the child who was being held by her nurse] a child who has been born in such bitter and cruel times, away from your home, away from your friends and away from your culture, it must be known to you that someday you will return to the home of your parents and, we hope, that you will join hands with the nations of the world, in their united march towards the ideals that have been created for mankind.[8]

Fireman Second Class Angle died early in a war that was fought against the tyranny and the rule of might that Consul General Pfeiffer wished for baby Bettina. The United States emerged from that war as the world's strongest power, capable of almost anything. It could dominate the world or help the world in healing. It could foster the rule of law and democracy or it could become a tyrant itself. What kind of world would America choose?

On November 16, 1945, the State Department loaded the Japanese at Bedford onto buses. They went to Cumberland, VA, boarded a B&O Railroad train that had Border Patrol agents on board for security, and traveled over several days, arriving in Seattle on November 20, 1945. They were taken to the docks and boarded the vessel USS *General GM Randall*, a troopship under contract to the navy and manned by a U.S. Coast Guard crew. Three months earlier this vessel had ferried 5,100 American troops from the European theater of war to the Pacific theater, in preparation for the anticipated invasion of Japan. The *GM Randall* left Seattle on November 21, 1945, taking the Japanese delegation, together with 1,300 other Japanese repatriates, to Japan to begin the long process of rebuilding their country.

Chapter Notes

Introduction

1. National Park Service, "Frequently Asked Questions: 'Why were the crewmembers' bodies never removed from the USS Arizona?'" *World War II Valor in the Pacific*, https://www.nps.gov/valr/faqs.htm, accessed May 8, 2016.
2. Erika Dreifus, "A 'Golden Prison' in Pennsylvania: The Hotel Hershey, 1942–43," *Pennsylvania History: A Journal of Mid-Atlantic Studies*, Vol. 69, No. 3 (Summer 2002): 431. https://journals.psu.edu/phj/article/download/25772/25541, accessed June 30, 2015.
3. Graham H. Stuart, "Special War Problems Division," *The Department of State Bulletin*, Publication 2148, Vol. XI, No. 262 (July 2, 1944): 7.
4. "The Department, Duties of the Special Division," *The Department of State Bulletin*, Publication 1877, Vol. VIII, No. 190 (February 13, 1943): 156.
5. Mike McCormick, "Historical Perspective: Pilot, under vigilant eye of FBI, made trip to Terre Haute," *Tribune Star*, June 18, 2007, http://www.tribstar.com/news/lifestyles/historical-perspective-pilot-under-vigilant-eye-of-fbi-made-trip/article_2a2e8cd9-e35f-5d31-bfbf-c5800b30f4e3.html, accessed May 8, 2016.
6. Letter to Lee from Hoover, March 11, 1942. Hot Springs, VA, Homestead Hotel. National Archives Identifier: 2530311. Office of Special Consular Services, 12/30/1954–1977. Department of State: Bureau of Security and Consular Affairs, Office of Protective Services, 1952–1953. General Records of the Department of State, 1763–2002. National Archives at College Park, Container ID: 107.
7. Edward F. Jones, "Nazi Embassy Privileges Are Suddenly Ended." *Times Herald*, Washington D.C., December 18, 1941.
8. Post by Vitesse, January 1, 2008, "Axis History Forum," http://forum.axishistory.com/viewtopic.php?t=132854, accessed June 14, 2015.
9. "History of the Bureau of Diplomatic Security of the United States Department of State," United States Department of State Bureau of Diplomatic Security, Printed October 2011, Global Publishing Solutions, First Edition, 54.
10. Arnold M. Krammer, "In Splendid Isolation: Enemy Diplomats in World War II," *Prologue, Journal of the National Archives*, Vol. 17, No. 1 (Spring 1985): 27.
11. Letter to Biddle from Hull, February 12, 1942. National Archives Identifier: 2529590. Record Group 59: General Records of the Department of State, 1763–2002. Office of Special Consular Services, 12/30/1954–1977. Department of State: Bureau of Security and Consular Affairs, Office of Protective Services, 1952–1953. General Records of the Department of State, 1763–2002. National Archives at College Park, Container ID: 72.
12. Telegram (701.6211/1599), Huddle to Secretary of State, March 5, 1942. "The Charge in Switzerland (Huddle) to the Secretary of State," *Foreign Relations*, 1942, Vol. 1, 327–328.
13. Lynn Grove, "The American Internee Experience in Nazi Germany," *Traces*, http://www.traces.org/americaninternees.html, accessed March 3, 2015.
14. Dispatch from Arthur F. Tower, September 12, 1942, Treatment of American Officials by Japanese Authorities. National Archives Identifier: 2529567. Department

Chapter Notes—One

of State, Bureau of Security and Consular Affairs: Office of Protective Services, 1952–1953. Record Group 59: General Records of the Department of State, 1763–2002. National Archives at College Park, Container ID: 70.

Chapter One

1. Letter to Fitch from Bannerman, dated December 16, 1941. "Subject: Hotel accommodations for the Diplomatic and Consular officials for Japan, Germany, Italy, Rumania and Bulgaria." Record Group 59: General Records of the Department of State, 1763–2002. National Archives Identifier: 2531043. Department of State: Bureau of Security and Consular Affairs, Office of Protective Services, 1952–1953. National Archives at College Park, Container ID: 179.
2. Ibid.
3. "The Homestead: A Great Hotel Entertains Jap Diplomats As Patriotic Duty," *Life Magazine*, Vol. 12, No. 7 (February 16, 1942): 73.
4. Bob Sibold, unpublished memorandum, "Report of the Axis Diplomats and Nationals at The Greenbrier, December 19th, 1941 to July 8th, 1942 (201 days stay)," 1–2.
5. Fay Ingalls, unpublished memorandum, "Japanese at Hot Springs," 1.
6. Telegram (123.0040/87b), Hull to Huddle, December 19, 1941, "Agreements With Enemy Countries For The Exchange Of Officials And Non-Officials," *Foreign Relations*, 1942, Vol. 1, 292.
7. "U.S. Announces Stand Towards Axis Diplomats," *The Asheville Citizen*, December 18, 1941, 1–2.
8. "Large Crowd at Defense Meeting," *White Sulfur Springs Sentinel*, December 19, 1941, 1.
9. "Gala New Year Is Planned at Resort," *White Sulfur Springs Sentinel*, December 19, 1941, 1.
10. "Internments," *White Sulfur Springs Sentinel*, December 19, 1941, 1.
11. Sibold, 1–2.
12. "Memorandum of agreement with respect to the detention of members of the German Embassy and Hungarian Legation at the Greenbrier Hotel, White Sulphur Springs, West Virginia," December 20, 1941. World War II: Letters, memos relating to foreign diplomats held at Greenbrier and FBI materials relating to their exchange (photocopies), 1941–1942. I Folder Ms 2009–006 Archives and History Library, WV Division of Culture and History.
13. Memorandum for Assistant Director E.A. Tamm, from A.N. Carlblom, December 23, 1941. World War II: Letters, memos relating to foreign diplomats held at Greenbrier and FBI materials relating to their exchange (photocopies), 1941–1942. I Folder Ms2009–006 Archives and History Library, WV Division of Culture and History.
14. "Axis Officials Interned Here," *White Sulfur Springs Sentinel*, December 26, 1941, 1.
15. "Greenbrier Denies Alien Objection," *White Sulfur Springs Sentinel*, December 26, 1941, 1.
16. Letter to Director Hoover from Carlblom regarding activities at the Greenbrier Hotel dated January 26, 1942. World War II: Letters, memos relating to foreign diplomats held at Greenbrier and FBI materials relating to their exchange (photocopies), 1941–1942. I Folder Ms2009–006 Archives and History Library, WV Division of Culture and History.
17. Ingalls, 4.
18. Daily Report from Special Agent Carson, January 15, 1942, RE: Joseph Krautlegger. Item 9—Memorandum on Joseph Krautlegger, Greenbrier Hotel Mission, Morgan, Roy L., 1908–1985. Special Collections, Arthur J. Morris Law Library, University of Virginia Law School: Inventory of the Papers of Roy L. Morgan, 1941–1966. http://lib.law.virginia.edu/special collections/ Box 9, Folder 13, MSS 93–4 1 mss93–4_b9_f13_i9_0001 tp/cdm16101.contentdm.oclc.org/cdm/search/searchterm/Springs.
19. Ibid.
20. "White Sulphur Aliens Taken into Custody," *The Greenbrier Independent*, February 13, 1942, 1.
21. Memorandum for the Director from R.L. Morgan, RE: Japanese Diplomatic Corps Internal Security, January 11, 1942, Greenbrier Hotel Mission, Morgan, Roy L., 1908–1985. Special Collections, Arthur J. Morris Law Library, University of Virginia Law School: Inventory of the Papers of Roy L. Morgan, 1941–1966. http://lib.law.

Chapter Notes—Two

virginia.edu/specialcollections/ Box 9, Folder 13, MSS 93-4 1 mss93-4_b9_f13_i9_0001 tp://cdm16101.contentdm.oclc.org/cdm/search/searchterm/Springs.

22. "Memorandum for Mr. E.A. Tamm," January 6, 1942, Greenbrier Hotel Mission, Morgan, Roy L., 1908–1985. Special Collections, Arthur J. Morris Law Library, University of Virginia Law School: Inventory of the Papers of Roy L. Morgan, 1941–1966. http://lib.law.virginia.edu/specialcollections/ Box 9, Folder 13, MSS 93-4 1 mss93-4_b9_f13_i9_0001 tp://cdm16101.contentdm.oclc.org/cdm/search/searchterm/Springs.

23. "Memorandum for the Attorney General," January 7, 1942, Greenbrier Hotel Mission, Morgan, Roy L., 1908–1985. Special Collections, Arthur J. Morris Law Library, University of Virginia Law School: Inventory of the Papers of Roy L. Morgan, 1941–1966. http://lib.law.virginia.edu/specialcollections/ Box 9, Folder 13, MSS 93-4 1 mss93-4_b9_f13_i9_0001 tp://cdm16101.contentdm.oclc.org/cdm/search/searchterm/Springs.

24. Handwritten Note on "Memorandum for the Attorney General," January 7, 1942, Greenbrier Hotel Mission, Morgan, Roy L., 1908–1985. Special Collections, Arthur J. Morris Law Library, University of Virginia Law School: Inventory of the Papers of Roy L. Morgan, 1941–1966. http://lib.law.virginia.edu/specialcollections/ Box 9, Folder 13, MSS 93-4 1 mss93-4_b9_f13_i9_0001 tp://cdm16101.contentdm.oclc.org/cdm/search/searchterm/Springs.

Chapter Two

1. Gwen Terasaki, *Bridge to the Sun* (Chapel Hill: University of North Carolina Press, 1957), 75.
2. *Ibid.*, 76.
3. Unsigned letter addressed to the Japanese Ambassador, Hotel Accommodations—Overflow. National Archives Identifier: 2530319. Department of State, Bureau of Security and Consular Affairs: Office of Protective Services, 1952–1953. Record Group 59: General Records of the Department of State, 1763–2002. National Archives at College Park, Container ID: 109.
4. Jane Eppings, "Pearl Harbor, Japanese Espionage and Arizona's Triangle T Ranch," *Prologue, The Magazine of the National Archives* (Spring 1997): 44.
5. Telegram, Postal Inspector Smith to Fitch, February 14, 1942. "23 Japanese from Hawaii via San Diego—S.S. President Hayes." National Archives Identifier: 2530394. Department of State: Bureau of Security and Consular Affairs, Office of Protective Services, 1952–1953. Record Group 59: General Records of the Department of State, 1763–2002. National Archives at College Park, Container ID: 115.
6. *Ibid.*
7. Letter to Fitch from Bannerman, February 25, 1942. "23 Japanese from Hawaii via San Diego—S.S. President Hayes." National Archives Identifier: 2530394. Department of State, Bureau of Security and Consular Affairs, Office of Protective Services, 1952–1953. Record Group 59: General Records of the Department of State, 1763–2002. National Archives at College Park, Container ID: 115.
8. Letter to Fitch from Bailey, Staff of the Japanese Consulate General, Honolulu, February 21, 1942. "23 Japanese from Hawaii via San Diego—S.S. President Hayes." National Archives Identifier: 2530394. Department of State: Bureau of Security and Consular Affairs, Office of Protective Services, 1952–1953. Record Group 59: General Records of the Department of State, 1763–2002. National Archives at College Park, Container ID: 115.
9. Memorandum, "Instructions for Representatives of Former Hungarian Consulate," New York, NY. December 24, 1941, Greenbrier Hotel Mission, Morgan, Roy L., 1908–1985. Special Collections, Arthur J. Morris Law Library, University of Virginia Law School: Inventory of the Papers of Roy L. Morgan, 1941–1966. http://lib.law.virginia.edu/specialcollections/ Box 9, Folder 13, MSS 93-4 1 mss93-4_b9_f13_i9_0001 tp://cdm16101.contentdm.oclc.org/cdm/search/searchterm/Springs.
10. Memorandum for Assistant Director D.M. Ladd, December 29, 1941, "Item 6—Remaining Guests at Greenbrier Hotel." Greenbrier Hotel Mission, Special Collections, Arthur J. Morris Law Library, University of Virginia Law School: http://lib.law.virginia.edu/specialcollections/ Box 10, Folder 4, MSS 93-4 Inventory of the Papers of Roy L. Morgan, 1941–1966 mss93_4_b10_f4_i6_0001.

Chapter Notes—Three

11. Memorandum for Assistant Director D.M. Ladd, January 10, 1942, "Item 17—Activities at the Greenbrier Hotel Greenbrier Hotel Mission." Special Collections, Arthur J. Morris Law Library, University of Virginia Law School: Inventory of the Papers of Roy L. Morgan, 1941–1966. http://lib.law.virginia.edu/special collections/ Box 10, Folder 4, MSS 93–4 mss93_4_b10_f4_i17_0001.

12. Memorandum for Assistant Director D.M. Ladd, January 30, 1942, "Item 35—Japanese Diplomatic Corps Internal Security Subject Greenbrier Hotel Mission." Special Collections, Arthur J. Morris Law Library, University of Virginia Law School: Inventory of the Papers of Roy L. Morgan, 1941–1966. http://lib.law.virginia.edu/specialcollections/ Contributors D.M. Ladd; Roy L. Morgan Date 1942–02–13 Type Text Format TIFF Source Box 10, Folder 1, MSS 93–4 Language EN Collection Title Page 1 Identifier mss93–4_b10_fl_i35_0001.

13. Telegram to Secretary of State from Wilson, December 24, 1941, "United States–Japanese Exchange Files." National Archives Identifier: 17343398. Department of State: Bureau of Security and Consular Affairs, Office of Protective Services, 1952–1953. Record Group 59: General Records of the Department of State, 1763–2002. National Archives at College Park, Container ID: 201.

14. Harold E. Davis, John J. Finan, and F. Taylor Peck, *Latin American Diplomatic History: An Introduction* (Baton Rouge: Louisiana State University, 1977): 225.

15. *Ibid.*, 241.

16. "History of the Bureau of Diplomatic Security of the United States Department of State," United States Department of State Bureau of Diplomatic Security, printed October 2011, Global Publishing Solutions, First Edition, 50.

17. Appendix, "Personal Justice Denied," Report of the Commission on Wartime Relocation and Internment of Civilians, Washington, D.C., June 1983, 305.

18. Memorandum to Mr. Duggan, May 4, 1942. National Archives Identifier: 2529590. Department of State: Bureau of Security and Consular Affairs, Office of Protective Services, 1952–1953. Record Group 59: General Records of the Department of State, 1763–2002. National Archives at College Park, Container ID: 72.

19. "Axis Diplomats in S. America Packing Bags," *The Times Recorder*, January 22, 1942, 1.

20. Letter Attention Mr. Bernard Gufler from Joachim Marggraff, September 6, 1942, Greenbrier Hotel—W.S.S., W.Va.–Poole. National Archives Identifier: 2530329. Department of State: Bureau of Security and Consular Affairs, Office of Protective Services, 1952–1953. Record Group 59: General Records of the Department of State, 1763–2002. National Archives at College Park, Container ID: 110.

21. Letter to Cabot, et al., from Green, May 9, 1942. Exchange—Official Personnel [2 Folders]. National Archives Identifier: 2529590. Department of State: Bureau of Security and Consular Affairs, Office of Protective Services, 1952–1953. Record Group 59: General Records of the Department of State, 1763–2002. National Archives at College Park, Container ID: 72.

22. Memo, To Secretary of State from Dawson, "Lists of Axis Nationals to be Repatriated from Bolivia," April 2, 1942, S.S. Drottningholm-Axis Removal from United States [Folder 5 of 5] National Archives Identifier: 2530353. Department of State: Bureau of Security and Consular Affairs, Office of Protective Services, 1952–1953. Record Group 59: General Records of the Department of State, 1763–2002. National Archives at College Park, Container ID: 113.

23. Memorandum, "Repatriation of Axis Officials and Nationals," April 9, 1942. Exchange—Official Personnel [2 Folders]. National Archives Identifier: 2529590. Department of State: Bureau of Security and Consular Affairs, Office of Protective Services, 1952–1953. Record Group 59: General Records of the Department of State, 1763–2002. National Archives at College Park, Container ID: 72.

Chapter Three

1. Sibold, 2.
2. Ingalls, 2.
3. Sibold, 2.
4. Memorandum for Mr. Kimball RE Duties at Greenbrier Hotel Mission, *Daily Report*, March 4, 1942. Inventory of the Papers of Roy L. Morgan, Special Collections, Arthur J. Morris Law Library, Uni-

Chapter Notes—Three

versity of Virginia Law School, http:/lib.law.virginia.ed/specialcollections/ Box 10, Folder 5, MSS 93–4.

5. Memorandum for Assistant Director D.M. Ladd, January 30, 1942, "Louis Toman Admts Taking Two Letters Out For Saporiti," Greenbrier Hotel Mission, Special Collections, Arthur J. Morris Law Library, University of Virginia Law School: Inventory of the Papers of Roy L. Morgan, 1941–1966. http://lib.law.virginia.edu/specialcollections/ Box 10, Folder 3, MSS 93–4 mss93_4_b10_f3_i5_0001.

6. Memorandum for Assistant Director D.M. Ladd, January 30, 1942, "Saporiti Will Be Intelligence Agent in Lisbon," Greenbrier Hotel Mission, Special Collections, Arthur J. Morris Law Library, University of Virginia Law School: Inventory of the Papers of Roy L. Morgan, 1941–1966. http://lib.law.virginia.edu/specialcollections/ Box 10, Folder 3, MSS 93–4 mss93_4_b10_f3_i5_0001.

7. Daily Report to Ladd from Lawler, March 1, 1942, "Item 1—The Greenbrier Hotel Mission Subject Greenbrier Hotel Mission." Special Collections, Arthur J. Morris Law Library, University of Virginia Law School: Inventory of the Papers of Roy L. Morgan, 1941–1966. http://lib.law.virginia.edu/specialcollections/ Contributors D.M. Ladd; J.E. Lawler Date 1942–03–01 Type Text Format TIFF Source Box 10, Folder 5, MSS 93–4 Language EN Collection Description Title Page 1 Identifier mss93_4_b10_f5_i1_0001.

8. Terasaki, 79–80.

9. Memorandum for the Director, Attn: Mr. Ladd, RE January 7, 1942, "Item 10—Japanese Diplomatic Corps Internal Security," Greenbrier Hotel Mission. Special Collections, Arthur J. Morris Law Library, University of Virginia Law School: Inventory of the Papers of Roy L. Morgan, 1941–1966. http://lib.law.virginia.edu/specialcollections/ Contributors D.M. Ladd; Roy L. Morgan Date 1942–01–07 Type Text Format TIFF Source Box 10, Folder 7, MSS 93–4 Language EN Collection Description Title Page 1 Identifier mss93_4_b10_f7_i10_0001.

10. Letter to Fitch from Poole, January 17, 1942, Hot Springs, Va., Homestead Hotel. National Archives Identifier: 2530311. Department of State: Bureau of Security and Consular Affairs, Office of Protective Services, 1952–1953. Record Group 59: General Records of the Department of State, 1763–2002. National Archives at College Park, Container ID: 107.

11. Memorandum for Assistant Director D.M. Ladd from Carlblom, January 19, 1942, "Item 25—Activities at the Greenbrier Hotel," Greenbrier Hotel Mission. Special Collections, Arthur J. Morris Law Library, University of Virginia Law School: Inventory of the Papers of Roy L. Morgan, 1941–1966. http://lib.law.virginia.edu/specialcollections/ Contributors D.M. Ladd; A.N. Carlblom; R.J. Untreiner Date 1942-01-19 Type Text Format TIFF Source Box 10, Folder 4, MSS 93–4 Language EN Collection Title Page 1 Identifier mss93_4_b10_f4_i25_0001.

12. Letter to R.L. Morgan from J. Edgar Hoover, May 12, 1942, "Item 40-German Diplomatic Corp Internal Security," Greenbrier Hotel Mission. Special Collections, Arthur J. Morris Law Library, University of Virginia Law School: Collection Inventory of the Papers of Roy L. Morgan, 1941–1966. http://lib.law.virginia.edu/specialcollections/ D.M. Ladd; Roy L. Morgan, J. Edgar Hoover; Alfred R. Nerz 1942–05–06 Box 10, Folder 4, MSS 93–4 mss93_4_b9_f4_i40_0004.

13. Fay Ingalls, "A Journal of the Sojourn of the Axis Diplomats at The Homestead," 5.

14. "Mrs. Roland A. (Lettie) Fleagle," National Border Patrol Museum, https://borderpatrolmuseum.com/interviews/mrs-roland-a-lettie-fleagle/, accessed May 8, 2016.

15. Memorandum for the Director, Attention Mr. Ladd, RE Japanese Diplomatic Corps Internal Security, Jan. 6, 1942, "Item 9—Japanese Diplomatic Corps Internal Security," Greenbrier Hotel Mission, Special Collections, Arthur J. Morris Law Library, University of Virginia Law School: Inventory of the Papers of Roy L. Morgan, 1941–1966. http://lib.law.virginia.edu/specialcollections/ D.M. Ladd; Roy L. Morgan Box 10, Folder 7, MSS 93–4 mss93_4_b10_f7_i9_0001.

16. "Our Axis Diplomats (Editorial)," *White Sulfur Springs Sentinel*, December 26, 1941, 1.

17. David Charay and William Wallace (as told to Warren Hall), "Interned Jap, German Envoys Hoard Supplies," *Times-Her-*

Chapter Notes—Four

ald, May 5, 1942. Special Collections, Arthur Morris Law Library, University of Virginia Law School, Box 9, Folder 11, MSS 93–4.

18. Ibid.

19. Letter to Fitch from Keeley, Assembly Inn. National Archives Identifier: 2530925. Department of State: Bureau of Security and Consular Affairs, Office of Protective Services, 1952–1953. Record Group 59: General Records of the Department of State, 1763–2002. National Archives at College Park, Container ID: 163.

20. Ibid.

21. Weekly Report, The Ursula Martin Case, "Item 6—Japanese Diplomatic Corps Internal Security," Special Collections, Arthur J. Morris Law Library, University of Virginia Law School: Inventory of the Papers of Roy L. Morgan, 1941–1966. http://lib.law.virginia.edu/specialcollections/ Contributors D.M. Ladd; Roy L. Morgan Date 1942–04–14 Type Text Format TIFF Source Box 9, Folder 7, MSS 93–4 Language EN Collection Description Title Page 1 Identifier mss93_4_b9_f7_i6_0001.

22. Letter to Fitch from Huskey, April 13, 1942, Grove Park Inn—Asheville, NC—Internment of Alien Enemies [3 Folders]. National Archives Identifier: 2531043. Department of State: Bureau of Security and Consular Affairs, Office of Protective Services, 1952–1953. Record Group 59: General Records of the Department of State, 1763–2002. National Archives at College Park, Container ID: 179.

23. Telegram (125.0040/134) Huddle to the Charge in Switzerland (Huddle) to the Secretary of State, February 28, 1942, "Agreements With Enemy Countries For The Exchange Of Officials And Non-Officials," Foreign Relations, 1942, Vol. 1, 319.

24. Sibold.

25. Ingalls.

26. Eppinga, 46.

27. Letter to Fitch from Bailey, May 30, 1942. National Archives Identifier: 2530351. Department of State: Bureau of Security and Consular Affairs, Office of Protective Services, 1952–1953. Record Group 59: General Records of the Department of State, 1763–2002. National Archives at College Park, Container ID: 112.

28. David Charay and William Wallace (as told to Warren Hall), "Interned Jap, German Envoys Hoard Supplies," Times-Herald, May 4, 1942. Special Collections, Arthur Morris Law Library, University of Virginia Law School, Box 9, Folder 11, MSS 93–4.

29. Memorandum for Mr. Ladd, "Von Stemple's Birthday Party," March 9, 1942, Item 10—The Greenbrier Hotel Mission. Special Collections, Arthur J. Morris Law Library, University of Virginia Law School: Inventory of the Papers of Roy L. Morgan, 1941–1966. http://lib.law.virginia.edu/specialcollections/ Contributors D.M. Ladd; J.E. Lawler Date 1942–03–09 Type Text Format TIFF Source Box 10, Folder 5, MSS 93–4 Language EN Collection Description Title Page 1 Identifier mss93_4_b10_f5_i10_0001.

30. Memorandum for Mr. Ladd, "Sievernich Domestic Difficulties," March 17, 1942. Greenbrier Hotel Mission. Special Collections, Arthur J. Morris Law Library, University of Virginia Law School: Inventory of the Papers of Roy L. Morgan, 1941–1966. http://lib.law.virginia.edu/special collections/ Contributors D.M. Ladd; J.E. Lawler Date 1942–03–17 Type Text Format TIFF Source Box 10, Folder 5, MSS 93–4 Language EN Collection Description Title Page 1 Identifier ss93_4_b10_f5_i18_0001.

Chapter Four

1. Memorandum of Conversation, by the Assistant Secretary of State (Long). Foreign Relations, 1942, Vol. 1, 302.

2. Memorandum for Mr Ladd, March 23, 1942, "Item 15—Activities at the Greenbrier Hotel," Special Collections, Arthur J. Morris Law Library, University of Virginia Law School: Inventory of the Papers of Roy L. Morgan, 1941–1966. http://lib.law.virginia.edu/specialcollections/ Contributors D.M. Ladd; A.N. Carlblom Date 1942–01–08 Type Text Format TIFF Source Box 10, Folder 4, MSS 93–4 Language EN Collection Description Title Page 1 Identifier m.

3. Ingalls, 9.

4. Fay Ingalls, The Valley Road (Cleveland and New York: World Publishing), 276.

5. Letter, Bannerman to Fitch, "Hotel Accommodations for the Japanese," Febru-

Chapter Notes—Four

ary 10, 1942. Department of State: Bureau of Security and Consular Affairs, Office of Protective Services, 1952–1953. Record Group 59: General Records of the Department of State, 1763–2002. National Archives at College Park, Container ID: 108.

6. *Ibid.*

7. Letter to Fitch from Bannerman, February 10, 1942, "Hotel Accommodations for the Japanese," Department of State: Bureau of Security and Consular Affairs, Office of Protective Services, 1952–1953. Record Group 59: General Records of the Department of State, 1763–2002. National Archives at College Park, Container ID: 108.

8. Letter to Fitch from Bannerman, "Hotel Accommodations for Japanese," February 13, 1942. Department of State: Bureau of Security and Consular Affairs, Office of Protective Services, 1952–1953. Record Group 59: General Records of the Department of State, 1763–2002. National Archives at College Park, Container ID: 166.

9. *Ibid.*

10. Memorandum, "Movement of Japanese from Homestead Hotel, Hot Springs, Virginia to Bon Air Hotel, Augusta, Georgia, tentatively fixed for March 12," Department of State: Bureau of Security and Consular Affairs, Office of Protective Services, 1952–1953. Record Group 59: General Records of the Department of State, 1763–2002. National Archives at College Park, Container ID: 108.

11. Letter to Fitch from Bannerman, March 11, 1942, "Possibility of moving the Japanese at Hot Springs to some other location," Department of State: Bureau of Security and Consular Affairs, Office of Protective Services, 1952–1953. Record Group 59: General Records of the Department of State, 1763–2002. National Archives at College Park, Container ID: 108.

12. "Virginia Hotel Is Left Holding the Bag," Newspaper clipping from Bath County Historical Society, File, Warm Springs, VA.

13. "The Japs Aren't Coming," Newspaper clipping from Bath County Historical Society, File, Warm Springs, VA.

14. Letter to Fitch from Bannerman, "Hotel Accommodations near the Greenbrier Hotel at White Sulphur Springs, to care for the expected overflow of Axis Ex-Diplomats," Department of State: Bureau of Security and Consular Affairs, Office of Protective Services, 1952–1953. Record Group 59: General Records of the Department of State, 1763–2002. National Archives at College Park, Container ID: 109.

15. Letter to Fitch from Bannerman, "Possibility of using Mount Weather, Virginia as a place to house the Japanese now at Hot Springs, Virginia," March 11, 1942. Department of State: Bureau of Security and Consular Affairs, Office of Protective Services, 1952–1953. Record Group 59: General Records of the Department of State, 1763–2002. National Archives at College Park, Container ID: 166.

16. Letter to Fitch from Bannerman, "Hotel Accommodations near the Greenbrier Hotel at White Sulphur Springs, to care for the expected overflow of Axis Ex-Diplomats," Department of State: Bureau of Security and Consular Affairs, Office of Protective Services, 1952–1953. Record Group 59: General Records of the Department of State, 1763–2002. National Archives at College Park, Container ID: 109.

17. Letter to Fitch, March 22, 1942, "Hotel Accommodations," National Archives Identifier: 2530319. Department of State: Bureau of Security and Consular Affairs, Office of Protective Services, 1952–1953. Record Group 59: General Records of the Department of State, 1763–2002. National Archives at College Park, Container ID: 109.

18. *Ibid.*

19. *ibid.*

20. Memo, "Hotel Accommodations," March 20, 1942. National Archives Identifier: 2530319 Department of State: Bureau of Security and Consular Affairs, Office of Protective Services, 1952–1953. Record Group 59: General Records of the Department of State, 1763–2002. National Archives at College Park, Container ID: 109.

21. Letter to Fitch from Bannerman, "Grove Park Inn, Asheville, North Carolina," March 20, 1942. Department of State: Bureau of Security and Consular Affairs, Office of Protective Services, 1952–1953. Record Group 59: General Records of the Department of State, 1763–2002. National Archives at College Park, Container ID: 179.

Chapter Notes—Four

22. "Resort is Leased by Government, Italians Rumanians, Bulgarians Will Come Here Soon," *Asheville Citizen*, March 30, 1942.
23. *Ibid.*
24. "City Buses Are Used to Carry 242 in Group From Special Trains," *Asheville Times*, April 3, 1942.
25. *Ibid.*
26. *Ibid.*
27. Newspaper Clipping, "Interned Enemy Envoys Plot and Fight in Grand Hotel," Greenbrier Hotel Mission. Special Collections, Arthur J. Morris Law Library, University of Virginia Law School: Inventory of the Papers of Roy L. Morgan, 1941–1966. http://lib.law.virginia.edu/special collections/ Contributors D.M. Ladd; Roy L. Morgan Date 1941–12–28 Type Text Format TIFF Source Box 10, Folder 2, MSS 93–4 Language EN Collection Title Page 1 Identifier mss93_4_b10_f2_i2_0001.
28. Letter, Sumner Welles to Senator Kilgore, April 3, 1942, "Transfer of Japanese from Homestead to Greenbrier," Greenbrier Hotel Mission. Special Collections, Arthur J. Morris Law Library, University of Virginia Law School: Inventory of the Papers of Roy L. Morgan, 1941–1966. http://lib.law.virginia.edu/special collections/ Harley M. Kilgore; Sumner Welles 1942-04-03 Box 10, Folder 5, MSS 93–4 mss93_4_b10_f5_i58_0001.
29. *The News Palladium*, Benton Harbor, Michigan, April 8, 1942, 1.
30. "Future Operation of Greenbrier Will Be In Interest of National Defense," *White Sulphur Springs Sentinel*, March 6, 1942.
31. Ingalls.
32. Memorandum for the Director, April 14, 1942, "Japanese Diplomatic Corps Internal Security," Greenbrier Hotel Mission. Special Collections, Arthur J. Morris Law Library, University of Virginia Law School: Inventory of the Papers of Roy L. Morgan, 1941–1966. http://lib.law.virginia.edu/specialcollections/ Contributors D.M. Ladd; Roy L. Morgan Date 1942–04–14 Type Text Format TIFF Source Box 9, Folder 7, MSS 93–4 Language EN Collection Description Title Page 1 Identifier mss93–4_b9_f7_i6_0001.
33. David Charay, William Wallace, "Nazi 'Guests' Taunt Hon. Japs At Greenbrier on Tokyo Raid," the *Times Herald*, May 4, 1942, Special Collections, Arthur J. Morris Law Library, University of Virginia Law School, box 9, folder 11 MSS 93–4.
34. Sibold.
35. Memorandum for the Director, April 6, 1942, "German Diplomatic Corps Internal Security," Greenbrier Hotel Mission. Special Collections, Arthur J. Morris Law Library, University of Virginia Law School: Inventory of the Papers of Roy L. Morgan, 1941–1966. http://lib.law.virginia.edu/ specialcollections/ Contributors D.M. Ladd; Roy L. Morgan Date 1942–04–06 Type Text Format TIFF Source Box 9, Folder 4, MSS 93–4 Language EN Collection Description Title Page 1 Identifier mss93–4_b9_f4_i20_0001.
36. Memorandum for Mr. Ladd, January 28, 1942, "Japanese Diplomatic Corps Internal Security," Greenbrier Hotel Mission. Special Collections, Arthur J. Morris Law Library, University of Virginia Law School: Inventory of the Papers of Roy L. Morgan, 1941–1966. http://lib.law.virginia.edu/ specialcollections/ Contributors D.M. Ladd; Roy L. Morgan Date 1942–04–14 Type Text Format TIFF Source Box 9, Folder 7, MSS 93–4 Language EN Collection Description Title Page 1 Identifier mss93–4_b9_f7_i6_0001.
37. Letter to Poole from Sievernich, May 4, 1942, Germans, Japs-Greenbrier Hotel, W.S.S., W.Va.-Poole [2 Folders] National Archives Identifier: 2530343. Department of State: Bureau of Security and Consular Affairs, Office of Protective Services, 1952–1953. Record Group 59: General Records of the Department of State, 1763–2002. National Archives at College Park, Container ID: 111.
38. Letter, Hoshide to Poole, January 20, 1942, Homestead- Japs Record Group 59: General Records of the Department of State, 1763–2002. Department of State: Bureau of Security and Consular Affairs, Office of Protective Services, 1952–1953. Record Group 59: General Records of the Department of State, 1763–2002. National Archives at College Park, Container ID: 107.
39. Daily Report, January 13, 1942, Memorandum for Assistant Director D.M. Ladd from Carlblom. Greenbrier Hotel Mission. Special Collections, Arthur J. Morris Law Library, University of Virginia Law School: Inventory of the Papers of Roy L. Morgan, 1941–1966. http://lib.law.virginia.edu/

Chapter Notes—Five

specialcollections/ Contributors D.M. Ladd; A.N. Carlblom Date 1942-01-13 Type Text Format TIFF Source Box 10, Folder 4, MSS 93-4 Language EN Collection Description Title Page 3 Identifier mss93_4_b10_f4_i18_0003.

Chapter Five

1. Telegram 701.6211/1482a, "The Secretary of State to the Charge in Switzerland (Huddle)," Washington, December 19, 1941, *Foreign Relations*, 1942, Vol. 1, 292.
2. Memo, "Diplomatic Exchange Europe," Department of State: Bureau of Security and Consular Affairs, Office of Protective Services, 1952-1953. Record Group 59: General Records of the Department of State, 1763-2002. ARC Identifier: 2530968. National Archives at College Park, Container ID: 170.
3. Telegram 125.0040/86, "The Secretary of State to the Charge in Switzerland (Huddle)," Washington, December 30, 1941, *Foreign Relations*, 1942, Vol. 1, 296.
4. Telegram 701.0211/1486a, "The Secretary of State to the Charge in Switzerland (Huddle)," Washington, *Foreign Relations*, 1942, Vol. 1 (December 30, 1941): 297.
5. Telegram 701.6511/1205 "The Charge in Switzerland (Huddle) to the Secretary of State," January 2, 1942, *Foreign Relations*, 1942, Vol. 1, 299.
6. Telegram 701.0211/1497, "The Charge in Switzerland (Huddle) to the Secretary of State," Bern, January 15, 1942, *Foreign Relations*, 1942, Vol. 1, 304.
7. Letter to Long from Green, January 24, 1942, Exchange—Official Personnel [2 Folders] National Archives Identifier: 2529590. Department of State: Bureau of Security and Consular Affairs, Office of Protective Services, 1952-1953. Record Group 59: General Records of the Department of State, 1763-2002. National Archives at College Park, Container ID: 72.
8. Letter to Saugstad from Long, February 18, 1942, Exchange—Official Personnel [2 Folders] National Archives Identifier: 2529590. Department of State: Bureau of Security and Consular Affairs, Office of Protective Services, 1952-1953. Record Group 59: General Records of the Department of State, 1763-2002. National Archives at College Park, Container ID: 72.
9. Telegram 701.0211/1642, "The Minister in Switzerland (Harrison) to the Secretary of State," *Foreign Relations*, 1942, Vol. 1 (March 31, 1942): 349.
10. Aide-Memoire 701.0010/211, "The British Embassy to the Department of State," *Foreign Relations*, 1942, Vol. 1 (February 2, 1942): 308.
11. *Ibid.*, 309.
12. Aide-Memoire 701.0011/385, "The British Embassy to the Department of State," *Foreign Relations*, 1942, Vol. 1, 332.
13. Intelligence Report, Issued by the Intelligence Division Office of Chief of Naval Operations Navy Department, December 20, 1942, Japanese from Peru—Background. National Archives Identifier: 2531333. Department of State: Bureau of Security and Consular Affairs, Office of Protective Services, 1952-1953. Record Group 59: General Records of the Department of State, 1763-2002. National Archives at College Park, Container ID: 194.
14. Memorandum 390.115A/1406, "The Spanish Embassy to the Department of State," *Foreign Relations*, 1942, Vol. 1, 448.
15. Telegram 701.0023/30, "The Acting Secretary of State to the Ambassador in Peru (Norweb)," *Foreign Relations*, 1942, Vol. 1, 323.
16. Telegram 701.0024/26, "The Acting Secretary of State to the Ambassador in Spain (Weddell)," *Foreign Relations*, 1942, Vol. 1, 330.
17. Telegram 701.0010/44, "The Acting Secretary of State to the Charge in Switzerland (Huddle)," *Foreign Relations*, 1942, Vol. 1, 334.
18. Telegram 701.0010/64a, "The Acting Secretary of State to the Charge in Switzerland (Huddle)," *Foreign Relations*, 1942, Vol. 1, 334."
19. *Ibid.*
20. Telegram 701.6224/76, "The Acting Secretary of State to the Ambassador in Spain (Waddell)," *Foreign Relations*, 1942, Vol. 1, 336.
21. Telegram 701.0010/105, "The Minister in Switzerland (Harrison) to the Secretary of State," *Foreign Relations*, 1942, Vol. 1, 361.
22. Telegram 701.0010/105, "The Secretary of State to the Minister in Switzerland (Harrison)," *Foreign Relations*, 1942, Vol. 1, 363.
23. Telegram 701.9411/1547a, "The Sec-

Chapter Notes—Six

retary of State to the Charge in Switzerland (Huddle)," *Foreign Relations*, 1942, Vol. 1, 378.

24. Telegram 701.9411/1630, "The Secretary of State to the Charge in Switzerland (Huddle)," *Foreign Relations*, 1942, Vol. 1, 397.

25. *Ibid.*, 394.

26. Telegram from Green, May 19, 1942, United (sic) States–Japanese Exchange Files. National Archives Identifier: 17343398. Department of State: Bureau of Security and Consular Affairs, Office of Protective Services, 1952–1953. Record Group 59: General Records of the Department of State, 1763–2002. National Archives at College Park, Container ID: 201.

Chapter Six

1. Telegram to Secretary of State, January 15, 1942. National Archives Identifier: 2529590. Department of State: Bureau of Security and Consular Affairs, Office of Protective Services, 1952–1953. Record Group 59: General Records of the Department of State, 1763–2002. Container ID: 72.

2. Memorandum 701.0010/211, "Memorandum of Conversation by the Under Secretary of State (Welles)," February 13, 1942, *Foreign Relations*, 1942, Vol. 1, 311.

3. Memorandum of Conversation by the Undersecretary of State (Welles), Rumbold, Clattenburg, Safe Conduct for Political Agents, January 16, 1942, United States–European Axis Exchange Files. National Archives Identifier: 17343391. Department of State: Bureau of Security and Consular Affairs, Office of Protective Services, 1952–1953. Record Group 59: General Records of the Department of State, 1763–2002. National Archives at College Park, Container ID: 200.

4. Letter to Long from Green, March 30, 1942, Unites (sic) States–Japanese Exchange Files. National Archives Identifier: 17343398. Department of State: Bureau of Security and Consular Affairs, Office of Protective Services, 1952–1953. Record Group 59: General Records of the Department of State, 1763–2002. National Archives at College Park, Container ID: 201.

5. Letter to Long from Green, March 31, 1942, Unites (sic) States–Japanese Exchange Files. National Archives Identifier: 17343398. Department of State: Bureau of Security and Consular Affairs, Office of Protective Services, 1952–1953. Record Group 59: General Records of the Department of State, 1763–2002. National Archives at College Park, Container ID: 201.

6. Letter to Halifax from Green, March 31, 1942. Unites (sic) States–Japanese Exchange Files, National Archives Identifier: 17343398. Department of State: Bureau of Security and Consular Affairs, Office of Protective Services, 1952–1953. Record Group 59: General Records of the Department of State, 1763–2002., ARC Identifier: 17343398, National Archives at College Park, Container ID: 201.

7. *Ibid.*

8. Memorandum of Conversation by the Undersecretary of State (Welles), Rumbold, Clattenburg, Safe Conduct for Political Agents, January 16, 1942, United States–European Axis Exchange Files. National Archives Identifier: 17343391.

9. *Ibid.*

10. *Ibid.*

11. Aide Memoire from British Embassy, February 2, 1942. United States–European Axis Exchange Files. National Archives Identifier: 17343391. Department of State: Bureau of Security and Consular Affairs, Office of Protective Services, 1952–1953. Record Group 59: General Records of the Department of State, 1763–2002. National Archives at College Park, Container ID: 200.

12. Memorandum, Groth to Green, May 15, 1942. National Archives Identifier: 2529590. Department of State: Bureau of Security and Consular Affairs, Office of Protective Services, 1952–1953. Record Group 59: General Records of the Department of State, 1763–2002. National Archives at College Park, Container ID: 72.

13. Memorandum, "Safe conduct for vessel to be used by United States Government in exchanging official and non-official person of Axis Nationality for American officials and others in Europe," February 16, 1942, United States-European Axis Exchange Files. National Archives Identifier: 17343391. Department of State: Bureau of Security and Consular Affairs, Office of Protective Services, 1952–1953. Record Group 59: General Records of the Department of State, 1763–2002. National

Chapter Notes—Six

Archives at College Park, Container ID: 200.

14. *Ibid.*

15. Memo to Warren and Long from Green, March 16, 1942, United States-European Axis Exchange Files. National Archives Identifier: 17343391. Department of State: Bureau of Security and Consular Affairs, Office of Protective Services, 1952–1953. Record Group 59: General Records of the Department of State, 1763–2002. National Archives at College Park, Container ID: 200.

16. Memorandum, February 25, 1942, Unites States–European Axis Exchange Files. National Archives Identifier: 17343391. Department of State: Bureau of Security and Consular Affairs, Office of Protective Services, 1952–1953. Record Group 59: General Records of the Department of State, 1763–2002. National Archives at College Park, Container ID: 200.

17. Confidential Intercept, "Treatment of German Travelling in Diplomatic Exchange Passport By Allied Government," November 7, 1942. National Archives Identifier: 2530968. Department of State: Bureau of Security and Consular Affairs, Office of Protective Services, 1952–1953. Record Group 59: General Records of the Department of State, 1763–2002. National Archives at College Park, Container ID: 170.

18. *Ibid.*

19. Memorandum of Conversation, February 16, 1942. National Archives Identifier: 2530598. Department of State: Bureau of Security and Consular Affairs, Office of Protective Services, 1952–1953. Record Group 59: General Records of the Department of State, 1763–2002. National Archives at College Park, Container ID: 129.

20. Appendix, "Personal Justice Denied," Report of the Commission on Wartime Relocation and Internment of Civilians, Washington, D.C., June 1983, 305.

21. Memorandum for Assistant Director D.M. Ladd, January 30, 1942, Greenbrier Hotel Mission. Special Collections, Arthur J. Morris Law Library, University of Virginia Law School: Inventory of the Papers of Roy L. Morgan, 1941–1966 http://lib.law.virginia.edu/specialcollections/ Box 10, Folder 3, MSS 93-4 mss93_4_b10_f3_i5_0001.

22. Thomas Connell, *America's Japanese Hostages: The World War II Plan For A Japanese Free Latin America* (Westport, CT: Praeger, 2002), 41.

23. Letter to Secretary of State from Long, April 9, 1942, SS Etolin. National Archives Identifier: 2529581. Department of State: Bureau of Security and Consular Affairs, Office of Protective Services, 1952–1953. Record Group 59: General Records of the Department of State, 1763–2002. National Archives at College Park, Container ID: 71.

24. Case File, Dirk, Albers, No. 22, Uruguay. National Archives Identifier: 2529561. Department of State: Bureau of Security and Consular Affairs, Office of Protective Services, 1952–1953. Record Group 59: General Records of the Department of State, 1763–2002. National Archives at College Park, Container ID: 69.

25. Case File, Arturo Albrecht, *Ibid.*

26. Memorandum regarding activities of the United States Government in removing from the other American Republics dangerous subversive aliens, November 3, 1942, National Archives Identifier: 2531068. Department of State: Bureau of Security and Consular Affairs, Office of Protective Services, 1952–1953. Record Group 59: General Records of the Department of State, 1763–2002. National Archives at College Park, Container ID: 180.

27. Memorandum, Long from Green, April 13, 1942, National Archives Identifier: 2529590. Department of State: Bureau of Security and Consular Affairs, Office of Protective Services, 1952–1953. Record Group 59: General Records of the Department of State, 1763–2002. National Archives at College Park, Container ID: 72.

28. *Ibid.*

29. Memorandum, Bannerman to Fitch, "Accommodations for the 500 Axis officials and non-officials arriving at New Orleans on the Transport ACADIA," April 16, 1942, National Archives Identifier: 2530937. Department of State: Bureau of Security and Consular Affairs, Office of Protective Services, 1952–1953. Record Group 59: General Records of the Department of State, 1763–2002. National Archives at College Park, Container ID: 166.

30. *Ibid.*, 2.

31. Letter to Woodward from Davis,

April 17, 1942. National Archives Identifier: 2530306. Department of State: Bureau of Security and Consular Affairs, Office of Protective Services, 1952–1953. Record Group 59: General Records of the Department of State, 1763–2002. National Archives at College Park, Container ID: 107.

32. *Ibid.*

33. Letter to Mr. Clattenburg, January 9, 1943, National Archives Identifier: 2530968. Department of State: Bureau of Security and Consular Affairs, Office of Protective Services, 1952–1953. Record Group 59: General Records of the Department of State, 1763–2002. National Archives at College Park, Container ID: 170.

34. "500 Axis Diplomats Stop-Over in U.S.," *Daily Illini*, April 28, 1942.

35. Robert Ernest Miller, *World War II Cincinnati: From the Front Line to the Home Front* (Charleston: History Press, 2014), 82.

36. Memorandum to Fitch from Bannerman, "Questions Raised by German group at Gibson Hotel, Cincinnati," as transmitted by Mr. Patton, April 28, 1942. National Archives Identifier: 2530306. Department of State: Bureau of Security and Consular Affairs, Office of Protective Services, 1952–1953. Record Group 59: General Records of the Department of State, 1763–2002. National Archives at College Park, Container ID: 107.

37. *Ibid.*

38. Letter to Mr. Clattenburg, January 9, 1943, National Archives Identifier: 2530968. Department of State: Bureau of Security and Consular Affairs, Office of Protective Services, 1952–1953. Record Group 59: General Records of the Department of State, 1763–2002.

Chapter Seven

1. "Axis Group Leaves Here to Return to Homelands," *Asheville Citizen*, May 7, 1942.

2. Memorandum for the Director, Attn: Mr. Ladd, May 8, 1942, Greenbrier Hotel Mission. Special Collections, Arthur J. Morris Law Library, University of Virginia Law School: Inventory of the Papers of Roy L. Morgan, 1941–1966. http://lib.law.virginia.edu/specialcollections/ Contributors D.M. Ladd; Roy L. Morgan Date 1942-05-08 Type Text Format TIFF Source Box 10, Folder 3, MSS 93–4 Language EN Collection Description Title Page 1 Identifier mss93_4_b10_f3_i61_0001.

3. "Germans Leave White Sulphur," *The Raleigh Register*, May 8, 1942.

4. Letter to Bill from Ed, May 14, 1942, Grove Park Inn, Asheville, NC National Archives Identifier: 2531043. Department of State: Bureau of Security and Consular Affairs, Office of Protective Services, 1952–1953. Record Group 59: General Records of the Department of State, 1763–2002. National Archives at College Park, Container ID: 179.

5. Memorandum for the Director, Attn: Mr. Ladd, May 15, 1942, Greenbrier Hotel Mission. Special Collections, Arthur J. Morris Law Library, University of Virginia Law School: Inventory of the Papers of Roy L. Morgan, 1941–1966. http://lib.law.virginia.edu/specialcollections/ Contributors D.M. Ladd; Roy L. Morgan Date 1942-05-15 Type Text Format TIFF Source Box 9, Folder 7, MSS 93–4 Language EN Collection Description Title Page 1 Identifier mss93–4_b9_f7_i22_0001.

6. "218 Japanese and Germans Interned at Grove Park Inn," *Asheville Citizen*, May 16, 1942.

7. "Aliens Depart; Grove Park Inn Open to Public," *Asheville Times*, June 12, 1942.

8. "Norwegian Girl Longs to Return Home," *Asheville Citizen*, June 12, 1942.

9. *Ibid.*

10. Memo to Mr. Clattenburg from Mr. Fitch, June 5, 1943. National Archives Identifier: 2531197. Department of State: Bureau of Security and Consular Affairs, Office of Protective Services, 1952–1953. Record Group 59: General Records of the Department of State, 1763–2002. National Archives at College Park, Container ID: 184.

11. "Japs Leave Here to Be Exchanged," *White Sulphur Springs Sentinel*, June 3, 1942, 1.

12. Memo for Mr. Ladd, RE Greenbrier Hotel Mission, March 6, 1942, Special Collection, Arthur J. Morris Law School, University of Virginia Law School, Box 10, folder 5, Mss 93–4.

Chapter Notes—Eight

13. "Last of Axis Internees Leave Here," *White Sulphur Springs Sentinel*, July 16, 1942, 1.
14. *Ibid.*
15. "Many of Group Had Resided in South America," *Asheville Times*, July 9, 1942, 1.
16. "Japs Badly Mistreat American Diplomats," *Statesville Record and Landmark*, August 27, 1942, 1.
17. "Look at This and This," *The Robesian*, August 4, 1942, 4.
18. "U.S. Ready for Second Exchange," *The Daily Mail*, August 21, 1943, 1.
19. Arthur E. Barbeau, "The Japanese at Bedford," *Western Pennsylvania Historical Magazine*, Vol. 64, Number 2 (April 1981): 155.
20. Letter, Bannerman to Fitch, April 15, 1943. National Archives Identifier: 2530968. Department of State: Bureau of Security and Consular Affairs, Office of Protective Services, 1952–1953. Record Group 59: General Records of the Department of State, 1763–2002. National Archives at College Park, Container ID: 170.

Chapter Eight

1. Ella Tomita, Japanese Internee, October 14, 2004, Interviewed by Kalei Ho and Mika Bailey, Japanese Cultural Center of Hawai'i. Japanese American Internment Unite for Modern History of Hawai'i (2008), Presented by the Japanese Cultural Center of Hawai'i October 14, 2004 http://hawaiiinternment.org/sites/default/files/Modern%20History%20of%20Hawaii_0.pdf.
2. Letter to Fitch form Bannerman, August 27, 1942. National Archives Identifier: 2530334. Department of State: Bureau of Security and Consular Affairs, Office of Protective Services, 1952–1953. Record Group 59: General Records of the Department of State, 1763–2002. National Archives at College Park, Container ID: 110.
3. Ella Tomita, *ibid.*
4. Newspaper clipping, "130 Japanese Brought Here from Hawaii," Grove Park Inn file, North Carolina Reading Room, Pack Memorial Library, Asheville, NC.
5. Letter to Keeley from Fitch, September 9, 1942. National Archives Identifier: 2530288. Department of State: Bureau of Security and Consular Affairs, Office of Protective Services, 1952–1953. Record Group 59: General Records of the Department of State, 1763–2002. National Archives at College Park, Container ID: 104.
6. List of Japanese Nationals From Hawaii Now Detained at Asheville Assembly Inn—Montreat, NC, National Archives Identifier: 2530937. Department of State: Bureau of Security and Consular Affairs, Office of Protective Services, 1952–1953. Record Group 59: General Records of the Department of State, 1763–2002. National Archives at College Park, Container ID: 166.
7. Memorandum to Green from Fitch, August 21, 1942. National Archives Identifier: 2530329. Department of State: Bureau of Security and Consular Affairs, Office of Protective Services, 1952–1953. Record Group 59: General Records of the Department of State, 1763–2002. National Archives at College Park, Container ID: 110.
8. Letter to Fitch from Briggs, October 13, 1942. National Archives Identifier: 2530937. Department of State: Bureau of Security and Consular Affairs, Office of Protective Services, 1952–1953. Record Group 59: General Records of the Department of State, 1763–2002. National Archives at College Park, Container ID: 166.
9. Letter to Keeley from Fitch, October 16, 1942. National Archives Identifier: 2530855. Department of State: Bureau of Security and Consular Affairs, Office of Protective Services, 1952–1953. Record Group 59: General Records of the Department of State, 1763–2002. National Archives at College Park, Container ID: 153.
10. Note to ALB, November 3, 1942. National Archives Identifier: 2530937. Department of State: Bureau of Security and Consular Affairs, Office of Protective Services, 1952–1953. Record Group 59: General Records of the Department of State, 1763–2002. National Archives at College Park, Container ID: 166.
11. Letter to Fitch from Briggs, November 3, 1942. National Archives Identifier: 2530855. Department of State: Bureau of Security and Consular Affairs, Office of

Chapter Notes—Eight

Protective Services, 1952–1953. Record Group 59: General Records of the Department of State, 1763–2002. National Archives at College Park, Container ID: 153.

12. Letter to Franklin from Fitch, December 22, 1942. National Archives Identifier: 2530855. Department of State: Bureau of Security and Consular Affairs, Office of Protective Services, 1952–1953. Record Group 59: General Records of the Department of State, 1763–2002. National Archives at College Park, Container ID: 153.

13. Letter to Chief from Miles, December 14, 1942. National Archives Identifier: 2530855. Department of State: Bureau of Security and Consular Affairs, Office of Protective Services, 1952–1953. Record Group 59: General Records of the Department of State, 1763–2002. National Archives at College Park, Container ID: 153.

14. Letter to Fitch from Bannerman, December 3, 1942. National Archives Identifier: 2530939. Department of State: Bureau of Security and Consular Affairs, Office of Protective Services, 1952–1953. Record Group 59: General Records of the Department of State, 1763–2002. National Archives at College Park, Container ID: 166.

15. "This Day in Presbyterian History," website accessed June 30, 2015. http://www/thisday.pcahistory.org/2012/04/aril-30-presbyterian-missionairies-freed/.

16. Letter to Keeley from Lyon, National Archives Identifier: 2530855. Department of State: Bureau of Security and Consular Affairs, Office of Protective Services, 1952–1953. Record Group 59: General Records of the Department of State, 1763–2002. National Archives at College Park, Container ID: 153.

17. *Ibid.*

18. Ella Tomita, Japanese Internee, *ibid.*

19. German American Internee Coalition, "The Mantel Family Story," posted October 2012, GAIC.com, accessed July 10, 2015.

20. Memorandum to Fitch, "Transfer of Montreat Detainees to the Immigration Service, March 22, 1943." National Archives Identifier: 2530968. Department of State: Bureau of Security and Consular Affairs, Office of Protective Services, 1952–1953. Record Group 59: General Records of the Department of State, 1763–2002. National Archives at College Park, Container ID: 170.

21. Letter to Fitch from Bailey, June 8, 1942. National Archives Identifier: 2530351. Department of State: Bureau of Security and Consular Affairs, Office of Protective Services, 1952–1953. Record Group 59: General Records of the Department of State, 1763–2002. National Archives at College Park, Container ID: 112.

22. Letter to Fitch from Bailey, June 8, 1942. National Archives Identifier: 2530351. Department of State: Bureau of Security and Consular Affairs, Office of Protective Services, 1952–1953. Record Group 59: General Records of the Department of State, 1763–2002. National Archives at College Park, Container ID: 112.

23. "Local Resort's Service to U.S. During War," *White Sulphur Springs Sentinel*, April 17, 1942.

24. Ingalls, 12.

25. *Life Magazine*, February 16, 1942, 68–69.

26. Letter to Fitch from Bannerman, June 7, 1943. National Archives Identifier: 2530925. Department of State: Bureau of Security and Consular Affairs, Office of Protective Services, 1952–1953. Record Group 59: General Records of the Department of State, 1763–2002. National Archives at College Park, Container ID: 163.

27. Letter to Fitch from LCF, May 18, 1943. National Archives Identifier: 2530925. Department of State: Bureau of Security and Consular Affairs, Office of Protective Services, 1952–1953. Record Group 59: General Records of the Department of State, 1763–2002. National Archives at College Park, Container ID: 163.

28. Letter to Fitch from Bannerman, "General Report on the Diplomatic Exchange, July 30." National Archives Identifier: 2531137. Department of State: Bureau of Security and Consular Affairs, Office of Protective Services, 1952–1953. Record Group 59: General Records of the Department of State, 1763–2002. National Archives at College Park, Container ID: 182.

29. *Ibid.*

Chapter Notes—Nine

30. Ibid.
31. Letter to Fitch from Bannerman, "Conference on the Diplomatic Exchange," September 2, 1942. Letter to Fitch From Bannerman, "General Report on the Diplomatic Exchange, July 30. National Archives Identifier: 2531137. Department of State: Bureau of Security and Consular Affairs, Office of Protective Services, 1952–1953. Record Group 59: General Records of the Department of State, 1763–2002. National Archives at College Park, Container ID: 182.
32. Letter to Fitch from Bannerman, October 30, 1944. National Archives Identifier: 2530281. Department of State: Bureau of Security and Consular Affairs, Office of Protective Services, 1952–1953. Record Group 59: General Records of the Department of State, 1763–2002. National Archives at College Park, Container ID: 104.

Chapter Nine

1. Hershey Archives, World War II: The Vichy Internment at the Hotel Hershey. http://www.hersheyarchives.org/essay/details.aspx?EssayId=22&Rurl=%2fresources%2fsearch-results.aspx%3fType%3dSearch%26Text%3dvichy%26StartMonth%3d%26EndMonth%3d%26StartDay%3d%26EndDay%3d%26StartYear%3d%26EndYear%3d.
2. Letter to Fitch from Bannerman, November 12, 1942. National Archives Identifier: 2531017. Department of State: Bureau of Security and Consular Affairs, Office of Protective Services, 1952–1953. Record Group 59: General Records of the Department of State, 1763–2002. National Archives at College Park, Container ID: 174.
3. Memorandum 125.0051/272a, "Memorandum by the Assistant Secretary of State (Long) for President Roosevelt," *Foreign Relations*, 1942, Vol. 1 (December 16, 1942): 378.
4. Ibid.
5. Letter, Bannerman to Fitch, November 13, 1942. National Archives Identifier: 2531017. Department of State: Bureau of Security and Consular Affairs, Office of Protective Services, 1952–1953. Record Group 59: General Records of the Department of State, 1763–2002. National Archives at College Park, Container ID: 174.
6. Hershey Archives, World War II: The Vichy Internment at the Hotel Hershey, accessed June 10, 2015. http://www.hersheyarchives.org/essay/details.aspx?EssayId=22&Rurl=%2fresources%2fsearch-results.aspx%3fType%3dSearch%26Text%3dvichy%26StartMonth%3d%26EndMonth%3d%26StartDay%3d%26EndDay%3d%26StartYear%3d%26EndYear%3d.
7. "Vichy Group to Leave Hershey," *The Indiana Gazette*, September 25, 1943, 3.
8. Memorandum from Fitch to Patton, "Transfer of the Vichy French Officials from Washington, D.C., to Hershey, Pennsylvania," November 18, 1942. National Archives Identifier: 2530270. Department of State: Bureau of Security and Consular Affairs, Office of Protective Services, 1952–1953. Record Group 59: General Records of the Department of State, 1763–2002. National Archives at College Park, Container ID: 103.
9. Memorandum, "Arrangements at Hotel Hershey for the French Officials," November 16, 1942. National Archives Identifier: 2531017. Department of State: Bureau of Security and Consular Affairs, Office of Protective Services, 1952–1953. Record Group 59: General Records of the Department of State, 1763–2002. National Archives at College Park, Container ID: 174.
10. Hershey Archives, World War II: The Vichy Internment at the Hotel Hershey. http://www.hersheyarchives.org/essay/details.aspx?EssayId=22&Rurl=%2fresources%2fsearch-results.aspx%3fType%3dSearch%26Text%3dvichy%26StartMonth%3d%26EndMonth%3d%26StartDay%3d%26EndDay%3d%26StartYear%3d%26EndYear%3d.
11. Erika Dreifus, "A Golden Prison in Pennsylvania: The Hotel Hershey, 1942–1943," *Pennsylvania History*, Vol. 69, No. 3 (Summer 2002). https://journals.psu.edu/phj/issue/view/1620.
12. Hershey Archives, World War II: The Vichy Internment at the Hotel Hershey. http://www.hersheyarchives.org/essay/details.aspx?EssayId=22&Rurl=%2fresources%2fsearch-results.aspx%3fType%3dSearch%26Text%3dvichy%26StartMonth%3d%26EndMonth%3d%26Start

Chapter Notes—Nine

Day%3d%26EndDay%3d%26StartYear%3d%26EndYear%3d.

13. Letter to Fitch from Steward, "Conditions at the Hershey Hotel," June 4, 1943. National Archives Identifier: 2530346. Department of State: Bureau of Security and Consular Affairs, Office of Protective Services, 1952–1953. Record Group 59: General Records of the Department of State, 1763–2002. National Archives at College Park, Container ID: 112.

14. Memorandum to Fitch from Bannerman, June 11, 1943. National Archives Identifier: 2530270. Department of State: Bureau of Security and Consular Affairs, Office of Protective Services, 1952–1953. Record Group 59: General Records of the Department of State, 1763–2002. National Archives at College Park, Container ID: 103.

15. Letter to Fitch, "Hotel Hershey," November 2, 1943. National Archives Identifier: 2530346. Department of State: Bureau of Security and Consular Affairs, Office of Protective Services, 1952–1953. Record Group 59: General Records of the Department of State, 1763–2002. National Archives at College Park, Container ID: 112.

16. Letter to Fitch from Innes, March 23, 1942, Subject: Report on Imbault-Huart Family, Hotel Hershey. National Archives Identifier: 2530859. Department of State: Bureau of Security and Consular Affairs, Office of Protective Services, 1952–1953. Record Group 59: General Records of the Department of State, 1763–2002. National Archives at College Park, Container ID: 154.

17. Letter to Fitch from Innes, March 10, 1943, Hotel Hershey. National Archives Identifier: 2530859. Department of State: Bureau of Security and Consular Affairs, Office of Protective Services, 1952–1953. Record Group 59: General Records of the Department of State, 1763–2002. National Archives at College Park, Container ID: 154.

18. Memorandum to Fitch, "Report on the Conditions at the Hershey Hotel," June 11, 1943. National Archives Identifier: 2530937. Department of State: Bureau of Security and Consular Affairs, Office of Protective Services, 1952–1953. Record Group 59: General Records of the Department of State, 1763–2002. National Archives at College Park, Container ID: 166.

19. Letter to Michelle from Deidre, Hershey Hotel. National Archives Identifier: 2530346. Department of State: Bureau of Security and Consular Affairs, Office of Protective Services, 1952–1953. Record Group 59: General Records of the Department of State, 1763–2002. National Archives at College Park, Container ID: 112.

20. Hershey Archives, World War II: The Vichy Internment at the Hotel Hershey. http://www.hersheyarchives.org/essay/details.aspx?EssayId=22&Rurl=%2fresources%2fsearch-results.aspx%3fType%3dSearch%26Text%3dvichy%26StartMonth%3d%26EndMonth%3d%26StartDay%3d%26EndDay%3d%26StartYear%3d%26EndYear%3d.

21. "French Group to Be Moved to Virginia," *Pittston Gazette*, September 25, 1943, 3.

22. Letter to Long et al. from Fitch, September 22, 1943. National Archives Identifier: 2530934. Department of State: Bureau of Security and Consular Affairs, Office of Protective Services, 1952–1953. Record Group 59: General Records of the Department of State, 1763–2002. National Archives at College Park, Container ID: 165.

23. Letter to Lyon, et al. from Fitch, September 16, 1943. National Archives Identifier: 2530926. Department of State: Bureau of Security and Consular Affairs, Office of Protective Services, 1952–1953. Record Group 59: General Records of the Department of State, 1763–2002. National Archives at College Park, Container ID: 163.

24. *Ibid.*

25. Letter to Long, Keeley, Lyon, Bonbright, from Fitch, September 22, 1942. National Archives Identifier: 2530303. Department of State: Bureau of Security and Consular Affairs, Office of Protective Services, 1952–1953. Record Group 59: General Records of the Department of State, 1763–2002. National Archives at College Park, Container ID: 107.

26. Letter to Brand, Frank and Plitt, from Fitch, October 30, 1943. National Archives Identifier: 2530303. Department of State: Bureau of Security and Consular Affairs, Office of Protective Services, 1952–

Chapter Notes—Ten

1953. Record Group 59: General Records of the Department of State, 1763–2002. National Archives at College Park, Container ID: 107.

27. Letter to Fitch, October 2, 1943. National Archives Identifier: 2530303. Department of State: Bureau of Security and Consular Affairs, Office of Protective Services, 1952–1953. Record Group 59: General Records of the Department of State, 1763–2002. National Archives at College Park, Container ID: 107.

28. Letter to Fitch from Mangels, Transfer of French diplomatic detainees from Hershey Pennsylvania to Three Hills, VA, October 4, 1942. National Archives Identifier: 2530303. Department of State: Bureau of Security and Consular Affairs, Office of Protective Services, 1952–1953. Record Group 59: General Records of the Department of State, 1763–2002. National Archives at College Park, Container ID: 107.

29. Memo from Bannerman and Plitt, "Inspection of Cascade Inn, Healing Springs, Virginia, October 25, 1943. National Archives Identifier: 2530934. Department of State: Bureau of Security and Consular Affairs, Office of Protective Services, 1952–1953. Record Group 59: General Records of the Department of State, 1763–2002. National Archives at College Park, Container ID: 165.

Chapter Ten

1. Letter to Fitch from Bannerman, Arrival of Italian Diplomatic Officials, June 19, 1943. National Archives Identifier: 2530931. Department of State: Bureau of Security and Consular Affairs, Office of Protective Services, 1952–1953. Record Group 59: General Records of the Department of State, 1763–2002. National Archives at College Park, Container ID: 165.

2. Letter to Fitch from Bannerman, February 11, 1943. National Archives Identifier: 2530968. Department of State: Bureau of Security and Consular Affairs, Office of Protective Services, 1952–1953. Record Group 59: General Records of the Department of State, 1763–2002. National Archives at College Park, Container ID: 170.

3. Letter to Miller from Fitch, February 20, 1943. National Archives Identifier: 2530286. Department of State: Bureau of Security and Consular Affairs, Office of Protective Services, 1952–1953. Record Group 59: General Records of the Department of State, 1763–2002. National Archives at College Park, Container ID: 104.

4. Letter to Lafcon from Fitch, February 19, 1943. National Archives Identifier: 2530930. Department of State: Bureau of Security and Consular Affairs, Office of Protective Services, 1952–1953. Record Group 59: General Records of the Department of State, 1763–2002 National Archives at College Park, Container ID: 164.

5. *Ibid.*

6. "Axis Diplomats Seized in Algiers Now Held in U.S. ... Exchange for Yanks in Germany Sought," *Chicago Tribune*, March 4, 1943.

7. Letter to Clattenburg from Fitch, March 3, 1943, Germans & Italians—Ingleside Hotel. National Archives Identifier: 2530930. Department of State: Bureau of Security and Consular Affairs, Office of Protective Services, 1952–1953. Record Group 59: General Records of the Department of State, 1763–2002. National Archives at College Park, Container ID: 164.

8. Letter to Fitch from Madden, "Attitude of the Staunton citizenry toward our detainees," June 12, 1943, Germans & Italians—Ingleside Hotel. National Archives Identifier: 2530930. Department of State: Bureau of Security and Consular Affairs, Office of Protective Services, 1952–1953. Record Group 59: General Records of the Department of State, 1763–2002. National Archives at College Park, Container ID: 164.

9. Letter to Clattenburg from Bannerman, August 18, 1943, Germans & Italians, Ingleside Hotel. National Archives Identifier: 2530931. Department of State: Bureau of Security and Consular Affairs, Office of Protective Services, 1952–1953. Record Group 59: General Records of the Department of State, 1763–2002. National Archives at College Park, Container ID: 165.

10. Letter to Hoover from Waldrop, July 14, 1942, Germans & Italians, Ingleside Hotel. National Archives Identifier: 2530931. Department of State: Bureau of

Chapter Notes—Ten

Security and Consular Affairs, Office of Protective Services, 1952–1953. Record Group 59: General Records of the Department of State, 1763–2002. National Archives at College Park, Container ID: 165.

11. Letter to Fitch from Bannerman, "Display of American flag," April 20, 1943, Germans & Italians, Ingleside Hotel. National Archives Identifier: 2530930. Department of State: Bureau of Security and Consular Affairs, Office of Protective Services, 1952–1953. Record Group 59: General Records of the Department of State, 1763–2002. National Archives at College Park, Container ID: 164.

12. Letter to Fitch from Madden, "Telephone conversation with local reporter," April 14, 1943, Germans & Italians—Ingleside Hotel . National Archives Identifier: 2530930. Department of State: Bureau of Security and Consular Affairs, Office of Protective Services, 1952–1953. Record Group 59: General Records of the Department of State, 1763–2002. National Archives at College Park, Container ID: 164.

13. Letter to Fitch from Madden, "Supplementary report to that submitted on the 14th of April 1943 relative to the display of the American flag at the Hotel Ingleside," April 29, 1943, Germans & Italians, Ingleside Hotel. National Archives Identifier: 2530931. Department of State: Bureau of Security and Consular Affairs, Office of Protective Services, 1952–1953. Record Group 59: General Records of the Department of State, 1763–2002. National Archives at College Park, Container ID: 165.

14. Letter to Fitch from Madden, Germans & Italians, Ingleside Hotel. National Archives Identifier: 2530931. Department of State: Bureau of Security and Consular Affairs, Office of Protective Services, 1952–1953. Record Group 59: General Records of the Department of State, 1763–2002. National Archives at College Park, Container ID: 165.

15. Letter to Long, Keeley, Lyon, Bonbright from Fitch, September 22, 1942, Three Hills Hotel—Warm Springs, Va.—French. National Archives Identifier: 2530303. Department of State: Bureau of Security and Consular Affairs, Office of Protective Services, 1952–1953. Record Group 59: General Records of the Department of State, 1763–2002. National Archives at College Park, Container ID: 107.

16. Memorandum, "The Secretary of State to President Roosevelt," 740.0021115 European War 1939/7127, *Foreign Relations*, 1942, Vol. 1, 378.

17. Memorandum, "The Secretary of State to the Swiss Charge (Feer)," *Foreign Relations*, 1942, Vol. 1, 107–108.

18. Memorandum, "The Secretary of State to the Minister in Switzerland (Harrison)," November 16, 1943. *Foreign Relations*, 1942, Vol. 1, 111.

19. Memorandum, "The Secretary of State to the Minister in Switzerland (Harrison)," November 16, 1943. *Foreign Relations*, 1942, Vol. 1, 112.

20. Letter to Fitch from Bannerman Hotel for housing French Officials, September 14, 1943, Italians—Shenvalee Hotel. National Archives Identifier: 2530926. Department of State: Bureau of Security and Consular Affairs, Office of Protective Services, 1952–1953. Record Group 59: General Records of the Department of State, 1763–2002. National Archives at College Park, Container ID: 163.

21. "Shenvalee In World War II," posted January 31, 2012, DNRonline.com http://www.dnronline.com/article/shenvalee ww2, accessed February 27, 2015.

22. Letter to Fitch from Bannerman, "Hunger Strike at the Shenvalee Hotel, February 23, 1944," National Archives Identifier: 2530928. Department of State: Bureau of Security and Consular Affairs, Office of Protective Services, 1952–1953. Record Group 59: General Records of the Department of State, 1763–2002. ARC Identifier: 2530928 National Archives at College Park, Container ID: 164.

23. Letter to Fitch from Madden, "Incident at the Shenvalee Hotel, New Market, Virginia," December 28, 1943, Italians—Shenvalee Hotel. National Archives Identifier: 2530926. Department of State: Bureau of Security and Consular Affairs, Office of Protective Services, 1952–1953. Record Group 59: General Records of the Department of State, 1763–2002. National Archives at College Park, Container ID: 163.

24. Letter to Fitch from Madden, "Supplemental Report to a Report Forwarded on April 7, 1944, titled 'Escape and Apprehension of Luigi Bosinco, a Italian Detainee,'" May 1, 1944, Italians—Shenvalee Hotel. National Archives Identifier: 2530927. Department of State: Bureau of Security

Chapter Notes—Eleven

and Consular Affairs, Office of Protective Services, 1952–1953. Record Group 59: General Records of the Department of State, 1763–2002. National Archives at College Park, Container ID: 164.

25. Letter to Keeley from Fitch, September 28, 1943, Italians—Shenvalee Hotel. National Archives Identifier: 2530926. Department of State: Bureau of Security and Consular Affairs, Office of Protective Services, 1952–1953. Record Group 59: General Records of the Department of State, 1763–2002. National Archives at College Park, Container ID: 164.

26. Letter to Keeley from Fitch, October 5, 1943, Italians—Shenvalee Hotel. National Archives Identifier: 2530926. Department of State: Bureau of Security and Consular Affairs, Office of Protective Services, 1952–1953. Record Group 59: General Records of the Department of State, 1763–2002. National Archives at College Park, Container ID: 163.

27. Letter to Fitch, "Parole of the Italian official Group," September 14, 1944, Italians—Shenvalee Hotel. National Archives Identifier: 2530927. Department of State: Bureau of Security and Consular Affairs, Office of Protective Services, 1952–1953. Record Group 59: General Records of the Department of State, 1763–2002. National Archives at College Park, Container ID: 164.

28. Letter to Fitch from Seward, "Attack on Mr. Ceccotti—Wednesday, Oct. 4, 1944," October 10, 1944, Italians—Shenvalee Hotel. National Archives Identifier: 2530927. Department of State: Bureau of Security and Consular Affairs, Office of Protective Services, 1952–1953. Record Group 59: General Records of the Department of State, 1763–2002. National Archives at College Park, Container ID: 164.

29. Letter to Fitch from Bannerman, Repatriation of Eighteen Italian Officials to Italy, December 11, 1944, Italians—Shenvalee Hotel. National Archives Identifier: 2530927. Department of State: Bureau of Security and Consular Affairs, Office of Protective Services, 1952–1953. Record Group 59: General Records of the Department of State, 1763–2002. National Archives at College Park, Container ID: 164.

30. "Swedish Motor Ship Gripsholm Sails for Lisbon to Exchange War Internees," *Daily Illini*, February 16, 1944.

Chapter Eleven

1. "Supreme Headquarters Allied Expeditionary Force, Office of Assistant Chief of Staff, Japanese Intelligence Report, June 8, 1945," Bedford Springs Hotel. National Archives Identifier: 2530861. Department of State: Bureau of Security and Consular Affairs, Office of Protective Services, 1952–1953. Record Group 59: General Records of the Department of State, 1763–2002. National Archives at College Park, Container ID: 154.

2. Telegram, Clattenburg to Murphy, May 15, 1945. National Archives Identifier: 2529777. Department of State: Bureau of Security and Consular Affairs, Office of Protective Services, 1952–1953. Record Group 59: General Records of the Department of State, 1763–2002. National Archives at College Park, Container ID: 81.

3. Letter to Fitch, "Hotel Accommodations for the Japanese, February 10, 1942," National Archives Identifier: 2530865. Department of State: Bureau of Security and Consular Affairs, Office of Protective Services, 1952–1953. Record Group 59: General Records of the Department of State, 1763–2002. National Archives at College Park, Container ID: 155.

4. "Citizens Get Talk on Quartering Foe," *The Fresno Bee*, July 23, 1945, 1.

5. "Plan to House Jap Group Does Not Include Coddling," *The Daily News*, July 9, 1945, 3.

6. Memorandum of Conversation, Accommodation of Japanese officials at Bedford Springs Hotel, July 5, 1945. National Archives Identifier: 2529777. Department of State: Bureau of Security and Consular Affairs, Office of Protective Services, 1952–1953. Record Group 59: General Records of the Department of State, 1763–2002. National Archives at College Park, Container ID: 81.

7. "Aren't We Being Too Nice?" *The Johnstown Tribune*, June 27, 1945, 6.

8. "[Copy of] Letter from Tribune Readers Veterans of World War II Protest," Editor of the Tribune, Bedford Springs Hotel. National Archives Identifier: 2530861. Department of State: Bureau of Security and Consular Affairs, Office of Protective Services, 1952–1953. Record Group 59: General Records of the Department of

Chapter Notes—Conclusion

State, 1763–2002. National Archives at College Park, Container ID: 154.

9. Newspaper Article, "Says Japs Used U.S. Prisoners of War for Bayonet Practice," Bedford Springs Hotel—Japanese Custody. National Archives Identifier: 2530201. Department of State: Bureau of Security and Consular Affairs, Office of Protective Services, 1952–1953. Record Group 59: General Records of the Department of State, 1763–2002. National Archives at College Park, Container ID: 99.

10. Memo from CSA to SWP, LE, July 4, 1945, Bedford Springs Hotel—Japanese. National Archives Identifier: 2530201. Department of State: Bureau of Security and Consular Affairs, Office of Protective Services, 1952–1953. Record Group 59: General Records of the Department of State, 1763–2002. National Archives at College Park, Container ID: 99.

11. "Plan to House Jap Group Does Not Include Coddling," *The Daily News*, July 9, 1945, 1.

12. "Calls Jap Diplomats 'Blue Chips of War,'" *Altoona Tribune*, July 20, 1945, 2.

13. *Ibid.*

14. *Ibid.*

15. Memo from Clark to Neal, et al., June 20, 1945, "Supreme Headquarters Allied Expeditionary Force, Office of Assistant Chief of Staff, Japanese Intelligence Report, June 8, 1945," National Archives Identifier: 2530861. Department of State: Bureau of Security and Consular Affairs, Office of Protective Services, 1952–1953. Record Group 59: General Records of the Department of State, 1763–2002. National Archives at College Park, Container ID: 154.

16. "Second Group of Japs Arrived," *Bedford Inquirer*, August 17, 1945, 3.

17. Memo, Holden to Fitch, "Activities of Mrs. Imgard Yomato, A Japanese Detainee the Bedford Springs Hotel," September 11, 1945. National Archives Identifier: 2529818. Department of State: Bureau of Security and Consular Affairs, Office of Protective Services, 1952–1953. Record Group 59: General Records of the Department of State, 1763–2002. National Archives at College Park, Container ID: 84.

18. Letter to Fitch from Madden, "Analysis of Internal Conditions at the Bedford Springs Hotel," September 28, 1945, Bedford Springs Hotel—Japanese Custody. National Archives Identifier: 2530201. Department of State: Bureau of Security and Consular Affairs, Office of Protective Services, 1952–1953. Record Group 59: General Records of the Department of State, 1763–2002. National Archives at College Park, Container ID: 99.

19. Letter to Fitch from Madden, "General Oshima," October 6, 1945, Bedford Springs Hotel—Japanese Custody. National Archives Identifier: 2530201. Department of State: Bureau of Security and Consular Affairs, Office of Protective Services, 1952–1953. Record Group 59: General Records of the Department of State, 1763–2002. National Archives at College Park, Container ID: 99.

20. Barbeau, 171.

21. *Ibid.*

22. "Jap Diplomats Leave Here On Journey Home," *Cumberland Evening Times*, November 17, 1945, 1.

Conclusion

1. The Homestead, Inter-Office Memorandum, "50th Anniversary of Pearl Harbor Attack," John M. Gassola, Jr., Director of Public Relations, December 2, 1991, 1.

2. "Supreme Headquarters Allied Expeditionary Force, Office of Assistant Chief of Staff, Japanese Intelligence Report, June 8, 1945," National Archives Identifier: 2530861. Department of State: Bureau of Security and Consular Affairs, Office of Protective Services, 1952–1953. Record Group 59: General Records of the Department of State, 1763–2002. National Archives at College Park, Container ID: 154.

3. *Ibid.*

4. "Gala New Year Is Planned at Resort," *White Sulfur Springs Sentinel*, December 19, 1941, 1.

5. Advertisement, "Benefit Dance," *White Sulfur Springs Sentinel*, July 24, 1942, 8.

6. James R. Young, "Top Flight Jap Officers Loll at Famed Pa. Resort," *The Portsmouth Herald*, October 5, 1945, 4.

7. "Victory Parade Held Around Japs' Hotel," *Altoona Tribune*, August 17, 1945, 1.

8. Memo to Fitch from Madden, "Christening of Hans Schwaraman's child," April 19, 1943, National Archives Identifier: 2530930. Department of State: Bureau of Security and Consular Affairs, Office of Protective Services, 1952–1953. Container ID: 164.

Bibliography

Books

Beck, Alfred M. *Hitler's Ambivalent Attaché: Lt. Gen. Friedrich Von Boetticher in America, 1933–1941.* Washington, D.C.: Potomac Books, 2005. http://search.ebscohost.com/login.aspx?direct=true&scope=site&db=nlebk&db=nlabk&AN=211763.
Bosworth, Allan R. *America's Concentration Camps.* New York: Norton, 1967.
Burdick, Charles Burton. *An American Island in Hitler's Reich: The Bad Nauheim Internment.* Menlo Park, CA: Markgraf Publications Group, 1987.
Connell, Thomas. *America's Japanese Hostages: The World War II Plan for a Japanese Free Latin America.* Westport, CT: Praeger, 2002.
Davis, Harold E., John J. Finan, and F. Taylor Peck. *Latin American Diplomatic History: An Introduction.* Baton Rouge: Louisiana State University Press, 1977.
Estlack, Russell W. *Shattered Lives, Shattered Dreams: The Disrupted Lives of Families in America's Internment Camps.* Springville, UT: Bonneville Books, 2011.
History of the Bureau of Diplomatic Security of the United States Department of State. United States Department of State Bureau of Diplomatic Security, Oct. 2011, Global Publishing Solutions, First Edition, 54.
Ingalls, Fay. *The Valley Road.* Cleveland; New York: The World Publishing Co., 1949.
Miller, Robert Ernest. *World War II Cincinnati: From the Front Line to the Home Front.* Charleston, SC: The History Press, 2014, 82.
Odo, Franklin. *The Columbia Documentary History of the Asian American Experience.* New York: Columbia University Press, 2002.
Terasaki, Gwen. *Bridge to the Sun.* Chapel Hill: University of North Carolina Press, 1957.

Periodical Articles

"Aide-Memoire." The British Embassy to the Department of State, 701.0010/211. "The British Ambassador to the Department of State." *Foreign Relations,* 1942, Vol. 1 (Feb. 2, 1942): 308.
"The Department, Duties of the Special Division." *The Department of State Bulletin,* Vol. 8, No. 190, Publication 1877, Feb. 13, 1943.
Dreifus, Erika. "A Golden Prison in Pennsylvania: The Hotel Hershey, 1942–43." *Pennsylvania History: A Journal of Mid-Atlantic Studies,* Vol. 69, No. 3 (Summer 2002). https://journals.psu.edu/phj/article/download/25772/25541.

Bibliography—Periodical Articles

Eppings, Jane. "Pearl Harbor, Japanese Espionage and Arizona's Triangle T Ranch." *Prologue, the Magazine of the National Archives*, Spring, 1997.
"The Homestead: A Great Hotel Entertains Jap Diplomats as Patriotic Duty." *Life Magazine*, Vol. 12, No. 7 (Feb. 16, 1942): 73.
Ingalls, Fay. *A Journal of the Sojourn of the Axis Diplomats at the Homestead*, Hot Springs, VA: 1943.
"Memorandum of Conversation by the Assistant Secretary of State (Long)." *Foreign Relations*, 1942, Vol. 1, 302.
"Memorandum of Conversation by the Under Secretary of State (Welles)." Feb. 13, 1942. *Foreign Relations*, 1942, Vol. 1, 311.
"Memorandum by the Assistant Secretary of State (Long) for President Roosevelt." *Foreign Relations*, 1942, Vol. 1 (Dec. 16, 1942): 378.
"The Secretary of State to President Roosevelt, 740.0021115 European War 1939/7127." *Foreign Relations*, 1942, Vol. 1, 378.
"The Secretary of State to the Minister in Switzerland (Harrison)." Nov. 16, 1943. *Foreign Relations*, 1942, Vol. 1, 111.
"The Secretary of State to the Swiss Charge (Feer)." *Foreign Relations*, 1942, Vol. 1, 107–108.
"The Spanish Embassy to the Department of State." *Foreign Relations*, 1942, Vol. 1, 448.
Stuart, Graham. "Special War Problems Division." *The Department of State Bulletin*, Publication 2148, Vol. XI, No. 262, July 2, 1944.
Telegram, "The Acting Secretary of State to the Ambassador in Peru (Norweb)." 701.0023/30. *Foreign Relations*, 1942, Vol. 1, 323.
Telegram, "The Acting Secretary of State to the Ambassador in Spain (Weddell)." 701.0024/26. *Foreign Relations*, 1942, Vol. 1, 330.
Telegram, "The Acting Secretary of State to the Ambassador in Spain (Waddell)." 701.6224/76. *Foreign Relations*, 1942, Vol. 1, 336.
Telegram, "The Acting Secretary of State to the Charge in Switzerland." 701.0010/64a, (Huddle). *Foreign Relations*, 1942, Vol. 1, 334.
Telegram, "The Acting Secretary of State to the Charge in Switzerland." 701.0010/44 (Huddle). *Foreign Relations*, 1942, Vol. 1, 334.
Telegram, "The Charge in Switzerland (Huddle) to the Secretary of State." 701.0211/1497, Jan. 15, 1942. *Foreign Relations*, 1942, Vol. 1, 304.
Telegram, "The Charge in Switzerland (Huddle) to the Secretary of State." 701.6511/1205. Jan. 2, 1942. *Foreign Relations*, 1942, Vol. 1, 299.
Telegram, Huddle to Secretary of State, 701.6211/1599, March 5, 1942. "The Charge in Switzerland (Huddle) to the Secretary of State." *Foreign Relations*, 1942, Vol. 1.
Telegram, Huddle to the Charge in Switzerland (Huddle) to the Secretary of State, 125.0040/134, Feb. 28, 1942. "Agreements with Enemy Countries for the Exchange of Officials and Non-Officials." *Foreign Relations*, 1942, Vol. 1, 319.
Telegram, Hull to Huddle, 123.0040/87b, Dec. 19, 1941. "Agreements with Enemy Countries for the Exchange of Officials and Non-Officials." *Foreign Relations*, 1942, Vol. 1.
Telegram, "The Minister in Switzerland (Harrison) to the Secretary of State." 701.0010/105. *Foreign Relations*, 1942, Vol. 1, 361.
Telegram, "The Minister in Switzerland (Harrison) to the Secretary of State." 701.0211/1642. *Foreign Relations*, 1942, Vol. 1, March 31, 1942.
Telegram, "The Secretary of State to the Charge in Switzerland (Huddle)." 125.0040/86, Dec. 30, 1941. *Foreign Relations*, 1942, Vol. 1, 296.

Bibliography—Newspaper Articles

Telegram, "The Secretary of State to the Charge in Switzerland (Huddle) Washington." 701.6211/1482a. Dec. 19, 1941. *Foreign Relations*, 1942, Vol. 1, 292.
Telegram, "The Secretary of State to the Charge in Switzerland (Huddle)." 701.0211/1486a. *Foreign Relations*, 1942, Vol. 1, Dec. 30, 1941, 297.
Telegram, "The Secretary of State to the Charge in Switzerland (Huddle)." 701.9411/1547a. *Foreign Relations*, 1942, Vol. 1, 378.
Telegram, "The Secretary of State to the Charge in Switzerland (Huddle)." 701.9411/1630. *Foreign Relations*, 1942, Vol. 1, 397.

Newspaper Articles

"Aliens Depart; Grove Park Inn Open to Public." *Asheville Times,* June 12, 1942.
"Aren't We Being Too Nice?" *The Jonestown Tribune,* June 27, 1945.
"Axis Diplomats in S. America Packing Bags." *The Times Recorder,* Zanesville, OH, Jan. 22, 1942.
"Axis Diplomats Seized in Algiers Now Held in U.S.—Exchange for Yanks in Germany Sought." *Chicago Tribune,* March 4, 1943.
"Axis Officials Interned Here." *White Sulphur Springs Sentinel,* Dec. 26, 1941.
"Calls Jap Diplomats 'Blue Chips of War,'" *Altoona Tribune,* July 20, 1945.
Charnay, David, and William Wallace (as told to Warren Hall). "Interned Jap, German Envoys Hoard Supplies." *Times-Herald,* May 5 1942, Special Collections, Arthur Morris Law Library, University of Virginia Law School, Box 9, Folder 11, MSS 93–4.
Charnay, David, and William Wallace. "Nazi 'Guests' Taunt Hon. Japs at Greenbrier on Tokyo Raid." *Times-Herald,* May 4, 1942, Special Collections, Arthur J. Morris Law Library, University of Virginia Law School, box 9, folder 11 MSS 93–4.
"Citizens Get Talk on Quartering Foe." *The Fresno Bee,* July 23, 1945.
"City Buses Are Used to Carry 242 in Group from Special Trains." *Asheville Times,* April 3, 1942.
"500 Axis Diplomats Stop-Over in U.S. *Daily Illini* (Champaign, Illinois) April 28, 1942.
"French Group to Be Moved to Virginia." *Pittston Gazette,* Sept. 25, 1943, 3.
"Future Operation of Greenbrier Will Be in Interest of National Defense." *White Sulphur Springs Sentinel,* March 6, 1942.
"Gala New Year Is Planned at Resort." *White Sulphur Springs Sentinel,* Dec. 19, 1941, 1.
"Germans Leave White Sulphur." *The Raleigh Register,* May 8, 1942.
"Greenbrier Denies Alien Objection." *White Sulphur Springs Sentinel,* Dec. 26, 1941.
"Jap Diplomats Leave Here on Journey Home." *Cumberland Evening Times,* Nov. 17, 1945.
"The Japs Aren't Coming." Newspaper clipping from Bath County Historical Society, File, Warm Springs, VA.
"Japs Badly Mistreat American Diplomats." *Statesville Record and Landmark,* Aug. 27, 1942, 1.
"Japs Leave Here to Be Exchanged." *White Sulphur Springs Sentinel,* June 3, 1942, 1.
Jones, Edward F. "Nazi Embassy Privileges Are Suddenly Ended." *Times Herald,* Washington, D.C., Dec. 18, 1941.
"Last of Axis Internees Leave Here." *White Sulphur Springs Sentinel,* July 16, 1942.
"Local Resort's Service to U.S. During War." *White Sulphur Springs Sentinel,* April 17, 1942.
"Look at This and This." *The Robesian,* Aug. 4, 1942, 4.

Bibliography—Archival Sources

"Many of Group Had Resided in South America." *Asheville Times*, July 9, 1942, 1.
McCormick, Mike. "Historical Perspective: Pilot, Under Vigilant Eye of FBI, Made Trip to Terre Haute." *Tribune Star*, June 18, 2007. http://www.tribstar.com/news/lifestyles/historical-perspective-pilot-under-vigilant-eye-of-fbi-made-trip/article_2a2e8cd9-e35f-5d31-bfbf-c5800b30f4e3.html. Accessed May 8, 2016.
The News Palladium, Benton Harbor, MI, April 8, 1942, 1
"Norwegian Girl Longs to Return Home." *Asheville Citizen*, June 12, 1942.
"Our Axis Diplomats (Editorial)." *White Sulphur Springs Sentinel*, Dec. 26, 1941, 1.
"Plan to House Jap Group Does Not Include Coddling." *The Daily News*, July 9, 1945, 1.
"Resort Is Leased by Government, Italians, Rumanians, Bulgarians Will Come Here Soon." *Asheville Citizen*, March 30, 1942.
"Second Group of Japs Arrived." *Bedford Inquirer*, Aug. 17, 1945.
"Swedish Motor Ship Gripsholm Sails for Lisbon to Exchange War Internees." *Daily Illini*, Feb. 16, 1944.
"218 Japanese and Germans Interned at Grove Park Inn." *Asheville Citizen*, May 16, 1942.
"U.S. Announces Stand Toward Axis Diplomats." *The Asheville Citizen*, Dec. 18, 1941.
"U.S. Ready for Second Exchange." *The Daily Mail*, Aug. 21, 1943, 1.
"Vichy Group to Leave Hershey." *The Indiana Gazette*, Sept. 25, 1943, 3.
"Victory Parade Held Around Japs' Hotel." *Altoona Tribune*, Aug. 17, 1945.
"Virginia Hotel Is Left Holding the Bag." newspaper clipping from Bath County Historical Society, File, Warm Springs, VA.
"White Sulphur Aliens Taken into Custody." *The Greenbrier Independent*, Feb. 13, 1942.
White Sulphur Springs Sentinel, Dec. 19, 1941.
Young, James R. "Top Flight Jap Officers Loll at Famed Pa. Resort." *The Portsmouth Herald*, Oct. 5, 1945.

Archival Sources

Albers, Dirk, Case File No. 22, Uruguay. National Archives Identifier: 2529561. Department of State, Bureau of Security and Consular Affairs, Office of Protective Services, 1952–1953. Record Group 59: General Records of the Department of State, 1763–2002. National Archives at College Park, Container ID: 69.
Daily Report, from Special Agent Carson, Jan. 15, 1942, RE: Joseph Krautlegger. Greenbrier Hotel Mission. Special Collections, Arthur J. Morris Law Library, University of Virginia Law School: Inventory of the Papers of Roy L. Morgan, 1941–1966 http://lib.law.virginia.edu/specialcollections/ Box 9, Folder 13, MSS 93–4 1 mss 93–4_b9_f13_i9_0001 tp://cdm16101.contentdm.oclc.org/cdm/search/searchterm/Springs.
Daily Report, to Ladd from Carlblom, Jan. 13, 1942, Greenbrier Hotel Mission. Special Collections, Arthur J. Morris Law Library, University of Virginia Law School: http://lib.law.virginia.edu/specialcollections/ Contributors D. M. Ladd; A. N. Carlblom Date 1942–01–13 Type Text Format TIFF Source Box 10, Folder 4, MSS 93–4 Language EN Collection Inventory of the Papers of Roy L. Morgan, 1941–1966 Description Title Page 3 Identifier mss93_4_b10_f4_i18_0003.
Daily Report, to Ladd from Lawler, March 1, 1942. The Greenbrier Hotel Mission. Special Collections, Arthur J. Morris Law Library, University of Virginia Law School: http://lib.law.virginia.edu/specialcollections/ Contributors D. M. Ladd; J. E. Lawler Date 1942–03–01 Type Text Format TIFF Source Box 10, Folder 5,

Bibliography—Archival Sources

MSS 93–4 Language EN Collection Inventory of the Papers of Roy L. Morgan, 1941–1966 Description Title Page 1 Identifier mss93_4_b10_f5_i1_0001.
"50th Anniversary of Pearl Harbor Attack." The Homestead, Inter-Office Memorandum. John M. Gassola, Jr., Director of Public Relations, Dec. 2, 1991. (From Bath Historical Society, Warm Springs, VA).
Handwritten note on "Memorandum for the Attorney General, Jan. 7, 1942." Greenbrier Hotel Mission. Special Collections, Arthur J. Morris Law Library, University of Virginia Law School: Inventory of the Papers of Roy L. Morgan, 1941–1966 http://lib.law.virginia.edu/specialcollections/ Box 9, Folder 13, MSS 93–4 1 mss 93–4_b9_f13_i9_0001 tp://cdm16101.contentdm.oclc.org/cdm/search/searchterm/ Springs.
Intelligence Report, Issued by the Intelligence Division Office of Chief of Naval Operations, Navy Department, Dec. 20, 1942. National Archives Identifier: 2531333. Department of State, Bureau of Security and Consular Affairs, Office of Protective Services, 1952–1953. Record Group 59: General Records of the Department of State, 1763–2002. National Archives at College Park, Container ID: 194.
"Interned Enemy Envoys Plot and Fight in Grand Hotel," newspaper clipping, Greenbrier Hotel Mission. Special Collections, Arthur J. Morris Law Library, University of Virginia Law School: http://lib.law.virginia.edu/specialcollections/ Contributors D. M. Ladd; Roy L. Morgan Date 1941–12–28 Type Text Format TIFF Source Box 10, Folder 2, MSS 93–4 Language EN Collection Inventory of the Papers of Roy L. Morgan, 1941–1966 Title Page 1 Identifier mss93_4_b10_f2_i2_0001.
Letter to Clattenburg, Jan. 9, 1943. National Archives Identifier: 2530968. Department of State, Bureau of Security and Consular Affairs, Office of Protective Services, 1952–1953. Record Group 59: General Records of the Department of State, 1763–2002. National Archives at College Park, Container ID: 170.
Letter to Fitch, "Hotel Accommodations for the Japanese." Feb. 10, 1942. National Archives Identifier: 2530865. Department of State, Bureau of Security and Consular Affairs, Office of Protective Services, 1952–1953. Record Group 59: General Records of the Department of State, 1763–2002. National Archives at College Park, Container ID: 155.
Letter to Fitch, "Hotel Hershey." Nov. 2, 1943. National Archives Identifier: 2530346. Department of State, Bureau of Security and Consular Affairs, Office of Protective Services, 1952–1953. Record Group 59: General Records of the Department of State, 1763–2002. National Archives at College Park, Container ID: 112.
Letter, Bannerman to Fitch, June 7, 1943. National Archives Identifier: 2530925. Department of State, Bureau of Security and Consular Affairs, Office of Protective Services, 1952–1953. Record Group 59: General Records of the Department of State, 1763–2002. National Archives at College Park, Container ID: 163.
Letter to Fitch, "Parole of the Italian Official Group." Sept. 14, 1944. National Archives Identifier: 2530927. Department of State, Bureau of Security and Consular Affairs, Office of Protective Services, 1952–1953. Record Group 59: General Records of the Department of State, 1763–2002. National Archives at College Park, Container ID: 164.
Letter to Fitch, March 22, 1942. National Archives Identifier: 2530319. Department of State, Bureau of Security and Consular Affairs, Office of Protective Services, 1952–1953. Record Group 59: General Records of the Department of State, 1763–2002. National Archives at College Park, Container ID: 109.
Letter to Fitch, Oct. 2, 1943. National Archives Identifier: 2530303. Department of

Bibliography—Archival Sources

State, Bureau of Security and Consular Affairs, Office of Protective Services, 1952–1953. Record Group 59: General Records of the Department of State, 1763–2002. National Archives at College Park, Container ID: 107.

Letter, Bailey to Fitch, "Staff of the Japanese Consulate General, Honolulu." Feb. 21, 1942. National Archives Identifier: 2530394. Department of State, Bureau of Security and Consular Affairs, Office of Protective Services, 1952–1953. Record Group 59: General Records of the Department of State, 1763–2002. National Archives at College Park, Container ID: 115.

Letter, Bailey to Fitch, June 8, 1942. National Archives Identifier: 2530351. Department of State, Bureau of Security and Consular Affairs, Office of Protective Services, 1952–1953. Record Group 59: General Records of the Department of State, 1763–2002. National Archives at College Park, Container ID: 112.

Letter, Bannerman to Clattenburg, Aug. 18, 1943. National Archives Identifier: 2530931. Department of State, Bureau of Security and Consular Affairs, Office of Protective Services, 1952–1953. Record Group 59: General Records of the Department of State, 1763–2002. National Archives at College Park, Container ID: 165.

Letter, Bannerman to Fitch, April 15, 1943. National Archives Identifier: 2530968. Department of State, Bureau of Security and Consular Affairs, Office of Protective Services, 1952–1953. Record Group 59: General Records of the Department of State, 1763–2002. National Archives at College Park, Container ID: 170.

Letter, Bannerman to Fitch, "Arrival of Italian Diplomatic Officials." June 19, 1943. National Archives Identifier: 2530931. Department of State, Bureau of Security and Consular Affairs, Office of Protective Services, 1952–1953. Record Group 59: General Records of the Department of State, 1763–2002. National Archives at College Park, Container ID: 165.

Letter, Bannerman to Fitch, Aug. 27, 1942. National Archives Identifier: 2530334. Department of State, Bureau of Security and Consular Affairs, Office of Protective Services, 1952–1953. Record Group 59: General Records of the Department of State, 1763–2002. National Archives at College Park, Container ID: 110.

Letter, Bannerman to Fitch, "Conference on the Diplomatic Exchange." Sept. 2, 1942. National Archives Identifier: 2531137 Department of State, Bureau of Security and Consular Affairs, Office of Protective Services, 1952–1953. Record Group 59: General Records of the Department of State, 1763–2002. National Archives at College Park, Container ID: 182.

Letter, Bannerman to Fitch, "Display of American Flag." April 20, 1943. National Archives Identifier: 2530930. Department of State, Bureau of Security and Consular Affairs, Office of Protective Services, 1952–1953. Record Group 59: General Records of the Department of State, 1763–2002. National Archives at College Park, Container ID: 164.

Letter, Bannerman to Fitch, Dec. 3, 1942. National Archives Identifier: 2530939. Department of State, Bureau of Security and Consular Affairs, Office of Protective Services, 1952–1953. Record Group 59: General Records of the Department of State, 1763–2002. National Archives at College Park, Container ID: 166.

Letter, Bannerman to Fitch, Feb. 11, 1943. National Archives Identifier: 2530968. Department of State, Bureau of Security and Consular Affairs, Office of Protective Services, 1952–1953. Record Group 59: General Records of the Department of State, 1763–2002. National Archives at College Park, Container ID: 170.

Letter, Bannerman to Fitch, Feb. 25, 1942. National Archives Identifier: 2530394. Department of State, Bureau of Security and Consular Affairs, Office of Pro-

Bibliography—Archival Sources

tective Services, 1952–1953. Record Group 59: General Records of the Department of State, 1763–2002. National Archives at College Park, Container ID: 115.

Letter, Bannerman to Fitch, "General Report on the Diplomatic Exchange." July 30, 1942. National Archives Identifier: 2531137. Department of State, Bureau of Security and Consular Affairs, Office of Protective Services, 1952–1953. Record Group 59: General Records of the Department of State, 1763–2002. National Archives at College Park, Container ID: 182.

Letter, Bannerman to Fitch, "Hotel Accommodations for Japanese." Feb. 13, 1942. National Archives Identifier: 2530937. Department of State, Bureau of Security and Consular Affairs, Office of Protective Services, 1952–1953. Record Group 59: General Records of the Department of State, 1763–2002. National Archives at College Park, Container ID: 166.

Letter, Bannerman to Fitch, "Hotel Accommodations for the Diplomatic and Consular Officials for Japan, Germany, Italy, Rumania and Bulgaria." Dec. 16, 1941. National Archives Identifier: 2531043. Department of State, Bureau of Security and Consular Affairs, Office of Protective Services, 1952–1953. Record Group 59: General Records of the Department of State, 1763–2002. National Archives at College Park, Container ID: 179.

Letter, Bannerman to Fitch, "Hotel Accommodations for the Japanese." Feb. 10, 1942. National Archives Identifier: 2530313. Department of State, Bureau of Security and Consular Affairs, Office of Protective Services, 1952–1953. Record Group 59: General Records of the Department of State, 1763–2002. National Archives at College Park, Container ID: 108.

Letter, Bannerman to Fitch, "Hotel Accommodations Near the Greenbrier Hotel at White Sulphur Springs, to Care for the Expected Overflow of Axis Ex-Diplomats." National Archives Identifier: 2530319. Department of State, Bureau of Security and Consular Affairs, Office of Protective Services, 1952–1953. Record Group 59: General Records of the Department of State, 1763–2002. National Archives at College Park, Container ID: 109.

Letter, Bannerman to Fitch, "Hotel for Housing French Officials." Sept. 14, 1943. National Archives Identifier: 2530926. Department of State, Bureau of Security and Consular Affairs, Office of Protective Services, 1952–1953. Record Group 59: General Records of the Department of State, 1763–2002. National Archives at College Park, Container ID: 163.

Letter, Bannerman to Fitch, "Hunger Strike at the Shenvalee Hotel, Feb. 23, 1944." National Archives Identifier: 2530928. Department of State, Bureau of Security and Consular Affairs, Office of Protective Services, 1952–1953. Record Group 59: General Records of the Department of State, 1763–2002. National Archives at College Park, Container ID: 164.

Letter, Bannerman to Fitch, March 20, 1942. National Archives Identifier: 2531043. Department of State, Bureau of Security and Consular Affairs, Office of Protective Services, 1952–1953. Record Group 59: General Records of the Department of State, 1763–2002. National Archives at College Park, Container ID: 179.

Letter, Bannerman to Fitch, Nov. 12, 1942. National Archives Identifier: 2531017. Department of State, Bureau of Security and Consular Affairs, Office of Protective Services, 1952–1953. Record Group 59: General Records of the Department of State, 1763–2002. National Archives at College Park, Container ID: 174.

Bibliography—Archival Sources

Letter, Bannerman to Fitch, Nov. 13, 1942. National Archives Identifier: 2531017. Department of State, Bureau of Security and Consular Affairs, Office of Protective Services, 1952–1953. Record Group 59: General Records of the Department of State, 1763–2002. National Archives at College Park, Container ID: 174.

Letter, Bannerman to Fitch, Oct. 30, 1944. National Archives Identifier: 2530281. Department of State, Bureau of Security and Consular Affairs, Office of Protective Services, 1952–1953. Record Group 59: General Records of the Department of State, 1763–2002. National Archives at College Park, Container ID: 104.

Letter, Bannerman to Fitch, "Possibility of Moving the Japanese at Hot Springs to Some Other Location." March 11, 1942. National Archives Identifier: 2530314. Department of State, Bureau of Security and Consular Affairs, Office of Protective Services, 1952–1953. Record Group 59: General Records of the Department of State, 1763–2002. National Archives at College Park, Container ID: 108.

Letter, Bannerman to Fitch, "Possibility of Using Mount Weather, Virginia as a Place to House the Japanese Now at Hot Springs, Virginia." March 11, 1942. National Archives Identifier: 2530937. Department of State, Bureau of Security and Consular Affairs, Office of Protective Services, 1952–1953. Record Group 59: General Records of the Department of State, 1763–2002. National Archives at College Park, Container ID: 166.

Letter, Bannerman to Fitch, "Repatriation of Eighteen Italian Officials to Italy." Dec. 11, 1944. National Archives Identifier: 2530927. Department of State, Bureau of Security and Consular Affairs, Office of Protective Services, 1952–1953. Record Group 59: General Records of the Department of State, 1763–2002. National Archives at College Park, Container ID: 164.

Letter, Briggs to Fitch (?), May 14, 1942. National Archives Identifier: 2531043. Department of State, Bureau of Security and Consular Affairs, Office of Protective Services, 1952–1953. Record Group 59: General Records of the Department of State, 1763–2002. National Archives at College Park, Container ID: 179.

Letter, Briggs to Fitch, Nov. 3, 1942. National Archives Identifier: 2530855. Department of State, Bureau of Security and Consular Affairs, Office of Protective Services, 1952–1953. Record Group 59: General Records of the Department of State, 1763–2002. National Archives at College Park, Container ID: 153.

Letter, Briggs to Fitch, Oct. 13, 1942. National Archives Identifier: 2530937. Department of State, Bureau of Security and Consular Affairs, Office of Protective Services, 1952–1953. Record Group 59: General Records of the Department of State, 1763–2002. National Archives at College Park, Container ID: 166.

Letter, Carlblom to Hoover, "Regarding Activities at the Greenbrier Hotel." Jan. 26, 1942. World War II. Letters, memos relating to foreign diplomats held at Greenbrier and FBI materials relating to their exchange (photocopies) 1941–1942. I Folder Ms2009–006 Archives and History Library, WV Division of Culture and History.

Letter, Davis to Woodward, April 17, 1942. National Archives Identifier: 2530306. Department of State, Bureau of Security and Consular Affairs, Office of Protective Services, 1952–1953. Record Group 59: General Records of the Department of State, 1763–2002. National Archives at College Park, Container ID: 107.

Letter, Deidre to Michelle, from Hershey Hotel. National Archives Identifier: 2530346. Department of State, Bureau of Security and Consular Affairs, Office

Bibliography—Archival Sources

of Protective Services, 1952–1953. Record Group 59: General Records of the Department of State, 1763–2002. National Archives at College Park, Container ID: 112.

Letter, Fitch to Brand, Frank, and Plitt, Oct. 30, 1943. National Archives Identifier: 2530303. Department of State. Bureau of Security and Consular Affairs, Office of Protective Services, 1952–1953. Record Group 59: General Records of the Department of State, 1763–2002. National Archives at College Park, Container ID: 107.

Letter, Fitch to Clattenburg, March 3, 1943. National Archives Identifier: 2530930. Department of State, Bureau of Security and Consular Affairs, Office of Protective Services, 1952–1953. Record Group 59: General Records of the Department of State, 1763–2002.1/1943–4/30/1943. National Archives at College Park, Container ID: 164.

Letter, Fitch to Franklin, Dec. 22, 1942. National Archives Identifier: 2530855. Department of State, Bureau of Security and Consular Affairs, Office of Protective Services, 1952–1953. Record Group 59: General Records of the Department of State, 1763–2002. National Archives at College Park, Container ID: 153.

Letter, Fitch to Keeley, Oct. 16, 1942. National Archives Identifier: 2530855. Department of State, Bureau of Security and Consular Affairs, Office of Protective Services, 1952–1953. Record Group 59: General Records of the Department of State, 1763–2002. National Archives at College Park, Container ID: 153.

Letter, Fitch to Keeley, Oct. 5, 1943. National Archives Identifier: 2530926. Department of State, Bureau of Security and Consular Affairs, Office of Protective Services, 1952–1953. Record Group 59: General Records of the Department of State, 1763–2002. National Archives at College Park, Container ID: 163.

Letter, Fitch to Keeley, Sept. 28, 1943. National Archives Identifier: 2530926. Department of State, Bureau of Security and Consular Affairs, Office of Protective Services, 1952–1953. Record Group 59: General Records of the Department of State, 1763–2002. National Archives at College Park, Container ID: 163.

Letter, Fitch to Keeley, Sept. 9, 1942. National Archives Identifier: 2530288. Department of State, Bureau of Security and Consular Affairs, Office of Protective Services, 1952–1953. Record Group 59: General Records of the Department of State, 1763–2002. National Archives at College Park, Container ID: 104.

Letter, Fitch to Lafcon, Feb. 19, 1943. National Archives Identifier: 2530930. Department of State, Bureau of Security and Consular Affairs, Office of Protective Services, 1952–1953. Record Group 59: General Records of the Department of State, 1763–2002. National Archives at College Park, Container ID: 164.

Letter, Fitch to Long, et al., Sept. 22, 1943. National Archives Identifier: 2530934. Department of State, Bureau of Security and Consular Affairs, Office of Protective Services, 1952–1953. Record Group 59: General Records of the Department of State, 1763–2002. National Archives at College Park, Container ID: 165.

Letter, Fitch to Long, Keeley, Lyon, and Bonbright, Sept. 22, 1942. National Archives Identifier: 2530303. Department of State, Bureau of Security and Consular Affairs, Office of Protective Services, 1952–1953. Record Group 59: General Records of the Department of State, 1763–2002. National Archives at College Park, Container ID: 107.

Letter, Fitch to Lyon, et al., Sept. 16, 1943. National Archives Identifier: 2530926. Department of State, Bureau of Security and Consular Affairs, Office of Protective Services, 1952–1953. Record Group 59: General Records of the Department of State, 1763–2002. National Archives at College Park, Container ID: 163.

Bibliography—Archival Sources

Letter, Fitch to Miller, Feb. 20, 1943. National Archives Identifier: 2530286. Department of State, Bureau of Security and Consular Affairs, Office of Protective Services, 1952–1953. Record Group 59: General Records of the Department of State, 1763–2002. National Archives at College Park, Container ID: 104.

Letter, Green to Cabot, et al., May 9, 1942. National Archives Identifier: 2529590. Department of State, Bureau of Security and Consular Affairs, Office of Protective Services, 1952–1953. Record Group 59: General Records of the Department of State, 1763–2002. National Archives at College Park, Container ID: 72.

Letter, Green to Halifax, March 31, 1942. National Archives Identifier: 17343398. Department of State, Bureau of Security and Consular Affairs, Office of Protective Services, 1952–1953. Record Group 59: General Records of the Department of State, 1763–2002. National Archives at College Park, Container ID: 201.

Letter, Green to Long, Jan. 24, 1942. National Archives Identifier: 2529590. Department of State. Bureau of Security and Consular Affairs. Office of Protective Services, 1952–1953. Record Group 59: General Records of the Department of State, 1763–2002. National Archives at College Park, Container ID: 72.

Letter, Green to Long, March 30, 1942. National Archives Identifier: 17343398. Department of State, Bureau of Security and Consular Affairs, Office of Protective Services, 1952–1953. Record Group 59: General Records of the Department of State, 1763–2002. National Archives at College Park, Container ID: 201.

Letter, Green to Long, March 31, 1942. National Archives Identifier: 17343398. Department of State, Bureau of Security and Consular Affairs, Office of Protective Services, 1952–1953. Record Group 59: General Records of the Department of State, 1763–2002. National Archives at College Park, Container ID: 201.

Letter, Hoover to Lee, March 11, 1942. National Archives Identifier: 2530311. Department of State, Bureau of Security and Consular Affairs, Office of Protective Services, 1952–1953. Record Group 59: General Records of the Department of State, 1763–2002. National Archives at College Park, Container ID: 107.

Letter, Hoover to Morgan, May 12, 1942. Greenbrier Hotel Mission. Special Collections, Arthur J. Morris Law Library, University of Virginia Law School: http://lib.law.virginia.edu/specialcollections/. D. M. Ladd; Roy L. Morgan; J. Edgar Hoover; Alfred R. Nerz 1942-05-06 Box 9, Folder 4, MSS 93-4 Collection Inventory of the Papers of Roy L. Morgan, 1941–1966 mss93-4_b9_f4_i40_0004.

Letter, Hoshide to Poole, Jan. 20, 1942. National Archives Identifier: 2530310. Department of State, Bureau of Security and Consular Affairs, Office of Protective Services, 1952–1953. Record Group 59: General Records of the Department of State, 1763–2002. National Archives at College Park, Container ID: 107.

Letter, Hull to Biddle, Feb. 12, 1942. National Archives Identifier: 2529590. Department of State, Bureau of Security and Consular Affairs, Office of Protective Services, 1952–1953. Record Group 59: General Records of the Department of State, 1763–2002. National Archives at College Park, Container ID: 72.

Letter, Huskey to Fitch, April 13, 1942. National Archives Identifier: 2531043. Department of State, Bureau of Security and Consular Affairs, Office of Protective Services, 1952–1953. Record Group 59: General Records of the Department of State, 1763–2002. National Archives at College Park, Container ID: 179.

Letter, Innes to Fitch, March 10, 1943. National Archives Identifier: 2530859. Department of State, Bureau of Security and Consular Affairs, Office of Protective Services, 1952–1953. Record Group 59: General Records of the Department of State, 1763–2002. National Archives at College Park, Container ID: 154.

Bibliography—Archival Sources

Letter, Innes to Fitch, March 23, 1942. National Archives Identifier: 2530859. Department of State, Bureau of Security and Consular Affairs, Office of Protective Services, 1952–1953. Record Group 59: General Records of the Department of State, 1763–2002. National Archives at College Park, Container ID: 154.

Letter, Keeley to Fitch. National Archives Identifier: 2530925. Department of State, Bureau of Security and Consular Affairs, Office of Protective Services, 1952–1953. Record Group 59: General Records of the Department of State, 1763–2002. National Archives at College Park, Container ID: 163.

Letter, LCF to Fitch, May 18, 1943. National Archives Identifier: 2530925. Department of State, Bureau of Security and Consular Affairs, Office of Protective Services, 1952–1953. Record Group 59: General Records of the Department of State, 1763–2002. National Archives at College Park, Container ID: 163.

Letter, Long to Saugstad, Feb. 18, 1942. National Archives Identifier: 2529590. Department of State, Bureau of Security and Consular Affairs, Office of Protective Services, 1952–1953. Record Group 59: General Records of the Department of State, 1763–2002. National Archives at College Park, Container ID: 72.

Letter, Long to Secretary of State, April 9, 1942. National Archives Identifier: 2529581. Department of State, Bureau of Security and Consular Affairs, Office of Protective Services, 1952–1953. Record Group 59: General Records of the Department of State, 1763–2002. National Archives at College Park, Container ID: 71.

Letter, Lyon to Keeley. National Archives Identifier: 2530855. Department of State, Bureau of Security and Consular Affairs, Office of Protective Services, 1952–1953. Record Group 59: General Records of the Department of State, 1763–2002. National Archives at College Park, Container ID: 153.

Letter, Madden to Fitch, "Analysis of Internal Conditions at the Bedford Springs Hotel." Sept. 28, 1945. National Archives Identifier: 2530201. Department of State, Bureau of Security and Consular Affairs, Office of Protective Services, 1952–1953. Record Group 59: General Records of the Department of State, 1763–2002. .National Archives at College Park, Container ID: 99.

Letter, Madden to Fitch, "Attitude of the Staunton Citizenry Toward Our Detainees." June 12, 1943. National Archives Identifier: 2530930. Department of State, Bureau of Security and Consular Affairs, Office of Protective Services, 1952–1953. Record Group 59: General Records of the Department of State, 1763–2002.1/1943–4/30/1943. National Archives at College Park, Container ID: 164.

Letter, Madden to Fitch, "General Oshima." Oct. 6, 1945. National Archives Identifier: 2530201. Department of State, Bureau of Security and Consular Affairs, Office of Protective Services, 1952–1953. Record Group 59: General Records of the Department of State, 1763–2002. National Archives at College Park, Container ID: 99.

Letter, Madden to Fitch, "Incident at the Shenvalee Hotel, New Market, Virginia." National Archives Identifier: 2530926. Department of State, Bureau of Security and Consular Affairs, Office of Protective Services, 1952–1953. Record Group 59: General Records of the Department of State, 1763–2002. National Archives at College Park, Container ID: 163.

Letter, Madden to Fitch, "Supplemental Report to a Report Forwarded on April 7, 1944, Titled 'Escape and Apprehension of Luigi Bosicn, a Italian Detainee,'" May 1, 1944. National Archives Identifier: 2530927. Department of State, Bureau of Security and Consular Affairs, Office of Protective Services, 1952–1953. Record Group 59: General Records of the Department of State, 1763–2002. National Archives at College Park, Container ID: 164.

Bibliography—Archival Sources

Letter, Madden to Fitch, "Supplementary report to that submitted on April 14, 1943, relative to the display of the American flag at the Hotel Ingleside." April 29, 1943. National Archives Identifier: 2530931. Department of State, Bureau of Security and Consular Affairs, Office of Protective Services, 1952–1953. Record Group 59: General Records of the Department of State, 1763–2002. National Archives at College Park, Container ID: 165.

Letter, Madden to Fitch, "Telephone Conversation with Local Reporter." April 14, 1943. National Archives Identifier: 2530930. Department of State, Bureau of Security and Consular Affairs, Office of Protective Services, 1952–1953. Record Group 59: General Records of the Department of State, 1763–2002.1/1943–4/30/1943. National Archives at College Park, Container ID: 164.

Letter, Madden to Fitch. National Archives Identifier: 2530931. Department of State, Bureau of Security and Consular Affairs, Office of Protective Services, 1952–1953. Record Group 59: General Records of the Department of State, 1763–2002. National Archives at College Park, Container ID: 165.

Letter, Marggraff to Gufler, Sept. 6, 1942. National Archives Identifier: 2530329. Department of State, Bureau of Security and Consular Affairs, Office of Protective Services, 1952–1953. Record Group 59: General Records of the Department of State, 1763–2002. National Archives at College Park, Container ID: 110.

Letter, Miles to Fitch, Dec. 14, 1942. National Archives Identifier: 2530855. Department of State, Bureau of Security and Consular Affairs, Office of Protective Services, 1952–1953. Record Group 59: General Records of the Department of State, 1763–2002. National Archives at College Park, Container ID: 153.

Letter, Poole to Fitch, Jan. 17, 1942. National Archives Identifier: 2530311. Department of State, Bureau of Security and Consular Affairs, Office of Protective Services, 1952–1953. Record Group 59: General Records of the Department of State, 1763–2002. National Archives at College Park, Container ID: 107.

Letter, Seward to Fitch, "Attack on Mr. Ceccotti—Wednesday, Oct. 4, 1944." Oct. 10, 1944. National Archives Identifier: 2530927. Department of State, Bureau of Security and Consular Affairs, Office of Protective Services, 1952–1953. Record Group 59: General Records of the Department of State, 1763–2002. National Archives at College Park, Container ID: 164.

Letter, Sievernich to Poole, May 4, 1942. National Archives Identifier: 2530343. Department of State, Bureau of Security and Consular Affairs, Office of Protective Services, 1952–1953. Record Group 59: General Records of the Department of State, 1763–2002. National Archives at College Park, Container ID: 111.

Letter, Steward to Fitch, "Conditions at the Hershey Hotel." June 4, 1943. National Archives Identifier: 2530346. Department of State, Bureau of Security and Consular Affairs, Office of Protective Services, 1952–1953. Record Group 59: General Records of the Department of State, 1763–2002. National Archives at College Park, Container ID: 112.

Letter, unsigned. Addressed to the Japanese Ambassador. National Archives Identifier: 2530319. Department of State, Bureau of Security and Consular Affairs, Office of Protective Services, 1952–1953. Record Group 59: General Records of the Department of State, 1763–2002. National Archives at College Park, Container ID: 109.

Letter, Waldrop to Hoover, July 14, 1942. National Archives Identifier: 2530931. Department of State, Bureau of Security and Consular Affairs, Office of Protective Services, 1952–1953. Record Group 59: General Records of the Department of State, 1763–2002. National Archives at College Park, Container ID: 165.

Bibliography—Archival Sources

Letter, Welles to Kilgore, April 3, 1942. Special Collections, Arthur J. Morris Law Library, University of Virginia Law School: http://lib.law.virginia.edu/special collections/ Harley M. Kilgore; Summer Welles 1942–04–03 Box 10, Folder 5, MSS 93-4 Inventory of the Papers of Roy L. Morgan, 1941–1966 mss93_4_b10_f5_i58_0001.

List of Japanese Nationals From Hawaii Now Detained at Asheville Assembly Inn—Montreat, N.C. National Archives Identifier: 2530937. Department of State, Bureau of Security and Consular Affairs, Office of Protective Services, 1952–1953. Record Group 59: General Records of the Department of State, 1763–2002. National Archives at College Park, Container ID: 166.

Memorandum for Assistant Director D. M. Ladd from Carlblom, Jan. 19, 1942. Greenbrier Hotel Mission. Special Collections, Arthur J. Morris Law Library, University of Virginia Law School: http://lib.law.virginia.edu/specialcollections/ Contributors D. M. Ladd; A. N. Carlblom; R. J. Untreiner Date 1942–01–19 Type Text Format TIFF Source Box 10, Folder 4, MSS 93-4 Language EN Collection Inventory of the Papers of Roy L. Morgan, 1941–1966 Title Page 1 Identifier mss93_4_b10_f4_i25_0001.

Memorandum for Assistant Director D. M. Ladd, Dec. 29, 1941. Greenbrier Hotel Mission. Special Collections, Arthur J. Morris Law Library, University of Virginia Law School: http://lib.law.virginia.edu/specialcollections/ Box 10, Folder 4, MSS 93-4 Inventory of the Papers of Roy L. Morgan, 1941–1966 mss93_4_b10_f4_i6_0001.

Memorandum for Assistant Director D.M. Ladd, Jan. 10, 1942. Greenbrier Hotel Mission. Special Collections, Arthur J. Morris Law Library, University of Virginia Law School: http://lib.law.virginia.edu/specialcollections/ Box 10, Folder 4, MSS 93-4 Inventory of the Papers of Roy L. Morgan, 1941–1966 mss93_4_b10_f4_i17_0001.

Memorandum for Assistant Director D.M. Ladd, Jan. 30, 1942. "Louis Toman Admits Taking Two Letters Out for Saporiti." Greenbrier Hotel Mission. Special Collections, Arthur J. Morris Law Library, University of Virginia Law School: http://lib.law.virginia.edu/specialcollections/ Box 10, Folder 3, MSS 93-4 Inventory of the Papers of Roy L. Morgan, 1941–1966 mss93_4_b10_f3_i5_0001.

Memorandum for Assistant Director D.M. Ladd, Jan. 30, 1942. "Saporiti Will Be Intelligence Agent in Lisbon." Greenbrier Hotel Mission. Special Collections, Arthur J. Morris Law Library, University of Virginia Law School: http://lib.law.virginia.edu/specialcollections/ Box 10, Folder 3, MSS 93-4 Inventory of the Papers of Roy L. Morgan, 1941–1966 mss93_4_b10_f3_i5_0001.

Memorandum for Assistant Director D.M. Ladd, Jan. 30, 1942. Greenbrier Hotel Mission. Special Collections, Arthur J. Morris Law Library, University of Virginia Law School: http://lib.law.virginia.edu/specialcollections/ Box 10, Folder 3, MSS 93-4 Inventory of the Papers of Roy L. Morgan, 1941–1966 mss93_4_b10_f3_i5_0001.

Memorandum for Assistant Director D.M. Ladd, Jan. 30, 1942. Greenbrier Hotel Mission. Special Collections, Arthur J. Morris Law Library, University of Virginia Law School: http://lib.law.virginia.edu/specialcollections/ Contributors D. M. Ladd; Roy L. Morgan Date 1942–02–13 Type Text Format TIFF Source Box 10, Folder 1, MSS 93-4 Language EN Collection Inventory of the Papers of Roy L. Morgan, 1941–1966 Title Page 1 Identifier mss93-4_b10_f1_i35_0001.

Bibliography—Archival Sources

Memorandum for Assistant Director E.A. Tamm, from A.N. Carlblom, Dec. 23, 1941. World War II. Letters, memos relating to foreign diplomats held at Greenbrier and FBI materials relating to their exchange (photocopies), 1941–1942. I Folder Ms2009–006 Archives and History Library, WV Division of Culture and History.

Memorandum for Mr. E.A.Tamm. Jan. 6, 1942, Greenbrier Hotel Mission. Special Collections, Arthur J. Morris Law Library, University of Virginia Law School: Inventory of the Papers of Roy L. Morgan, 1941–1966 http://lib.law.virginia.edu/specialcollections/ Box 9, Folder 13, MSS 93–4 1 mss93–4_b9_f13_i9_0001 tp://cdm16101.contentdm.oclc.org/cdm/search/searchterm/Springs.

Memorandum for Mr. Kimball Re Duties at Greenbrier Hotel Mission. *Daily Report*, March 4, 1942. Inventory of the Papers of Roy L. Morgan, Special Collections, Arthur J. Morris Law Library, University of Virginia Law School, http:/lib.law.virginia.ed/specialcollections/ Box 10, Folder 5, MSS 93–4.

Memorandum for Mr. Ladd, Jan. 28, 1942. Greenbrier Hotel Mission. Special Collections, Arthur J. Morris Law Library, University of Virginia Law School: http://lib.law.virginia.edu/specialcollections/ Contributors D. M. Ladd; Roy L. Morgan Date 1942–04–14 Type Text Format TIFF Source Box 9, Folder 7, MSS 93–4 Language EN Collection Inventory of the Papers of Roy L. Morgan, 1941–1966 Description Title Page 1 Identifier mss93–4_b9_f7_i6_0001.

Memorandum for Mr. Ladd, March 23, 1942. Greenbrier Hotel Mission. Special Collections, Arthur J. Morris Law Library, University of Virginia Law School: http://lib.law.virginia.edu/specialcollections/ Contributors D. M. Ladd; A. N. Carlblom Date 1942–01–08 Type Text Format TIFF Source Box 10, Folder 4, MSS 93–4 Language EN Collection Inventory of the Papers of Roy L. Morgan, 1941–1966 Description Title Page 1.

Memorandum for Mr. Ladd, RE Greenbrier Hotel Mission, March 6, 1942. Special Collection, Arthur J. Morris Law Library, University of Virginia Law School, Box 10, folder 5, Mss 93–4.

Memorandum for Mr. Ladd. "Sievernich Domestic Difficulties, March 17, 1942." Greenbrier Hotel Mission. Special Collections, Arthur J. Morris Law Library, University of Virginia Law School: http://lib.law.virginia.edu/specialcollections/ Contributors D. M. Ladd; J. E. Lawler Date 1942–03–17 Type Text Format TIFF Source Box 10, Folder 5, MSS 93–4 Language EN Collection Inventory of the Papers of Roy L. Morgan, 1941–1966 Description Title Page 1 Identifier ss93_4_b10_f5_i18_0001.

Memorandum for Mr. Ladd. "Von Stemple's Birthday Party." March 9, 1942. Greenbrier Hotel Mission. Special Collections, Arthur J. Morris Law Library, University of Virginia Law School: http://lib.law.virginia.edu/specialcollections/ Contributors D. M. Ladd; J. E. Lawler Date 1942–03–09 Type Text Format TIFF Source Box 10, Folder 5, MSS 93–4 Language EN Collection Inventory of the Papers of Roy L. Morgan, 1941–1966 Description Title Page 1 Identifier mss93_4_b10_f5_i10_0001.

Memorandum for the Attorney General. Jan. 7, 1942 Greenbrier Hotel Mission. Special Collections, Arthur J. Morris Law Library, University of Virginia Law School: Inventory of the Papers of Roy L. Morgan, 1941–1966 http://lib.law.virginia.edu/specialcollections/ Box 9, Folder 13, MSS 93–4 1 mss93–4_b9_f13_i9_0001 tp://cdm16101.contentdm.oclc.org/cdm/search/searchterm/Springs.

Memorandum for the Director from R L Morgan, RE: Japanese Diplomatic Corps

Bibliography—Archival Sources

Internal Security, Jan. 11, 1942. Greenbrier Hotel Mission. Special Collections, Arthur J. Morris Law Library, University of Virginia Law School: Inventory of the Papers of Roy L. Morgan, 1941–1966 http://lib.law.virginia.edu/special collections/ Box 9, Folder 13, MSS 93–4 1 mss93–4_b9_f13_i9_0001 tp://cdm16101.contentdm.oclc.org/cdm/search/searchterm/Springs.

Memorandum for the Director, April 14, 1942. Greenbrier Hotel Mission. Special Collections, Arthur J. Morris Law Library, University of Virginia Law School: http://lib.law.virginia.edu/specialcollections/ Contributors D. M. Ladd; Roy L. Morgan Date 1942-04-14 Type Text Format TIFF Source Box 9, Folder 7, MSS 93–4 Language EN Collection Inventory of the Papers of Roy L. Morgan, 1941–1966 Description Title Page 1 Identifier mss93–4_b9_f7_i6_0001.

Memorandum for the Director, April 6, 1942. Greenbrier Hotel Mission. Special Collections, Arthur J. Morris Law Library, University of Virginia Law School: http://lib.law.virginia.edu/specialcollections/ Contributors D. M. Ladd; Roy L. Morgan Date 1942-04-06 Type Text Format TIFF Source Box 9, Folder 4, MSS 93–4 Language EN Collection Inventory of the Papers of Roy L. Morgan, 1941–1966 Description Title Page 1 Identifier mss93–4_b9_f4_i20_0001.

Memorandum for the Director, Attention Mr. Ladd, RE Japanese Diplomatic Corps Internal Security, Jan, 6 1942. Greenbrier Hotel Mission. Special Collections, Arthur J. Morris Law Library, University of Virginia Law School: http://lib.law.virginia.edu/specialcollections/ D. M. Ladd; Roy L. Morgan Box 10, Folder 7, MSS 93–4 Inventory of the Papers of Roy L. Morgan, 1941–1966 mss93_4_b10_f7_i9_0001.

Memorandum for the Director, Attn Mr. Ladd, May 15, 1942. Greenbrier Hotel Mission. Special Collections, Arthur J. Morris Law Library, University of Virginia Law School: http://lib.law.virginia.edu/specialcollections/ Contributors D. M. Ladd; Roy L. Morgan Date 1942-05-15 Type Text Format TIFF Source Box 9, Folder 7, MSS 93–4 Language EN Collection Inventory of the Papers of Roy L. Morgan, 1941–1966 Description Title Page 1 Identifier mss93–4_b9_f7_i22_0001.

Memorandum for the Director, Attn Mr. Ladd, May 8, 1942. Greenbrier Hotel Mission. Special Collections, Arthur J. Morris Law Library, University of Virginia Law School: http://lib.law.virginia.edu/specialcollections/ Contributors D. M. Ladd; Roy L. Morgan Date 1942-05-08 Type Text Format TIFF Source Box 10, Folder 3, MSS 93–4 Language EN Collection Inventory of the Papers of Roy L. Morgan, 1941–1966 Description Title Page 1 Identifier mss93_4_b10_f3_i61_0001.

Memorandum for the Director, Attn: Mr. Ladd, RE Jan. 7, 1942. Greenbrier Hotel Mission. Special Collections, Arthur J. Morris Law Library, University of Virginia Law School: http://lib.law.virginia.edu/specialcollections/ Contributors D. M. Ladd; Roy L. Morgan Date 1942-01-07 Type Text Format TIFF Source Box 10, Folder 7, MSS 93–4 Language EN Collection Inventory of the Papers of Roy L. Morgan, 1941–1966 Description Title Page 1 Identifier mss93_4_b10_f7_i10_0001.

Memorandum from Bannerman and Plitt. "Inspection of Cascade Inn Healing Springs, Virginia." Oct. 25, 1943. National Archives Identifier: 2530934. Department of State, Bureau of Security and Consular Affairs, Office of Protective Services, 1952–1953. Record Group 59: General Records of the Department of State, 1763–2002. National Archives at College Park, Container ID: 165.

Memorandum from Clark to Neal, et al., June 20 1945. "Supreme Headquarters Allied

Bibliography—Archival Sources

Expeditionary Force, Office of Assistant Chief of Staff, Japanese Intelligence Report, June 8, 1945." National Archives Identifier: 2530861. Department of State, Bureau of Security and Consular Affairs, Office of Protective Services, 1952–1953. Record Group 59: General Records of the Department of State, 1763–2002. National Archives at College Park, Container ID: 154.

Memorandum from CSA to SWP, LE, July 4, 1945. National Archives Identifier: 2530201. Department of State, Bureau of Security and Consular Affairs, Office of Protective Services, 1952–1953. Record Group 59: General Records of the Department of State, 1763–2002. National Archives at College Park, Container ID: 99.

Memorandum from Fitch to Patton. "Transfer of the Vichy French Officials from Washington, D.C., to Hershey Pennsylvania, Nov. 18, 1942. National Archives Identifier: 2530270. Department of State, Bureau of Security and Consular Affairs, Office of Protective Services, 1952–1953. Record Group 59: General Records of the Department of State, 1763–2002. National Archives at College Park, Container ID: 103.

Memorandum from Mangels to Fitch. "Transfer of French Diplomatic Detainees from Hershey, Pennsylvania, to Three Hils, VA." Oct. 4, 1942. National Archives Identifier: 2530303. Department of State, Bureau of Security and Consular Affairs, Office of Protective Services, 1952–1953.Record Group 59: General Records of the Department of State, 1763–2002. National Archives at College Park, Container ID: 107.

Memorandum of Agreement with Respect to the Detention of Members of the German Embassy and Hungarian Legation at the Greenbrier Hotel, White Sulphur Springs, West Virginia, Dec. 20, 1941 World War II." Letters, memos relating to foreign diplomats held at Greenbrier and FBI materials relating to their exchange (photocopies), 1941–1942. I Folder Ms2009–006 Archives and History Library, WV Division of Culture and History.

Memorandum of Conversation by the Undersecretary of State (Welles), Rumbold, Clattenburg. "Safe Conduct for Political Agents." Jan. 16, 1942. National Archives Identifier: 17343391. Department of State, Bureau of Security and Consular Affairs, Office of Protective Services, 1952–1953. Record Group 59: General Records of the Department of State, 1763–2002. National Archives at College Park, Container ID: 200.

Memorandum of Conversation, Feb. 16, 1942. National Archives Identifier: 2530598. Department of State, Bureau of Security and Consular Affairs, Office of Protective Services, 1952–1953. Record Group 59: General Records of the Department of State, 1763–2002. National Archives at College Park, Container ID: 129.

Memorandum of Conversation. "Accommodation of Japanese Officials at Bedford Springs Hotel." July 5, 1945. National Archives Identifier: 2529777. Department of State, Bureau of Security and Consular Affairs, Office of Protective Services, 1952–1953. Record Group 59: General Records of the Department of State, 1763–2002. National Archives at College Park, Container ID: 81.

Memorandum regarding activities of the Unites States Government in removing from the other American Republics dangerous subversive aliens, Nov. 3, 1942. National Archives Identifier: 2531068. Department of State, Bureau of Security and Consular Affairs, Office of Protective Services, 1952–1953. Record Group 59: General Records of the Department of State, 1763–2002. National Archives at College Park, Container ID: 180.

Bibliography—Archival Sources

Memorandum Repatriation of Axis Officials and Nationals, April 9 1942. National Archives Identifier: 2529590. Department of State, Bureau of Security and Consular Affairs, Office of Protective Services, 1952–1953. Record Group 59: General Records of the Department of State, 1763–2002. National Archives at College Park, Container ID: 72.

Memorandum , Bannerman to Fitch, June 11, 1943. National Archives Identifier: 2530270. Department of State, Bureau of Security and Consular Affairs, Office of Protective Services, 1952–1953. Record Group 59: General Records of the Department of State, 1763–2002. National Archives at College Park, Container ID: 103.

Memorandum , Bannerman to Fitch. "Questions Raised by German Group at Gibson Hotel, Cincinnati as Transmitted by Mr. Patton." April 28, 1942. National Archives Identifier: 2530306. Department of State, Bureau of Security and Consular Affairs, Office of Protective Services, 1952–1953. Record Group 59: General Records of the Department of State, 1763–2002. National Archives at College Park, Container ID: 107.

Memorandum to Fitch from Madden. "Christening of Hans Schwaraman's Child." April 19, 1943. National Archives Identifier: 2530930. Department of State, Bureau of Security and Consular Affairs, Office of Protective Services, 1952–1953. Container ID: 164.

Memorandum to Fitch. "Report on the Conditions at the Hershey Hotel." June 11, 1943. National Archives Identifier: 2530937. Department of State, Bureau of Security and Consular Affairs, Office of Protective Services, 1952–1953. Record Group 59: General Records of the Department of State, 1763–2002. National Archives at College Park, Container ID: 166.

Memorandum to Fitch. "Transfer of Montreat Detainees to the Immigration Service." March 22, 1943. National Archives Identifier: 2530968. Department of State, Bureau of Security and Consular Affairs, Office of Protective Services, 1952–1953. Record Group 59: General Records of the Department of State, 1763–2002. National Archives at College Park, Container ID: 170.

Memorandum to Green from Fitch, Aug. 21, 1942. National Archives Identifier: 2530329. Department of State, Bureau of Security and Consular Affairs, Office of Protective Services, 1952–1953. Record Group 59: General Records of the Department of State, 1763–2002. National Archives at College Park, Container ID: 110.

Memorandum to Long from Green, April 13, 1942. National Archives Identifier: 2529590. Department of State, Bureau of Security and Consular Affairs, Office of Protective Services, 1952–1953. Record Group 59: General Records of the Department of State, 1763–2002. National Archives at College Park, Container ID: 72.

Memorandum to Mr. Clattenbury from Mr. Fitch, June 5, 1943. National Archives Identifier: 2531197. Department of State, Bureau of Security and Consular Affairs, Office of Protective Services, 1952–1953. Record Group 59: General Records of the Department of State, 1763–2002. National Archives at College Park, Container ID: 184.

Memorandum to Mr. Duggan, May 4, 1942. National Archives Identifier: 2529590. Department of State, Bureau of Security and Consular Affairs, Office of Protective Services, 1952–1953. Record Group 59: General Records of the Department of State, 1763–2002. National Archives at College Park, Container ID: 72.

Bibliography—Archival Sources

Memorandum to Secretary of State from Dawson. "Lists of Axis Nationals to Be Repatriated from Bolivia." April 2, 1942. National Archives Identifier: 2530353. Department of State, Bureau of Security and Consular Affairs, Office of Protective Services, 1952–1953. Record Group 59: General Records of the Department of State, 1763–2002. National Archives at College Park, Container ID: 113.

Memorandum to Warren and Long from Green. National Archives Identifier: 17343391. Department of State, Bureau of Security and Consular Affairs, Office of Protective Services, 1952–1953. Record Group 59: General Records of the Department of State, 1763–2002. National Archives at College Park, Container ID: 200.

Memorandum, "Arrangements at Hotel Hershey for the French Officials." Nov. 16, 1942. National Archives Identifier: 2531017. Department of State, Bureau of Security and Consular Affairs, Office of Protective Services, 1952–1953. Record Group 59: General Records of the Department of State, 1763–2002. National Archives at College Park, Container ID: 174.

Memorandum, "Instructions for Representatives of Former Hungarian Consulate, New York, New York." Dec. 24, 1941. Greenbrier Hotel Mission. Special Collections, Arthur J. Morris Law Library, University of Virginia Law School: Inventory of the Papers of Roy L. Morgan, 1941–1966 http://lib.law.virginia.edu/special collections/ Box 9, Folder 13, MSS 93–4 1 mss93–4_b9_f13_i9_0001 tp://cdm16101.contentdm.oclc.org/cdm/search/searchterm/Springs.

Memorandum, "Movement of Japanese from Homestead Hotel, Hot Springs, Virginia, to Bon Air Hotel, Aug.a Georgia, Tentatively Fixed for March 12." National Archives Identifier: 2530313. Department of State, Bureau of Security and Consular Affairs, Office of Protective Services, 1952–1953. Record Group 59: General Records of the Department of State, 1763–2002. National Archives at College Park, Container ID: 108.

Memorandum, "Safe conduct for vessel to be used by United States Government in exchanging official and non-official person of Axis Nationality for American officials and others in Europe, Feb. 16, 1942." National Archives Identifier: 17343391. Department of State, Bureau of Security and Consular Affairs, Office of Protective Services, 1952–1953. Record Group 59: General Records of the Department of State, 1763–2002. National Archives at College Park, Container ID: 200.

Memorandum, Bannerman to Fitch. "Accommodations for the 500 Axis Officials and Non-Officials Arriving at New Orleans on the Transport ACADIA, April 16, 1942." National Archives Identifier: 2530937. Department of State, Bureau of Security and Consular Affairs, Office of Protective Services, 1952–1953. Record Group 59: General Records of the Department of State, 1763–2002. National Archives at College Park, Container ID: 166.

Memorandum, Diplomatic Exchange. National Archives Identifier: 2530968. Department of State, Bureau of Security and Consular Affairs, Office of Protective Services, 1952–1953. Record Group 59: General Records of the Department of State, 1763–2002. National Archives at College Park, Container ID: 170.

Memorandum, Feb. 25, 1942. National Archives Identifier: 17343391. Department of State, Bureau of Security and Consular Affairs, Office of Protective Services, 1952–1953. Record Group 59: General Records of the Department of State, 1763–2002. National Archives at College Park, Container ID: 200.

Memorandum, Groth to Green, May 15, 1942. National Archives Identifier: 2529590. Department of State, Bureau of Security and Consular Affairs, Office of Pro-

Bibliography—Archival Sources

tective Services, 1952–1953. Record Group 59: General Records of the Department of State, 1763–2002. National Archives at College Park, Container ID: 72.

Memorandum, Holden to Fitch. "Activities of Mrs. Imgard Yomato, a Japanese Detainee at the Bedford Springs Hotel." Sept. 11, 1945. National Archives Identifier: 2529818 Department of State, Bureau of Security and Consular Affairs, Office of Protective Services, 1952–1953. Record Group 59: General Records of the Department of State, 1763–2002. National Archives at College Park, Container ID: 84.

Memorandum, hotel accommodation, March 20 1942. National Archives Identifier: 2530319. Department of State, Bureau of Security and Consular Affairs, Office of Protective Services, 1952–1953. Record Group 59: General Records of the Department of State, 1763–2002. National Archives at College Park, Container ID: 109.

Memorandum, unpublished. "Japanese at Hot Springs." Fay Ingalls. ((From Bath Historical Society, Warm Springs, VA)

Memorandum, unpublished. "Report of the Axis Diplomats and Nationals at the Greenbrier, Dec. 19th, 1941 to July 8th, 1942 (201 Days Stay)." Bob Sibold. (From Greenbrier Hotel.)

Note to ALB, Nov. 3, 1942. National Archives Identifier: 2530937. Department of State, Bureau of Security and Consular Affairs, Office of Protective Services, 1952–1953. Record Group 59: General Records of the Department of State, 1763–2002. National Archives at College Park, Container ID: 166.

"130 Japanese Brought Here from Hawaii," newspaper clipping, Grove Park Inn file, North Carolina Reading Room, Pack Memorial Library, Asheville.

"Report Says Japs Used U.S. Prisoners of War for Bayonet Practice." National Archives Identifier: 2530201. Department of State, Bureau of Security and Consular Affairs, Office of Protective Services, 1952–1953. Record Group 59: General Records of the Department of State, 1763–2002. National Archives at College Park, Container ID: 99.

Supreme Headquarters Allied Expeditionary Force, Office of Assistant Chief of Staff, Japanese Intelligence Report, June 8, 1945, National Archives Identifier: 2530861. Department of State. Bureau of Security and Consular Affairs, Office of Protective Services, 1952–1953. General Records of the Department of State, 1763–2002. National Archives at College Park, Container ID: 154.

Supreme Headquarters Allied Expeditionary Force, Office of Assistant Chief of Staff, Japanese Intelligence Report, June 8, 1945, National Archives Identifier: 2530861. Department of State, Bureau of Security and Consular Affairs, Office of Protective Services, 1952–1953. Record Group 59: General Records of the Department of State, 1763–2002. National Archives at College Park, Container ID: 154.

Telegram, Clattenburg to Murphy, May 15, 1945. National Archives Identifier: 2529777. Department of State, Bureau of Security and Consular Affairs, Office of Protective Services, 1952–1953. Record Group 59: General Records of the Department of State, 1763–2002. National Archives at College Park, Container ID: 81.

Telegram, Postal Inspector Smith to Fitch, Feb. 14, 1942. National Archives Identifier: 2530394. Department of State, Bureau of Security and Consular Affairs, Office of Protective Services, 1952–1953. Record Group 59: General Records of the Department of State, 1763–2002. National Archives at College Park, Container ID: 115.

Telegram from Green, May 19, 1942. National Archives Identifier: 17343398. Depart-

Bibliography—Internet Sources

ment of State, Bureau of Security and Consular Affairs, Office of Protective Services, 1952–1953. Record Group 59: General Records of the Department of State, 1763–2002. National Archives at College Park, Container ID: 201.

Telegram to Secretary of State from Wilson, Dec. 24, 1941. National Archives Identifier: 17343398. Department of State, Bureau of Security and Consular Affairs, Office of Protective Services, 1952–1953. Record Group 59: General Records of the Department of State, 1763–2002. National Archives at College Park, Container ID: 201.

Telegram to Secretary of State, Jan. 15, 1942. National Archives Identifier: 2529590. Department of State, Bureau of Security and Consular Affairs, Office of Protective Services, 1952–1953. Record Group 59: General Records of the Department of State, 1763–2002. Container ID: 72.

Tower Arthur, F., dispatch from, Sept. 12, 1942, Treatment of American Officials by Japanese Authorities. National Archives Identifier: 2529567. Department of State, Bureau of Security and Consular Affairs, Office of Protective Services, 1952–1953. Record Group 59: General Records of the Department of State, 1763–2002. National Archives at College Park, Container ID: 70.

"Treatment of German Travelling in Diplomatic Exchange Passport By Allied Government, Date of letter Nov. 7, 1942." Confidential Intercept, National Archives Identifier: 2530968. Department of State, Bureau of Security and Consular Affairs, Office of Protective General Records of the Department of State, 1763–2002. National Archives at College Park, Container ID: 170.

The Ursula Martin Case, Weekly Report. Special Collections, Arthur J. Morris Law Library, University of Virginia Law School: http://lib.law.virginia.edu/specialcollections/ Contributors D. M. Ladd; Roy L. Morgan Date 1942-04-14 Type Text Format TIFF Source Box 9, Folder 7, MSS 93-4 Language EN Collection Inventory of the Papers of Roy L. Morgan, 1941–1966 Description Title Page 1 Identifier mss93-4_b9_f7_i6_0001.

"Veterans of World War II Protest." Letter from Tribune Readers, Editor of the Tribune, Bedford Springs Hotel. National Archives Identifier: 2530861. Department of State, Bureau of Security and Consular Affairs, Office of Protective Services, 1952–1953. Record Group 59: General Records of the Department of State, 1763–2002. National Archives at College Park, Container ID: 154.

Internet Sources

"FAQ—'Why Were the Crewmembers' Bodies Never Removed from the USS *Arizona*?'" National Park Service. *World War II Valor in the Pacific*, accessed June 30, 2015. http://www.nps.gov/valr/faq.htm.

German American Internee Coalition. "The Mantel Family Story." posted Oct. 2012, GAIC.com. Accessed July 10, 2015. http://gaic.info/mantel-family/.

Grove, Lynn. "The American Internee Experience in Nazi Germany." *Traces*, Accessed March 3, 2015. http://www.traces.org/americaninternees.html.

Hershey Archives, World War II: The Vichy Internment at the Hotel Hershey. Accessed March 4, 2015 http://www.hersheyarchives.org/essay/details.aspx?EssayId=22&Rurl=%2Fresources%2Fsearch-results.aspx%3FType%3DBrowseEssay.

"Mrs. Roland A (Lettie) Fleagle." National Border Patrol Museum, BorderPatrolMuseusm.com accessed May 8, 2016. https://borderpatrolmuseum.com/interviews/mrs-roland-a-lettie-fleagle/.

Bibliography—Internet Sources

Post by Vitesse, Jan. 1, 2008. "Axis History Forum." Accessed July 9, 2015 http://forum.axishistory.com/viewtopic.php?t=132854.

"Shenvalee in World War II." posted Jan. 31, 2012, DNRonline.com, accessed Feb. 27, 2015. www.dnronline.com/article/shenvaleeww2.

"This Day in Presbyterian History." website accessed Jun 30, 2015. http://www/thisday.pcahistory.org/2012/04/aril-30-presbyterian-missionairies-freed/.

Tomita, Ella, Japanese Internee, Oct. 14, 2004, Interviewed by Kalei Ho and Mika Bailey, Japanese Cultural Center of Hawai'i. Japanese American Internment Unite for Modern History of Hawai'i (2008). Presented by the Japanese Cultural Center of Hawai'i, Oct. 14, 2004. (page 55) Accessed Feb. 22, 2015. http://hawaiiinternment.org/sites/default/files/Modern%20History%20of%20Hawaii_0.pdf.

Index

Acadia 39, 81, 87, 90–92, 98, 114, 133
Albers, Dirk 88
Albrecht, Arturo 88–89
Anderson, Robert 116–117
Angle, Ernest 6, 21, 54, 156
Argentina 35–36, 72–75, 85, 88
Arizona 1, 5–6, 30, 49, 71, 79, 101
Armistice Committee 131–132, 135
Asama Maru 103
Asheville 60–61, 91, 95, 98–102, 104, 106, 108–111, 113–114, 153
Assembly Inn 2, 110, 112, 114–116
Augusta 57–58

Bad Gastein 145, 153
Bad Nauheim 15–16, 50, 66, 77, 97, 103
Baden-Baden 4, 127, 129, 131–132, 134, 137, 142
Bannerman, Robert 18, 23, 30, 56–60, 85, 91–93, 106, 108, 111–112, 117–118, 131, 134–135
Barbeur, Arthur 106, 151
Bedford 148–150
Bedford Springs Hotel 145–147, 149–150, 154–156
Biddle, Francis 13, 22, 27
Blum, Adolph 95
Bolivia 34, 39, 74–76, 81–82, 85, 87, 90–91, 96–97, 100, 113
Bombieri, Enrico 138, 141–142
Bon Air Hotel 57–58, 131
Border Patrol 5, 19, 23, 47–49, 51, 71, 94, 123, 156
Bosinco, Luigi 139–140
Brazil 34–37, 72–74, 89, 102
Buddha 113
Buddhist 107, 113
Buenos Aires 36, 75, 138
Bureau of Immigration and Naturalization Service 7, 22–24, 31–32, 45–47, 51, 88, 108–110, 112, 115, 117, 127, 129, 134, 139, 150, 153

Caribbean 89, 91
Carlblom, A.N. 23, 25
Cascades 130, 142
Chile 34–35, 75
China 107
Cincinnati 2, 92–95, 98, 133
Clifton Forge 49
Colombia 35, 38, 52, 74, 80–81, 85–88, 90, 96–97, 100, 113–114
Colonna, Ascanio 54, 91, 95
Cuba 34, 36, 96–97, 119
Cultrera, Alessandro 133

Dalmatian 125
Davis, Nathaniel 8, 92
Dominican Republic 96–97
Doolittle Raid 63, 106
Dragoon 30, 101
Dreifus, Erika 7, 124
Drottningholm 4, 76–77, 91–94, 96–97, 99–104, 114, 117, 133

Ecuador 76, 80–82, 87–91, 96–97, 100
England 73
Eppinga, Jane 29
Espionage 9, 29, 35, 40, 70, 83, 87, 105
Etolin 39, 81, 88, 91

FBI 2, 4–5, 7, 9, 17, 19–20, 22–29, 32–33, 35, 42–49, 51–54, 58, 63, 71, 82, 88, 108, 134, 153
Fitch, Thomas 23, 58, 60, 85, 91, 106, 108–109, 115, 117–118, 126, 128–129, 131–132, 135, 150
Fleagle, Roland 47
France 3, 7, 10, 99, 121–123, 127, 133, 137, 143
Frederick Johnson 118–119

199

Index

Gassler, Joseph 123
Georgia 58, 128
Gestapo 16
Glider 9, 51, 71
Greece 10
Green, Joseph 35, 68–69, 81, 84, 91
Greenbrier 1–2, 4–6, 8–9, 18–21, 23–27, 32–33, 36–37, 41–48, 50–52, 54–55, 58, 60–65, 85–87, 92, 94–99, 101–102, 104, 109, 114–115, 128, 153–154
Grew, Joseph 11, 104, 106
Gripsholm 4, 79, 89, 102–105, 107–109, 113–114, 117, 142
Grove Park Inn 2, 60–61, 95–96, 99, 101–102, 104, 106, 108–110, 112–114, 153
Guatemala 36, 38, 96–97, 101

Haiti 34, 36, 96
Hamburg 88, 113
Hawaiian 11, 71, 101–102, 108–109
Henri-Haye, Gaston 121–123, 127, 129–130
Hiroshima 155
Hoover, J. Edgar 10, 22, 25, 27, 29, 46–47, 134
Hotel Gibson 92–94, 96–98, 133
Hotel Hershey 121–125, 127–130, 132, 137
Hull, Cordell 78
Hungary 33, 95, 99, 101, 115

Iceland 68
Immigration 7, 22–24, 31–32, 45–47, 51, 88, 108–109, 112, 115, 117, 127, 129, 134, 139, 150, 153
Immunity 13, 83, 127, 131, 144, 156
India 105
Informant 43–45, 52–53, 62–63, 65
Ingalls, Fay 20, 25, 42, 47, 51, 56, 62, 116
Ingleside Hotel 5, 132–138, 142, 156
Internment 4, 7, 22–23, 31, 71, 76, 80, 88, 90, 92–93, 95, 99, 102, 104, 107, 113, 115, 118, 127, 137, 139, 148, 153
Italy 3, 10, 15, 18, 36–38, 44, 70, 73, 95, 99, 115, 131, 133, 135–137, 141–143, 145

Jeschke Grand Hotel 16

Korea 105
Krammer, Arnold 13
Kungsholm 55, 76, 103

Ladd, D.M. 86, 91
Lake Lure 110, 128, 132

Lake Placid 2, 57
Laredo 36
Laupahoehoe 107
Lawler, J.E. 43–44, 86
Lewisburg 24
Lima 71, 133
Lisbon 15, 39, 44, 67, 69, 72–73, 75–76, 97, 99, 103, 142
London 11–12, 81–82, 84
Louisiana 113, 118
Lourdes 121–122, 127, 131, 136
Lourenço Marques 15, 39, 69, 73, 78, 103
Luftwaffe 154
Luxemburg 10

Madden, Frank 135, 138, 140, 151
Mantel, Mary 113
Marggraff, Joachim 38
Measles 94
Mexico 36, 78, 90, 96–97, 99–100, 104
Miami 23, 57
Microphones 149
Miller, Ernest 93
Minner, Robert 33, 64, 101
Missouri 155
Montana 71
Montreat 2, 109–116
Morgan, Robert 26, 45–46, 48, 63–64
Morris, Leland 10, 50, 77
Mount Weather 59
Mozambique 15
Myrtle Beach 18

Nagasaki 155
Nertz, Alfred 46
Netherlands 10
New Orleans 36, 87, 90–93, 98, 114, 118–119, 133
Newark 10
Nicaragua 36, 96–97
Norfolk 69
North Carolina 2, 60, 108–110, 113–114, 123, 128
Norway 10, 101

Oahu 107
Oath 43
Ohio 20, 36
Oklahoma 113

Panama Canal 34–35, 74, 80, 114
Paraguay 36–37, 72–74, 89, 102
Pardon 52
Paris 147
Parole 2–3, 101, 127–128, 140–141
Patagonia 30

Index

Pearl Harbor 1, 10–11, 21, 29, 36, 87, 102, 147–148, 154–155
Pennsylvania 3, 7, 33, 96, 102, 123, 146–150
Peru 1, 4, 39, 71, 74, 76, 80–82, 86–87, 89–91, 96–97, 100, 113, 133
Philippines 103, 149
Phoenix 30
Ping Pong 32, 124, 155
Poole, E.P. 58, 64, 98
Portugal 69–70, 73, 99, 142
POW 147
Press 12, 32, 47, 58, 67, 93, 123, 150
Protocol 22, 24, 55

Quinwood 6
Quito 81

Relocation 3, 108
Repatriation 8, 13, 35–36, 38–39, 69, 74–76, 81, 84, 86, 90–91, 103, 117, 137, 142
Ribbentrop, Joachim 137
Richmond 18
Riedel, Peter 9, 51, 71
Rio de Janeiro 36, 69, 72–73, 76, 102
Rome 1, 11, 16, 44, 69, 76, 82
Roosevelt, Franklin 1, 9–10, 34–35, 122, 136
Rotterdam 12
Rudall, Jon 26
Rumania 18, 99

Sabotage 1, 8, 35, 70, 80, 83, 88, 120
Sanatorium 110
Saporiti, Piero 43–45
Savannah 2, 59
Seagoville 115
Seattle 65, 156

Serpa Pinto 102–103, 117
Shawanee 90
Shenvalee Hotel 128–129, 136–140, 142
Sibold, Roy 20, 22, 41, 51, 63, 115
Singapore 16, 108–109, 116
Sjogreen, Margrete 101
South Carolina 145
Spain 13, 73
Spying 1, 8–10
Staunton 132–135, 138, 153
Sweden 92, 144
Switzerland 99, 139, 144

Terasaki, Gwen 28, 44–45
Texas 36, 113, 115, 139
Thailand 149–150
Thomsen, Hans 53, 95, 98
Three Hills Estates 129–130
Tokyo 1, 11, 14, 16, 28–29, 63, 82, 99, 105, 151, 155
Triangle T 29–30, 37, 47, 51, 101–102, 115
Tucson 30, 49
Tunis 131, 138

Uruguay 36–37, 72–74, 88–89, 102

Venezuela 70, 82, 88–91, 96–97
Vichy 3, 7, 121–125, 127, 129, 142–143
Virginia 1, 3–7, 18, 24, 26, 28, 33, 48–49, 58–59, 62, 95–96, 114, 126, 128–129, 132, 134, 138–140, 142

Wainwright, Gen. George 3, 149, 154
Warren, Ara 87, 91
Wehrmacht 154

Yamamoto, Irmgard 150–151
Yugoslavia 10

www.ingramcontent.com/pod-product-compliance
Ingram Content Group UK Ltd.
Pitfield, Milton Keynes, MK11 3LW, UK
UKHW042007140426
5217IPUK00015B/1039